nff
Catriona Windle

Normal for Fife

NFF is a fictionalised account of my experiences training as a nurse in Fife, Scotland from 1982-1985. The language and medical terminology is consistent with that period in time.

Page

5 Urban Explorers

8 Victoria Hospital, Ward 1 Geriatrics, 1982 June - August

22 Victoria Hospital, Ward 2 General Medical, 1982 October - December

59 Victoria Hospital, Ward 3 Surgical/Gynaecology, 1983 January - March

67 Path House, Kirkcaldy, 1983 February

92 Victoria Hospital, Accident and Emergency, 1983 May - July

99 Forth Park Maternity Hospital, 1983 September - December

108 Springfield Woods, 1983 November

118 Path house, Kirkcaldy, 1983 December

128 Stratheden Psychiatric Hospital, 1984 January

133 Stratheden Psychiatric Hospital, Ward 4 Men's Long Stay, 1984 January - March

163 Stratheden Psychiatric Hospital, Ward 5 Women's Long Stay, 1984 April - June

- *170* Carstairs State Mental Hospital, 1984 June

- *176* Stratheden Psychiatric Hospital,
  Ward 5 Women's Long Stay

- *190* Stratheden Psychiatric Hospital, Playfield House,
  Department of Child and Adolescent Psychiatry,
  1984 July - August

- *199* Stratheden Psychiatric Hospital, Community
  Psychiatric Nursing, 1984 September - November

- *219* Stratheden Psychiatric Hospital, Ward 6
  Psychogeriatrics, November 1984 - January 1985

- *229* Stratheden Psychiatric Hospital, Ward 7 Acute
  Psychiatry/Female, 1985 February

- *236* Stratheden Psychiatric Hospital, Ward 8 Acute
  Psychiatry/Female, 1985 February - April

- *265* Stratheden Psychiatric Hospital, Ward 7 Acute
  Psychiatry/Female, May 1985

- *274* Stratheden Psychiatric Hospital, Sick Unit/Female,
  1985 June - September

- *294* Goodmayes Hospital London, Psychogeriatrics,
  1985 September

- *296* Littlemore Hospital, Oxford, 1985 September

- *305* Stratheden Psychiatric Hospital, Sick Unit/Female,
  1985 October

- *310* Queen Charlotte Rooms, Leith Edinburgh,
  2020 December

- *312* Thorngrove House Sheltered Housing Complex,
  Aberdeen, 2023 February

- *314* (& Cover) Springfield Woods

- *316* Glossary

The Nursing Hierarchy...
Chief Nursing Officer
Matron / Nursing Officer
Sister / Charge Nurse
Staff Nurse / Registered Nurse
Enrolled Nurse
Student Nurse (training for registration)
Pupil Nurse (training for enrolment)
Nursing Assistant

The Medical Hierarchy...
Consultant
Senior Registrar
Registrar
Houseman
Junior Houseman
Medical Student

Urban Explorers

I went back to Stratheden with my husband last winter. We were a bit hungover having been to an art school reunion the night before. It was my husband that went to art school, not me. Anyway, we wandered around the grounds of the old part of the hospital, the bit they don't use any more - the bit that I worked in. I kept thinking that someone would come out and shoo us off, tell us we don't belong here - but nobody seemed to care.

It was snowing, so everything was quiet and still, in that muffled, snowy way. We were taking photos for this book. I stood outside Ward 4 smiling at the camera, looking down the sloping path ahead of me. I remember pushing a body down that path. It was dark - I guess I was on nights. It was snowing then too. They must have been short of porters; nurses wouldn't normally be pushing bodies around. It was hard work keeping that trolley on track and upright in the snow.

I remember the morgue - transferring the patient into a mortuary drawer. I think there might have been some kind of device that allowed us to do that quite easily. We had a smoke after we'd finished - sitting on the white porcelain autopsy table chatting. What did we talk about? The porter must have been twice my age - hospital gossip I suppose - there was never any shortage of that. I remember the cigarettes - Raffles 100s. They were longer than normal cigarettes - better value for money.

Strange how some memories come back so vividly while others seem to scuttle off in fear. I felt kind of sick standing there smiling at the camera, and it wasn't just the hangover. The voices of the men who lived in Ward 4 were snaking their way back into my conscious mind, as if they had been hiding there, suspended in time, quietly waiting to be remembered.

We didn't stay long. It was too cold and we couldn't actually get into the buildings. Back at home, in the comfort of my own living room, I Googled Stratheden and was surprised to find a series of films by a group of people that call themselves *Urban Explorers*. They seem to operate all over the world - finding their way into derelict buildings, taking care not to damage or break anything. They never steal, they make that very clear. They are not thieves - they are explorers.

They are children - these time travelling adventurers. Thrill seekers, wriggling through narrow passages, dank and dusty portals to the past. My past - in this case. Well, a past I played a small part in. Pretty insignificant, my role in the history of Stratheden, in the scheme of things - but far from insignificant to me.

I felt the thrill too, I must confess, watching that first film- seeing the long corridors and high ceilinged rooms with tattered 1970's curtains. There's a surprising amount of clinical debris lying around amongst the rubble and bird droppings: trolleys; hoists; screens; commodes; scales - the kind that you sit on; hydraulic beds and baths. Imagine that! Hydraulic baths!

They are in Women's Long Stay now. I recognize the corridor that leads from the kitchen up to the wards. "These cells are quite nice," an explorer declares. "Maybe it wasn't so bad being an inmate here." They weren't inmates, they were patients! And those weren't cells - they were rooms! And they were not for patients! I want to shout. Those sunny little rooms were offices; for doctors, matrons, sisters and charge nurses. Our patients didn't sleep in rooms. They slept in dormitories; in neat, nightingale style rows with fresh white linen sheets, striped pyjamas or long flowery nightgowns - all hospital issue. Our patients didn't have rooms - unless, perhaps, if they were dying.

Watching the films though, I can see how things moved on after I left; mixed sex wards with snappy, modern names (Tarvitt); partitions between the beds in the dormitories; a sign on a cupboard door that says: *Patients Council tea and coffee.*

Sometimes the Urban Explorers go out filming at night. They have a little machine as well as their camera - an EVP recorder - a ghost detector - for recording electronic voice phenomena. "Speak to us spirits. Use your energy to send us a message." They hold their little machine out hopefully; standing, stock still, in the long, gloomy corridors - young and strong, pale and terrified, listening for voices in empty rooms.

Victoria Hospital
Ward 1 Geriatrics
1982 June - August

Sister Bonnyface sits, legs crossed, arms folded in her dark blue uniform, a froth of blonde curls surrounding her frilly white cap. Only Sisters have frills on their caps, and they have white puffy cuffs on their uniforms too, like little girl's party dresses. She watches attentively as we sprinkle talcum powder over the pink and white marble patterned waterproof mattress that looks like a giant slab of meat. We snap out a starched cotton sheet and cover it all up as if we are making a pie. Sister has our little red books in her hand, our assessment books. Today she is assessing our bed making skills.

We smooth the bottom sheet down and pull it tight - creases cause bedsores and bedsores can be deadly. Then we put on the draw sheet, the top sheet and two pastel coloured cellular blankets that remind me of my little brother's baby blankets, except Mum always sewed a satin trim round the edge of those. "Your hospital corners are beautiful," Sister announces, clasping her hands together. She seems genuinely moved.

Samira and I stand back to admire our handiwork. "It looks like a wedding cake," I say. Sister laughs and gets up. "But not for much longer I'm afraid. Remember the toe tuck." I hadn't forgotten, but it seems such a shame to spoil such smooth perfection. I lean forward and pull the blankets up into a peak at the bottom of the bed, shake everything loose a bit. "And why do we need the toe tuck?" Sister asks. "To prevent foot-drop," Samira says quickly, then looks a little embarrassed. "That's right," says Sister. "You girls are doing grand." She turns and marches towards her office, leaving us to the rest of the beds.

Every new admission has a total immersion bath; not a shower or a bed bath - a big bath. "It's surprising what you learn when you take people's clothes off," Staff Nurse Munsaka says as we lower a pale and trembling old man into warm salted water. "The salt will heal any wounds and rashes." I have never seen old bodies naked before. I have only ever seen babies and children, and a few young men who, like me, are not yet twenty.

I learn that tattoos of anchors look like bruises on old skin, and hearts, broken, or with arrows through the middle, look like dog bites. I learn that elderly women have tattoos too - though not so often. I learn that old men's legs are smooth and bald, and women sometimes have hairy chests, just below their throat, or around the nipples. "Loss of secondary sexual characteristics," Staff Nurse Munsaka explains as she pours a jug of cold water over the old man's erection. He calls out in protest, looks up at me as if I should know better.

It is a mixed ward, men on one side, women on the other, with the bathrooms, sluice and treatment rooms down the middle. There are two single rooms either side of Sister's office for patients who need to be closely monitored - they have windows all around them. We have a married couple coming in today who are deaf and speak only in sign language. Sister tells us to put an extra bed into one of the single rooms. "It's a lonely world for people who are deaf, and they've kept each other company all their lives. Why should they stop now?" She says it loud for the older nurses to hear. They tut and turn away in disapproval. "But what about the hospital corners?" I ask, imagining the difficulties the old couple will have cuddling up. "Just make the beds up as usual and push them together. We can leave the rest to them. You can pull their curtains too. I'm sure they won't want an audience." One of the older nurses flounces off with her arms in the air.

Sister welcomes the deaf couple in as if it is their honeymoon suite. They look pleased and a little abashed. "We will leave you to unpack, then Nurse will come and help you with your baths." She's talking about me. I am filled with a mixture of pride and apprehension. When I go in later to fetch them for their baths they are both naked and the husband is kneeling on the floor trimming his wife's pubic hair.

:♡: :♡: :♡:

The catering staff are on strike. We've been sent twenty salads for the evening meal. The patients who are able to make it to the table at the top of the ward sit there looking furious. "I'M NOT EATING IT!" A frail and shaky old man shouts, throwing his plate across the room. I can't believe it;

he's a retired high court judge - but then, maybe that kind of behaviour is normal for men like him. Memories of Muirfield golf club flit through my mind - The Honourable Society of Edinburgh Golfers; I worked there for a while - my first weekend job. They wouldn't have tolerated salad either: "MORE BUTTER ON THE GENTLEMAN'S CRUMPET!" The bad tempered cook screamed in my ear that first Sunday afternoon shift. "AND REMEMBER YOU MUST ALWAYS APPROACH THE GENTLEMEN FROM THE RIGHT."

"SUPERB!" The crumpet loving gentleman proclaimed, rubbing his hands together as I approached him from the right with my little white apron and heavily laden tray. He leant towards his companion in a way that made me think he was going to make a comment about me or the food I was setting before him. But he was simply continuing their conversation, as if I was deaf or not actually there: "Well old chap, I hate to be the one to tell you, but you've really put your cock in the custard this time."

Anyway, the geriatric judge is not the only one to kick up a stink today. The other patients are swift to follow his example. Crockery is flying. Cutlery is thrown to the floor. There is salad everywhere except on people's plates. Even the jam has travelled at speed across the room and is sliding down the wall like a scene from a horror movie. "Oh dear," says Sister. "Looks like I'm going to have to send you girls to the chippy."

We have chippy food for the next three days - the nurses and

the patients, except Samira, who brings her own food in.
You can have: a fish supper; a chicken supper; a steak pie
supper; a sausage supper; a white pudding supper - or just
chips. We sit around the table at the top of the ward, Sister at
the head and Enrolled Nurse Nieson - Tam, who everyone
says is her favourite, next to her on the right.

When I worked at Muirfield the staff would sit round the
table like this to eat at the end of every shift, Upstairs
Downstairs style, whether we liked it or not - I did not. This
feels different though. I don't mind it at all. "You're a cheap
date," says Tam, because I only eat chips. "I've never met a
vegetarian before," says Sister. "Why don't you try the white
pudding supper? That's not got any meat in it." I am
doubtful, but I can see she's keen for me eat something more
than chips. I stick my fork in the long sausage shaped
pudding and hold it in the air. "Remind you of anything?"
Tam says, with a wink and a cheeky grin, so I bare my teeth
like a dog and bite the top off with a snap. There is a roar of
laughter from around the table. "I can see I'm going to have
to keep my eye on you," says Sister loudly, her light blue eyes
sparkling, her hands clasped in that rapturous way of hers.

Later Samira and I are getting changed in the locker room
and I ask if she wants to go for a drink. "I can't. I have to get
Donald's shirts ironed. I'm way behind with them." - "I can't
believe you are married," I say to her. There were girls from
my school that got married at sixteen - *child brides* my father
calls them. Samira waited until she was eighteen, but she
looks very young - even younger than me. "There's nothing

weird about being married. You're the weird one, with your mad jokes and your funny colour schemes." She sits with her jeans on, her uniform bunched around her waist, buttoning up a white lacy blouse that looks good against her dark skin. I look down at my wine coloured jersey and petrol blue peasant skirt wondering if I've got it all wrong again.

Enrolled Nurse Ketchen - Shirley, never complains about us being slow or forgetting to do things. She never whines about being tired either. She always seems a little bored with life and doesn't go out of her way to be friends with any of the other trained nurses, except Tam, who often stops to hug her in the corridor, maybe because they are both enrolled nurses.

If Shirley hears the older nurses being nasty to Samira and me, telling us to pull our fingers out, or saying we don't know what hard work is, she tells them to shut up and they back off immediately. When she found me crying in the locker room because I had just heard that my mum has been diagnosed with breast cancer she put her arm around me and took me to see Sister.

It's Shirley's job to check the controlled drugs each Sunday. She always picks me to help. I stand next to her, trying to look as if I'm not staring at her. I have a bad habit of staring at people. She looks like Miss Turnstiles in *On the Town*; honey blonde ringlets pulled up in a pert little pony tail; long black eyelashes, looking down intently. She pours the colourful tablets into a tablet counter; a small metal triangle, like a snooker triangle, but with a base. I try to concentrate on what she's doing, but her hands move so fast I can't really keep track of it all. "So that's forty two, 50mg Morphine. Yes?" She writes 42 in the book, tips the tablets from the triangular counter back into the bottle, not even looking to see if I agree, then we move onto the liquids for oral use.

We've been talking as we work, about her cousin, who I've been seeing the last few weeks. I met him in the bar of the hotel that is our nurses' home, since the real nurses' home was burnt down. "He's my favourite cousin," she tells me. "More like a brother really. I'm glad he's met you. You could be just what he needs."

※ ※ ※

His name is Rab and he looks like Roy Harper. He's kind of grumpy, but he likes the same music as me, and he loves reading too. So we have things in common, which matters a lot, as I've not met many people I have things in common with since I came to live in Kirkcaldy - in fact, not any, except for him.

He's quite a bit older than me - in his late twenties. He was a miner for a while, but now he works in the Alcan factory in Burntisland. He's a union man and he sometimes gets a bit angry when we talk about politics. I am learning what subjects to avoid - "What's it like being a miner?" - "Let's talk about something else."

Mostly we talk about books. Like me, he loves Sunset Song, though he hasn't read it quite as many times as I have. We talk about Chris Guthrie as a character. "She's a man's invention," I say decisively - though I've never really thought about her that way before. "She's a man's idea of a woman." I say it more to myself than Rab really, testing this new notion in my head. "What's wrong with that?" He snaps back. He points at my empty glass, shouts over to the barmaid - "Another gin and lime here when you're ready."

He has his own council flat. He was given it after his mum died a few years ago; a swap for the three bedroomed house that he and his sister were raised in. His dad left when his mum was pregnant with his sister - "And good riddance to him." I can see from his expression that I shouldn't ask why.

His flat hasn't got a lot of furniture, but everywhere you look there are plants, including two cannabis plants that he calls Smith and Jones after the TV show. There are black and white photos on the walls that he has taken himself. They are mostly Scottish landscapes, but there's some of his mum and one of his sister, Eileen, looking beautiful and moody, like something really bad is about to happen.

He has lots of records, quite a few that I have, but some classical too. "I have very catholic tastes," he tells me the first time I visit. I nod knowingly. My first boyfriend told me the same thing, so I understand what it means, and that it has nothing to do with monks or religion. "Where's your sister now?" - "Burntisland. With two screaming weans and a total prick for a husband." I frown at his harsh assessment and he seems to soften. "You'd like her. She's a reader too. And she was good at art in school - really good. She could have been something if it hadn't been for him." - "Why didn't you try for university or art school?" I prepare myself for some caustic response, but in fact, he seems pleased that I've asked. He laughs, in a surprised kind of way. "That was never an option. We left school the day we were sixteen, Eileen and me. We had to work; Mum needed the money. Well, we all needed the money. My uncle - Shirley's dad - he arranged a job down the pit for me. I don't think I was even asked. It was just assumed that's what I would do and I went along with it. I didn't really like school anyway - too many teachers eh?" We both laugh then, because I hated school too - something else we have in common.

He tells me about the history of mining, as we sit among the plants, smoking joints, drinking home brewed beer. He tells me about families being threatened with eviction if even one of them tried to leave the pit to better themselves. Children as young as six being lowered down mines in cages in the middle of the night. "It was slavery, and there's plenty still living off the profits." He tells me that when the mines were nationalised back in 1947 the government paid the pit owners compensation. They are still receiving annuities to this day and will do so for many years to come. "And what for?" His top lip curls beneath his beard. "For working people to death and running the pits to ruin."

"We have a patient on Ward 1 who used to be a miner," I tell him. "He was in the Michael Pit when it went on fire in 1967. He was trapped in the Dysart Main Seam. He's got dementia now and he relives it, over and over. He hallucinates the whole thing - begs and screams for us to help. He clutches on to us really hard. Look." I show him the finger shaped bruises on my arms where Mr Fyall clung to me a few days ago, shouting and pointing behind him. "It's as if he thinks we could run into the past and save those men that died down there." Rab looks at me with great concern. Well, he looks kind of angry to be honest, but I think that's how he shows concern. "Poor bastard. Poor fucking bastard." His hand seems to tighten round his glass and for a moment I think he might throw his drink at the wall. But he sets it down carefully on the coffee table, gets up and goes through to the kitchen. He comes back with a bottle of home brew. "Here, give this to your patient. Jesus Christ it sounds like he needs it." The next day I start reading Sunset Song again, fall in love with Chris Guthrie again. Who cares if she's a man's invention.

When we go out we generally go to the pub at the end of his road - three times we've been there. It's huge, with a bright blue carpet and lots of pool tables. Everyone knows everyone else and I don't feel welcome there. His friends are all ages; men and women he has been brought up with - neighbours and cousins, their parents, grandparents, great grandparents. The men are friendly enough, but the women eye me suspiciously. It's not helped by the fact that Rab insists on buying all my drinks, fussing over me, making sure I am comfortable and warm - as if I am some kind of princess. After he has me settled in, he disappears for ages, leaving me sitting on the edge of whichever multi-generational group he has selected. The girls and women look me up and down with disdain - my long skirts, Dad's old jumpers, the luminous green plastic cracker ring that my wee brother gave me last Christmas. I tried to chat to them the first time I was there, but the conversation was flat and pointless. Now I just take my book and read, knowing full well they'll hate me all the more for it.

"It's like I'm actually living in a DH Lawrence book," I grumble as he walks me home. "Lady Chatterley's Lover?" He asks, pulling me close to him. "No - Women in Love." I break free of his hold, laughing and quoting, in a loud dramatic voice - "It's such an inheritance of a universe of dark reality."

~ ~ ~

It's Sunday and I'm checking the controlled drugs with Shirley again. She's telling me that Rab really likes me. He's a bit upset that I haven't been answering his calls the last few days. I squirm as she counts the ampoules of morphine. I enjoy the time I spend with Rab, but I have a vague, uneasy feeling about him, like I'm not seeing something that I maybe should be seeing. Maybe it's just because he's older. I don't know what to say to Shirley so I just say, "Yes." She looks at me a little quizzically, then goes back to counting. "So you're going to ring him then?" - "Yes," I say again. She looks relieved. "Good. He's a sound bloke - honest."

I don't ring him. Sister has arranged some time off for me, so that I can go back to Gullane and see my mum who is out of hospital after finishing five days intensive radiation therapy. As she tells me about the time off she hands me a basket of home baking - fruit scones and a Victoria Sponge. "Mum will need building up," she says. "Dad too most likely. All that worry. Poor man." I start crying and Tam gets up and gives me a cuddle, his cigarette still smoking in the ashtray. "Yer mam'll be fine pet," he says. "Just you go and get yourself on that train." I cry even harder, maybe because I'm scared for my mum or maybe just because Sister and Tam are so kind.

Back home things are much the same as usual. Dad has invited my godfather to stay and Mum is annoyed with him for that, but she's up and dressed and determined to act as normal. They love that Sister Bonnyface has baked for them. They love her name and ask me if she does have a bonny face. "Well, she isn't exactly pretty - but her eyes are so kind and friendly. And she's always smiling. She has lovely rosy cheeks. She kind of glows with goodness. I think that's better then pretty, don't you?" - "Well it certainly sounds it," Mum says, laughing. "Victoria sponge from the Victoria hospital!" Dad says. He takes a big bite - "My God it's almost as good as your mother's!"

When we sit down for dinner later my godfather looks at me

and says - "So - geriatrics, the cleaning of the orifices." Dad laughs, I don't; it doesn't feel right to me - thinking about my patients in that way. I tell them about the salad episode - they laugh a lot at that. "I'm with the auld yins," says my godfather. "Who the hell likes salad for Christ's sake?" He has salad on his plate right now.

Mum doesn't want to talk about the cancer, so I just try to be helpful; hoovering and dusting and polishing, helping with the cooking now and again. I hate helping with the cooking because she stands over me tutting so much that I get all anxious and make a mess of things. It's better just to stick to the housework and taking the dogs out. I smoke when I'm out with the dogs. If my clothes smell of cigarettes I blame my godfather.

Travelling back to Fife on the train, looking out on the cold grey sea, I decide I will speak to Shirley about Rab. I want to know if he really likes me. Maybe if I'm honest with her about how I feel she'll tell me something more about him. I'm disappointed the next day though, because there's no sign of her on the ward, though her shifts usually match mine. I go into the office, knocking quietly first. "Excuse me Sister, where is Shirley today?" - "She's gone," Sister says, looking up from her notes. "You won't be seeing her again. Now, tell me all about Mum. How is she doing?"

Later, when we're washing the admission beds down Samira leans towards me and whispers, "Have you heard about Shirley? Everyone's talking about it. She's been stealing the controlled drugs - selling them on." I stand there staring at Samira in disbelief. Images of Shirley pouring tablets from the pill counter back into the little brown bottles flit through my mind. Was she pouring some up her cardigan sleeve? Surely I would have noticed? Maybe I was too busy looking at her long eyelashes, thinking about old Hollywood movies, or her cousin Rab. Was she writing the wrong numbers in the book - 42 instead of 52, going back to take the extra tablets later? Samira throws a pillow at me - "Wake up Dozy. We've got beds to make."

"Have you girls ever seen a dead body?" I jump. Sister is standing right behind me. I'm still reeling from Samira's news and I feel kind of disorientated. "I know this won't be easy," Sister says. "But it's best to get it over with. Mr Fyall has just passed away and I think you should come and see what's done."

The curtains are closed, Tam and Staff Nurse Munsaka stand on either side of the bed. Nurse Munsaka isn't awfully pleased; she believes that bodies should not be washed for at least four hours after death. She looks rather stern as she tells us this. "I'm afraid we need the bed," Sister says quietly. "I'm sorry for it, because he does look peaceful." She turns to Samira and I. "This is what we mean girls, when we call death a mercy." Tam and Nurse Munsaka wash Mr Fyall's body for the last time, gently and without talking. "Watch carefully," says Sister. "You'll be doing a lot of this."

Victoria Hospital
Ward 2 General Medical
1982 October to December

Sister Bonnyface gave us our daily instructions as we sat drinking tea around the table at the top of the ward. Here, we stand in the office and wait patiently for our orders while Sister Jardine finishes her round with the night staff. Nobody talks. There are seats, but nobody sits on them. Shona, who is a student in the year above me and my new room mate at the hotel, keeps touching her hat. It is stuck to her head with parcel tape because her hair is too short for grips. One of the staff nurses gives it a push and the tape comes unstuck, Shona turns and glares at her.

Sister Jardine comes in and sits at her desk without acknowledging us - a short, slight woman, with permed grey hair and old fashioned wing tip glasses. She starts reading aloud, going through the Kardex, telling us about each patient. She calls out their name, age and diagnosis, even if we know them quite well because they have been with us a while. At the end of each report she says, BIG BATH or BED BATH or SHOWER. We scribble as she talks and beside each name write, big or bed or S. She takes her glasses off, looks up, points at each of us in turn - "YOU, YOU, YOU - bed baths." She points again, "YOU, YOU, YOU, big baths. YOU and YOU, showers." We shuffle out into the ward with our lists.

Shona and I have been put to work with a nurse called Linda

Dunsire. She is only young, probably about twenty one, but she hates students. Usually it's the nursing assistants, the older ones, that hate us, but apparently Linda failed her staff nurse training and got downgraded to enrolled nurse - so she's maybe a bit bitter about that I suppose. "You two work together," Linda commands. "I don't want to be saddled with you. I'll start at that end." She points to the first bay of the women's side of the ward - the easiest side. "Fair enough, since she's working alone," says Shona. "The men are better fun anyway."

We start with Mr Golinski who was admitted last night with a stroke. He is unconscious and has a catheter in. He seems perfectly clean to me, in a fresh, stripey cotton nightshirt, but still we must wash and shave him. He doesn't stir at all. We move on to Mr Dickson, a small, thin man in his early fifties who is smoking a cigarette, using a cardboard sick bowl for an ash tray. "Yer a bit of a fire hazard are ye no?" Shona stands with her hands on her hips. "Have ye no got an ashtray?" - "Dinnae you fire hazard me," Mr Dickson protests. "Ave been told there's to be no more smokin' in this bay - HE'S GOING ON OXYGEN." He points to the man in the opposite bed, Mr Travis, who holds his hands up in a gesture of apology, but says nothing - probably because he's too breathless. "OCH YER ALL RIGHT PAL," Mr Dickson shouts over. "Poor old bugger," he says, under his breath to Shona. "OLD! He's younger than you!" Shona wags her finger. "You're the old bugger." - "Not too old to put you over my knee ye cheeky wee rascal," Mr Dickson laughs. "I'd like 'tae see ye try," Shona says, brandishing a warm soapy flannel. He makes a grab for her, but is stopped by a fit of coughing. Shona leans him forward, rubs his back gently, holding the cardboard dish under his chin. "Aye yer probably right love," he says when the coughing stops. He leans back into his pillows, his face grey and hollow looking, "I think ma spanking days are over." He is quiet as we wash him down, closes his eyes, as most of our patients do, while we sponge his lower body.

Our next patient is a new admission; a GP who has suffered a small heart attack - a myocardial infarction - after breaking his leg. He's in a side room. Usually it's only people who are dying that get put in the side rooms - to give them and their relatives some privacy. There are only four on each ward; two on the women's side and two on the men's. The GP isn't dying though - he's in a side room because he's a private patient. When we go in Sister is there, and the consultant, and Dr Chowdhury, the registrar. They are chatting and laughing as if they are at a cocktail party. The GP doesn't seem very ill at all. He is pink and healthy looking - quite a good looking man, in a smooth, well groomed way that doesn't appeal to me. He is young to have had a heart attack though, only in his early forties, and his leg is in traction - so he needs to be bed bathed. Sister and the doctors leave to let us get on with our work.

Shona disappears into the adjoining bathroom to fill our basin with warm water. The GP smiles and lies back, staring at me. His hand slithers down the bed and he pushes the blankets away so that I can see his penis. I pull the blankets back over him. "We'll wash your face and shoulders first." He gives an unpleasant little laugh. Shona comes back in and together we pull the doctor forward in the bed to lay a towel over his pillows. We are quiet as we work, washing his lower body quickly with no chatter at all. When we leave Shona says, "Did he flash his bits at you?" I nod, feel my face flush with embarrassment. "I thought so. Dirty old git. Bloody private an' all. We shouldn't even have to work with him if you ask me. It's not like we'll get paid any extra, like his bloody consultant does. And him taking up a single room when he doesn't need it. Bloody disgusting."

I'm working with Linda Dunsire today - just me and her. She's in a terrible mood, scowling and avoiding eye contact, only speaking to me when absolutely necessary. A new patient is being admitted as an emergency. She is wheeled in at great speed by two doctors and Staff Nurse Mayes, who is the best staff nurse on the ward and everyone's favourite. Sister stands waiting for them at the ward entrance.

As they wheel the new patient into a side room Sister calls out to me to get the defibrillator trolley and bring it in right away. I run for the trolley and wheel it up there as fast as I can, knock on the door and wait. Nurse Mayes pulls the door open. Her patient's screams ring out into the ward. I push the trolley towards her and she spins it into the room. Her face is flushed, her eyes big and bright - it's like she's high on something. "THANK YOU SWEETHEART," she shouts. I turn to go but she catches me by the arm. "We're going to have to leave the ward to you students and Nurse Dunsire this morning okay? Don't bother answering the phone. If there's any problem with the other patients just come and get me - but knock first please, like you did before. Okay darling?" - "She looks young," I hear myself say. "She is," says Nurse Mayes, standing in front of the now closed side room door. "And she's got three little kids. I don't know if there's anything we can do for her, but…"

Nurse Mayes is never usually so nice to me. Until today she seems to have viewed me with a good deal of suspicion. I'm really quite scared of her - much more so than I am of Linda Dunsire. This new, friendly attitude is kind of reassuring and I feel more confident than usual as I walk back towards the main ward to continue with the bed baths.

We do our round quietly. The whole ward is quiet. We start with the GP in the side room first, hoping he will be too sleepy to expose himself. "He's a dirty pig," says Linda, as we walk towards his room. For once I agree with her. We wash him quickly with lots of towels to keep him covered. Even so, he manages to manoeuvre himself so that his penis is always exposed. At one point it touches the back of my hand and rises into an erection. I look at Linda and see her grimace of discomfort. I motion to the jug of cold water on his locker but she shakes her head. As we leave she says, "It's not a trick I'd use with a private patient. He might report us and we could get into real trouble."

After the men we move on to the women's bays. Our first patient is a sixty five year old lady who is recovering from a right sided stroke. Her white hair is all curly and bouncy and she has a very fresh complexion. She looks like a picture book granny. "You're far too fat," says Linda. "If you weren't so fat you might not have had a stroke and we wouldn't be struggling to get you on this bed pan." The woman's face turns crimson. Tears spring to her eyes. I squeeze her shoulder, "You're okay. You're on now. I'll keep hold of you so you don't fall off."

The phone is ringing and ringing. "Nurse Mayes said just to ignore it," I say to Linda. I thought she might be a bit friendlier since our experience with the GP, but she glares at me and struts off towards the office. Our patient starts weeping. "It's all so awful," she says, teetering on the bedpan. It takes all my strength to keep her steady. "That poor woman they've brought in. And me needing help with the toilet like this. I feel like such a nuisance. It's so humiliating. Then that one being so nasty. She's cruel - that's what she is. Does she not think I've tried to keep slim? I do try Nurse. Honestly. I do." - "Well I don't think you're too fat," I say. "I think you look lovely." She smiles down at me, tears still flowing. "You're a nice wee thing. You'll be a fine nurse. Not like that other one."

I could tell her that - although I don't like Linda, I do feel a bit sorry for her. I could tell her about the terrible snobbery between enrolled nurses, who do two years training, and registered nurses, who do three years. It seems to me that good nursing and bad nursing has nothing to do with whether you are enrolled or registered. The whole thing is a nonsense. You can be a really good enrolled nurse with twenty years experience and get paid less than a registered nurse with a couple of years experience. I could say that Linda is angry because she wants to be the one in that side room saving the woman who is too young to die and has three children to raise. That's what she did her training for - and if there were no registered nurses available she would be expected to do it, but she wouldn't get paid any extra, and the next day she would be back with me on big baths and bed baths.

I don't say any of those things; usually when I say things like that people look at me a bit strangely - as if I'm not understanding something really obvious. Rab would have been interested - if I'd still been seeing him. That's the kind of conversation he enjoys, being a union man. He would have put me right if I was being stupid - but I haven't heard from Rab since Shirley disappeared. I did try to phone him a few times; there was no answer. I miss him a bit; it would be quite nice to see him again - and I want to know about Shirley.

I don't even know if Samira's story is true - not that she would lie - but it could just be gossip. I can't believe Shirley is a criminal - a drug dealer, who might end up in prison - may well be in prison now. Miss Turnstyles - a drug dealer! The idea of it seems totally ridiculous. There's been nothing in the local newspapers about it. Samira's husband would know - he's a policeman, maybe she would ask him for me. I could just go to Rab's flat and knock on the door. I don't know though - something is telling me not to do either of those things.

Linda has disappeared. I carry on with the bed baths on my own. It was obvious that she would rather be in the side room with Nurse Mayes and Sister and the doctors. I could tell by the way she kept staring at the door; as if she would eventually see right through it. I can't say that I have any desire to be in there, and that is making me wonder if nursing is the right job for me. It's easy enough right now mind you, working alone, without Linda or Shona; washing and drying people, making them comfortable, filling up their water jugs and chatting to them about their lives at home. I love talking to patients when it's just me and them. This is exactly how I thought nursing would be.

Ever since I was a child reading Doctor David and Sister Susan in the *Twinkle* I've imagined myself in this role. My teddies and dolls always had a long list of ailments for me to remedy - through love and bed rest and a good quantity of bossiness. Whenever a grown up asked me what I wanted to do I would say, "I'm going to be a nurse." My parents used to laugh. "She's very consistent," my father always said. I had a sense of being mocked - but no amount of mocking was going to change my mind. I wanted to be kind and helpful - to make sick people better. I never imagined not being able to make them better.

Nurse Mayes comes into the sluice, shuts the door and leans against it. "Could you spare a fag?" I've never seen her smoke before. "I don't usually," she says. She bows her head and starts crying. "We lost her. I knew we would, but…" I give her a cigarette and we stand in silence puffing. "Better not let Sister see I've been crying," she says, throwing her half smoked fag into the sluice. She washes her hands and splashes cold water onto her face, dries it with a paper towel, then turns and smiles, "Thanks honey. You've done well today."

Wandering back to the hotel at the end of my shift I feel comforted by her kindness, proud to be the recipient of it. *You've done well today* - the words ring in my ears. I didn't do anything really, but her praise is like medicine - and of course I want to be a nurse. I want to be just like her.

I am shaving Mr Golinski when he opens his eyes. It's the first time I've seen him awake. He is Polish and I'm not sure how good his English is. He glares at me and says, "McVitie's Jamaican Ginger cake." I stand back, holding the soapy razor in the air. "Do you want some?" - "Yes." He looks a little irritated. "I'm sorry, I can only give you porridge or scrambled egg." He closes his eyes like he's going to sleep again. I finish shaving him then tidy up and leave to fetch some porridge.

While I am in the kitchen a new admission arrives. I hear

him roaring in German. I don't know what he's saying, but it sounds like swear words. I come out into the ward and see Linda and Dr Chowdhury trying to calm him down. He grabs Dr Chowdhury by the tie and starts winding it round his fist. Sister comes out of her office and stands staring. "MR WOLF! I MUST ASK YOU TO BEHAVE YOURSELF!" I look at Linda and she smiles. She is trying not to laugh.

"I WILL NOT TOLERATE THIS KIND OF BEHAVIOUR ON MY WARD," Sister barks. Mr Wolf sits up and rubs his hands together. "AH SISTER!" He has a definite twinkle in his eye - "COME, COME…" He pats the bed for the tiny Sister to come and sit by him. He is quite a distinguished looking man, in his late fifties, a bit overweight - but he looks strong despite his illness. Dr Chowdhury is looking very relieved to be free of his grip. "Nurse Dunsire, go and fetch Mr Wolf some coffee - NO SUGAR." Sister commands as she pulls the curtains closed.

The ward goes quiet as Sister does Mr Wolf's admission. Linda takes his coffee in then comes over to help me with Mr Golinski. As she is walking over we hear another roar - "DIESER KAFFEE SCHMECKT WIE PISSE!" Linda pulls the curtains round us quickly and we sit on Mr Golinski's bed laughing into our cupped hands. Mr Golinski is still feigning sleep, but every now and again I see one of his eyes opening. A head pops through the curtains, it's Staff Nurse Mayes. "Hello Hello, has anyone got the time, or shall I go and ask Mr Wolf?" She comes in and looks at Mr Golinski and says, "He's awake!" I don't know how she knows that, because his eyes are still closed. Mr Golinski must wonder too because he opens both eyes and stares at her, he doesn't look very pleased.

"What's wrong with Mr Wolf?" I ask Nurse Mayes later, while we are doing the weekly check of controlled drugs. She carefully records the number of tablets we counted then puts her hands on her hips like she means business. "He had open heart surgery eight weeks ago and has been drinking ever since he was discharged. Smoking too. Just not following any of the rules. It's a miracle he has survived. God knows what damage he's done. We're going to have to keep a very close eye on him." - "Well that'll be fun." - "Quite - though he seems to have taken a shine to Sister Jardine. So perhaps we have a fighting chance."

A young woman has been admitted who is the same age as me. She has Type I Diabetes, but she doesn't follow her diabetic diet. She goes out drinking and eats whatever she feels like, then doesn't take any insulin. She was brought in after being found lying behind someone's sofa. They'd had a party the night before. They didn't even know who she was. She doesn't look like she eats much of anything. Her breath smells strongly of alcohol. "Why does her breath smell of alcohol?" Nurse Mayes asks me in the office later. "Hyperglycemia," I respond, quick as a flash. "Correct," she says. "Plus, she's drunk."

She won't speak to me at all, the new patient. I am disappointed because I am curious about her. She completely ignores me when I ask her if she would like a drink of water. She has vomit all down her neck and chest. I try to help her clean up, but she fights me off. Linda tries too, but it's no good. She ignores our questions as if we are invisible and hits out if we go too near. I put a bowl of warm soapy water on her locker and she sends it flying. Nurse Mayes manages to wash her and settle her down. "As soon as we get her sorted out she'll discharge herself, Nurse Mayes says with a sigh, as we carry the basin and towels through to the sluice. "She does it every time." - "But why?" I ask. Nurse Mayes shrugs, "Who knows. She won't tell us anything. Seems like she doesn't much want to live though."

I go to Mr Golinski next, I've left him until last to give me plenty of time. I don't care if I miss my break for him. I make his porridge exactly as he likes it and use a small spoon because I know he won't take much; five small spoons feel better than two large.

Mr Wolf has been moved to a side room. He's been yelling and shouting all night, keeping the other patients awake. I'm on big baths and he's last on my list. I'm working on my own today. I go into his room. He isn't in bed. He's in the bathroom, but he isn't using the toilet - he is crawling around on the floor. He looks up at me in alarm as I enter, then ducks as if there's something flying around his head.

He's talking in German, so I don't know what he's trying to tell me. He puts his finger to his mouth and says, "Shhhh!" - "You have to have a bath," I whisper, bending down so he can hear me. He looks at me in disbelief. I start running the bath, gesturing for him to undress - but he's too busy dodging his invisible enemy.

He rushes forwards and grabs a towel from the pile on the window sill, throws it into the bath, then dives back down onto the ground and starts slithering along the floor. He climbs up into the bed and cowers beneath the blankets. He points at the curtains, making a sign like he wants me to close them, though it's a beautiful blue sky day and nobody can see him, given we are four floors up. He seems absolutely terrified so I quickly close the curtains. He jabbers away in German, still swiping his arms from time to time.

I go into the bathroom and pull the plug out. Sister comes in as I am wringing out the towel. She stands staring at Mr Wolf, tries to approach him, but he starts shouting wildly. I walk towards her, "Mr Wolf seems a bit confused today. I think he might be hallucinating." - "Has he had his bath?" - "Yes." She leaves without saying anything more and I don't really know what to do. Mr Wolf is still hiding under the blankets so I stay with him a while, wiping his locker, tidying things away. After a bit I hear him snoring. I fold the blankets down under his chin and tuck him up like a baby, then I leave to get Mr Golinski's breakfast.

Mr Golinski refuses to eat. I try to persuade him with

scrambled egg but he closes his mouth tight. He doesn't take one single spoonful. Later at lunch I ask Nurse Mayes what is wrong with him. "He's probably depressed," she says. "It happens after a stroke sometimes." - "And what about Mr Wolf?" - "Oh he's in the DT's," she says. "Delirium Tremens - alcohol withdrawal. We didn't realise how much he'd been drinking. He'll be all right. We've given him some Diazepam. Don't worry. He'll be fine."

Our GP patient is very constipated despite large quantities of laxatives and two regular enemas. Sister has prescribed a high treacle enema. The junior doctors laugh when they see the prescription but the consultant treats the decision with his usual gravity. "This is an unusual option. Not a course of action we would normally advise. But Sister Jardine has been around long enough. She knows her stuff. We must bow to her wisdom."

Sister shows us how to prepare the enema, warming it gently on the small kitchen stove, using a thermometer to ensure that it doesn't get too hot. We take it down to our patient's room. I am told to stand and hold a long tube, with a wide funnel attached to it, up high above my head. Sister stands on a chair and pours the sugary mixture into the funnel slowly and steadily. The tube falls down below the level of the bed then back up and into the doctor's anus. "This'll sort him out," Sister says loudly. "This'll do the trick." Shona and Linda have rolled the doctor on to his side, as far as his traction will allow. His head is bowed and he shudders a little every time Sister speaks. Nurse Mayes holds Sister's chair steady. I smile at her and she gives me a wink. After we've tidied up the enema paraphernalia Sister sends me on my break so I don't even have to deal with the results, which I've been told were quite spectacular.

Mr Golinski is still refusing to eat. Sister tells me to try him with some ginger cake, which is definitely his favourite thing. I brought it in the first time but Sister seems to buy it now - there's always some in the office anyway. He hardly takes any today though, despite my pleading.

The other students tease me about Mr Golinski, because I said he was a handsome man - which is true, even if he is in his sixties. He's not so handsome now mind you - being so thin. Some of the nurses don't like foreign patients; they say that they come over here when they are ill - to get free NHS care. They say that about Mr Wolf, but they can hardly say that about Mr Golinski; he's been here since the Second World War.

I like his Polish accent, his pale, winter sky eyes, and the way he speaks - so stern and formal. I like that he asks me for such particular things; his Marks and Spencers suit; his silver pocket watch; a packet of Melrose tea. I imagine the watch ticking in the silence of his home, his black suit hanging on the back of a door, grey dust settling on the shoulders. Nobody has visited him and nobody has phoned to ask how he is.

There is a woman dying of cancer in one of the female side rooms. She is forty seven years old - the same age as my mum. Nurse Mayes looks after her mostly, but today, because I'm on bed baths she has asked me to go in and help. Our patient can't speak. Every time she opens her mouth black, foul smelling stuff comes out. I am cleaning her up, wiping her throat and chest. I think I'm going to be sick. Dr Chowdhury and Nurse Mayes are muttering over her medicine chart. Perhaps I've made a noise - Dr Chowdhury and Nurse Mayes look up at me suddenly. Our patient is looking at me too, with huge pitiful eyes. I run out of the room, still holding her sick bowl, and head for the sluice.

I empty the sick bowl then vomit into the sluice myself, stand over the water shaking, crying. Dr Chowdhury comes in and offers me a cigarette, lights one up for himself. "How do you do it?" I ask, after blowing my nose and wiping my face. He stands, leaning against the warm door of the bedpan washer, stroking the ends of his neat black moustache, then smiles kindly. "It's not your tragedy," he says. "It's hers. And she doesn't need you to take part in it. You must stand on the outside and observe. Don't intrude on her grief. Distance yourself. Observe, and consider what you can do to ease her suffering. You are not the one who is suffering. You are not ill, or in pain, or dying. You can be strong. That is your job. That is what she needs you to do."

We go back into the room. Sister has joined Nurse Mayes. They are leaning on the window sill, still looking at the medicine chart. Nurse Mayes looks up and clears her throat - "Sister and I think that it's time for more morphine." Dr Chowdhury stares at her for a few moments then nods. Sister draws up the injection and hands it to the doctor. Nurse Mayes holds our patient's hand and we stand in silence observing as the pain slips from her eyes at last.

Shona and I have been on a late shift. The ward is full and lots of nurses are off with flu. We worked right through without a break and can't be bothered getting changed to go home; we still have our uniforms on under our coats. I'm wearing my white moccasin shoes but Shona has put on her stilettos. "I wouldn't be seen dead in them outdoors," she says, throwing her smelly moccasins to the back of her locker. I never had smelly feet before, but nurses shoes always stink.

We stop at the chippy on the way home. I ask for chips. Shona asks for a sausage supper. We lean against the big glass fryer watching our food sizzling in the fat. I feel myself turning pink with the heat. I have a big scarf on, and a cosy knitted hat. Shona is still wearing her nurses cap. "Ocht I'll leave it on," she says. "I cannae be bothered carrying it."

Shona is the same height as me in her high heels. She looks pale in the bright light. I wonder if her head gets cold with her hair being so short - it stands up around her cap in little blonde spikes. She turns to me and makes a funny face, wiggling her heavy, dark eyebrows in the direction of the stainless steel counter. I look down and see a newspaper open at page three. I know a girl from home who is a page three model. She's a bit of a celebrity in our village. I used to work with her when I was a waitress. She is younger than me by two years, very shy and timid. "What's the time?" she asked me once and I nodded at the clock. "Could you tell me the time?" Her dark cheeks reddened prettily as she stood waiting for me to understand her problem. I'm glad it isn't her breasts lying there on the counter waiting to get wrapped round my chips.

We had planned to eat our food at Shona's granny and grandpa's house, which is on our way back to the hotel, but we are too hungry so we ask for the pokes to be left open; we will eat as we walk. The newspaper packages feel heavy and warm in our hands. I love the smell of the fat soaked inky paper. Shona takes her sausage out and holds it high with two fingers, chewing it from the bottom up. She looks kind of funny. I want to laugh at her, but I'm too tired and busy eating my chips. A man appears before us in a coat not dissimilar to our black woollen nurses' coats. He stands right in front of us with his hands in his pockets - then his coat is open and his penis is out and fully erect. It looks big and strangely golden because the orange light of a lamp post is shining on it.

Shona screams and I jump. She starts shaking her sausage at

him, shouting - "I'M TRYING TAE EAT MA SAUSAGE SUPPER." The sausage slips from her fingers and falls onto the pavement. Shona looks furious. She bends down and I think she's going to pick the sausage up. Maybe the flasher thinks that too, because he's stepped back and is looking a bit surprised. But she leaves the sausage lying and takes off one of her shoes, then runs at him with the high heel pointed at his head. The flasher takes off and I stand watching as Shona hirples down the street after him, her chips in one hand, her shoe in the other other screaming - "I'LL GET YE, YE FILTHY BUGGER. I'LL GET YE."

I can't eat any more chips because I am laughing so much I'm crying and my face and tummy muscles hurt. Shona puts her shoe back on and tries to eat some of hers, but it seems she's lost her appetite too. We stop in at her grandparents anyway. She tells them all about the flasher in a high, indignant voice. Her grandpa is furious. He paces up and down saying, "The filthy bugger," just like his grand daughter had done only ten minutes earlier, then he wants to phone the police.

"Och just forget it Grandpa," Shona shouts, as we stand in the kitchen washing the newspaper ink from our hands. "What are the police going to do anyway? Bloody nothing. Same as usual." - "She's right," says her granny, taking the phone from her husband's hand. "They'll take all night getting a statement then they'll do nothing. Just forget it." Her grandpa isn't pleased but he reluctantly agrees. "Shame about your sausage though eh?" I say to Shona. She starts laughing - sets me off again. Her grandpa puts his head in his hands.

Her granny makes a pot of tea and we sit on the big comfy sofa eating snowballs, the Tunnocks kind with coconut and sweet sticky cream, then her grandpa makes us the alcoholic kind. We have a couple of them and I get Shona to re-enact the chasing of the flasher, brandishing her white stiletto in the air, shouting: "I'm just trying tae eat ma sausage supper." She does it really well - so like the real thing that, in the end, even her grandpa laughs.

◯ ◯ ◯

Mrs Meston is being brought up from Accident and Emergency at the same time as I arrive on the ward for night duty. Andy, the porter is very friendly and familiar with her. "She's had a rough ride today," he says loudly. "Haven't you Nellie?" Mrs Meston smiles up at him, takes hold of his hand, looking dreamy. "She's been in a lot of pain," Andy says, as we transfer her from trolley to bed. "But she's had some Diamorph and that's settled her - hasn't it Nellie? You're a wee bit better now eh?" Her eyes are locked on him as if he's her only reference point. Andy takes both her hands in his - "I'm going to leave you with this lovely lass then Nellie." He gives me her hand, rests his own on my shoulders, stands behind me looking at our patient. "She's a nice lassie. You'll be fine with her." Nellie has hold of my hand now and she doesn't seem to want to let go. Staff Nurse Gowans, who I'll be working with overnight, comes across and says, "You just go ahead with her admission. I'll get the handover report."

I ask her to confirm her name, address, date of birth - then do her observations; blood pressure, pulse, respiration, temperature. I write my recordings in her chart. Everything seems okay, though I thought the morphine might have brought things lower. "How are you feeling Nellie?" - "Cold," she says, with a theatrical shiver. I go off to fetch another blanket, popping into the office on the way to the linen cupboard, to tell Nurse Gowans that the obs are fine. "Good," she says. "I was thinking it might be a good idea for you to do your case study on this lady - since you've met her right from the start? You'll need to ask her permission - get her to sign your wee book."

I go back to Nellie with the blanket and my little blue assessment book, ask her if she will agree to be my case study. "Me? Really? I'd love that." - "I'll change your name," I tell her. "Nobody will know it's you." - "Och you don't have to do that," she says, looking a bit disappointed. I prop her up with pillows so she can sign my book. "Have you got a good pen? I want it to look nice." She signs in large, shoogly letters that slope to the right. Her name is barely legible but she underlines it and adds a shaky curl at the end. She seems pleased with the result.

I leave her to rest, go back to the main ward to help Nurse Gowans with the nine o'clock medicine round. "She has a peptic ulcer," Nurse Gowans tells me. "My husband has one -

bloody agony. She seems quite settled now though. We'll change her to thirty minute obs, until eleven, then decrease to hourly - let her get some sleep."

Nellie settles in well. She seems to like being here. "I'm a widow," she tells me, as I stand taking her pulse once more. "The kids are all up and gone their own different ways. I get awful lonely. Will you put that in your case study?" - "Yes - why not?" We have a wee laugh. I sit on her bed since Sister isn't around and Nurse Gowans isn't the kind of staff nurse that minds these things. She tells me about her children; where they live and what they do. I notice her face becoming paler, lean forward to ask if she is okay. She vomits all over me - bright red, bloody vomit. "Oh," she groans. "Oh hen. I'm sorry." Then she does it again. I am covered in blood. I run for Nurse Gowans and some towels and a basin. Nurse Gowans jumps when she sees me. "My God you look like something from The Exorcist. Go and get washed and changed. I'll see to Nellie."

I shower and change at top speed and am back in the ward within ten minutes. Nellie is lying on her side now, in fresh white linen and new blankets. She takes my hand. "I'm sorry," she says, then does it again – vomits, right down my front. Nurse Gowans comes in through the curtain and looks at me in disbelief. This time I have to run down to the laundry for a clean uniform. "What happened?" The laundry lady looks me up and down. "Peptic ulcer - perforated - I think." She winces and shakes her head in sympathy with my patient. "We're awful short of uniforms. I've got one more in your size then it's fourteen's and up - and I've only a few of them." She hands me the pristine white tunic, still warm from being pressed. She seems a bit reluctant to let go of it. "Please try and keep it clean," she says - like my mum when I was little, going out in my second set of clothes that day. When I get back to the ward there are two doctors and a medical student round Nellie's bed. Amazingly she's still conscious. I take her hand and she looks at me - all nice and clean again. "Don't speak!" I tell her, standing as far from her as I can while still holding her hand. She smiles weakly.

Andy comes up and we wheel her down to theatre. On the way she vomits over me again. It comes out of her like a fountain. I never knew anyone had so much blood. While we are waiting for the surgeon the doctors give her a transfusion. There are bags of blood and tubes going into almost every vein in her body: her arms; her neck; her ankles. "I need to get another uniform," I shout, knowing I must look a ghastly sight. "Go in there and put some scrubs on," says the Consultant. "Nurse Gowans has asked if you can come into theatre. I understand this woman is your case study?" A medical student leads me through to the locker room and sorts me out with a set of scrubs. "Just copy me," she says, turning the tap on with her elbows to wash her hands.

I don't have to do anything at all after that - just keep quiet and watch as the surgeon cuts through Nellie's soft white belly and starts to operate. There are lots of little bubbles just below the surface of her skin. "That's fat," the surgeon says to me, as if he's giving me some kind of warning. No-one except him and the anaesthetist talk. It feels very calm and peaceful after the mayhem of the vomiting and the blood transfusion. The surgeon points a few more things out to me. I nod and try to look like I'm feeling absolutely fine with the situation and don't just want it all to be over as soon as possible. He lifts what seems to be half of Nellie's insides out of her body and places them carefully on a green sterile cloth right next to the gaping wound. Peering into the cavity of her half empty belly he locates the source of bleeding. "My God it's huge. I've never seen anything like it!" It doesn't look so huge to me; a tiny hole, about the size of a five pence coin. I can't believe it's caused all that bleeding - that such an insignificant looking thing could actually kill someone.

It feels like I've been in theatre for hours, but it can't have been that long because people are still coming off their breaks when Andy and I wheel Nellie back to the ward. Nurse Gowans tells me I should go for my break - have something to eat. I look at her in horror. "Can't I just go to the sluice for a fag?" She laughs and nods, gently pushes me in that direction.

My hands shake so much I can barely light my cigarette. I'm still not convinced that Nellie will survive. I'm trying not to cry, telling myself that this is not my tragedy - I must stand on the outside and observe; I am not ill; I must be the strong one. I light a second cigarette, praying silently that Nellie will be okay, though I don't believe in God at all. When I come out of the sluice Staff Nurse Gowans has made coffee and toast and banana. The nurses from the male end come up and we all sit together eating. Everyone wants to know about the operation. Everyone is telling me what a great case study it's going to be.

When all the work is done I wander over and stand at the window looking across the sea to Gullane - my parents and my little brother are over there, tucked up in their cosy beds. I give them a little wave. The Nairns linoleum factory siren goes off. I watch the hunched Lowry like figures of the morning shift shuffle reluctantly through the gates to start their day of labour. They look cold and underdressed. I fold my arms round myself and shiver. I hadn't noticed I was cold until now. Nurse Gowans comes over. She thinks I'm looking at the old nurses home. "I remember the night of the fire," she says. "It was terrible, seeing those girls throwing themselves out the windows and nothing we could do - just standing here watching." I imagine the fire - the heat of it. I know some girls who were in it; one who was in a coma for ten months after jumping. I'm glad it happened before my time.

The day shift nurses come drifting in. Sister Jardine asks me to come into the office and tell them all about the operation. I'm still wearing scrubs because of the shortage of uniforms. I can sense the envy of the other students as I tell my tale, but I don't feel proud, and I know for sure that I don't want to work in theatre. Maybe my parent's were right - they wanted me to go to art school like my older brother. I think they hoped I would grow out of the nursing idea. It's hard to think about that; I feel so tired. I feel cold and hollow and empty - like somebody lifted my guts out of my body and forgot to put them back in again.

I arrive early and go to Nellie's bed as soon as I get in. She's in a side room now, sitting up, tired and pale, but she waves and smiles. "Oh my God Nellie. I can't believe you survived." She laughs. "Oh hen I'm sorry. What a night for you." - "What a night for both of us! Just because I asked you to be my case study - you didn't have to go all accident and emergency on me." She smiles and shakes her head - "I'm looking forward to seeing this case study. I can't wait to read all about me."

It's a quiet night so Nurse Gowan lets me sit in the office and do my college work. Nellie's awake by six am. I make her some tea and toast and sit by her bed reading. "Is that what happened?" she says. "I just remember being sick all over you. After that it's just a blur." - "You were sick on me five times Nellie." - "Oh for God's sake! I'm awful sorry about that. But I like your story. I'm not sure what it all means but it sounds very impressive - all that Latin and things. Is there any chance I could keep it? I think it might help me - knowing what happened." - "I could write it up for you Nellie, but I'll have to ask Sister first."

I go home and re-write Nellie's tale in my best writing, add a few explanatory notes and take it in that night. I don't ask Sister. I don't ask Staff Nurse Gowans either; I just give it to

Nellie - it's her story after all.

He comes in about midnight screaming and yelling. He is only in his thirties but looks much older - very emaciated. His long black hair is thin and straggly, though his beard is fairly thick. He is dying but he doesn't want morphine. "I WANT TO SAY GOODBYE TO MY WIFE AND I WANT TO BE RATIONAL." He roars and shouts all through the night, calling for his wife over and over - "NADIA. NADIA. NADIA." His wife doesn't come.

Dr Chowdhury tries to persuade him to take the morphine, or Diazepam at least, but he fights like a wild animal every time we approach him. I sit with him throughout my shift. He is still trying to shout when Sister Jardine comes in in the morning. His voice is raw and hoarse. Sister stands staring at him, with her frilly white cap and her big black cape with the red lining. He stares back, his eyes full of hostility. She leaves and returns five minutes later with Dr Chowdhury and a syringe on a tray. "You can go now," she says to me.

Walking back to the hotel I smoke five cigarettes in a row, then feel sick and ashamed. I put the rest of the pack in the bin and walk away, then I go back and fish them out again. When I get in I put on my pyjamas, boil an egg in the kettle. I haven't any bread. I never bother with it because we aren't allowed toasters. I have another cigarette then get into bed. The curtains aren't very thick. The sun shines right through them, bathing the room in a warm, dappled gold. I bury my head beneath the duvet, manage a few hours sleep on and off. I can hear people's voices in the street, or maybe it's the hotel bar. I keep thinking I can hear someone saying the name Nadia. I suppose I must be dreaming.

When I get back to the ward that night he is dead.

Mr Wolf is being discharged so he can go home for Christmas. It's funny to see him dressed. His clothes hang off him but his eyes are bright and he's lost that florid, heavy drinker's complexion; he looks ten years younger than he did when he came in. His daughter has come over from Germany to collect him. She is plump and blonde, tall like her father. She seems quite cheerful when she talks to us, but keeps shouting and wagging her finger at him. They are slowly interpreting the leaflet that Sister gave him with all the rules for people recovering from heart surgery. It's the same leaflet my dad got after he had heart surgery a few years ago. I remember the rules - no alcohol, no smoking, no intercourse.

When they get to that last bit Mr Wolf throws his arms up in rage and rips the leaflet in two "QUATSCH!" he shouts. Sister comes marching down the corridor to see what's going on. She picks up the torn leaflet and joins in with the daughter, wagging her finger at Mr Wolf. He moves towards the door as if to leave. Sister steps in his way to stop him, feet apart hands on hips, standing her ground - her patient towering above her. "MR WOLF I DO NOT WANT TO SEE YOU IN MY WARD AGAIN!" She turns to me - "GO AND GET MR WOLF ANOTHER LEAFLET. NOW."

When I get back he is asking Sister if she will go to Germany with him. "I will do everything you tell me," he says. "I will be your most most obedient and humble man. You will be treated like the English royalty. You will be the most royal of all. Every day will be Christmas for you." I have never seen Sister laugh before, but she is laughing now. She extends her hand for him to shake. He turns it in his and kisses it, then pulls her up into to his arms for a hug. "MR WOLF. REALLY!" Sister shouts, straightening her hat, laughing heartily. The other nurses come over to join us, the doctors too; everyone happy and tearful at the same time. It feels good to be waving him off, though we will all miss him.

It's Saturday night and everyone on our floor of the hotel who is not working is going to Jackie O's. I don't really like the idea of a nightclub, but Shona has persuaded me to go. We have been out shopping. I bought some new clothes - the kind of things you could wear to a club. I bought a turquoise jumpsuit which I have on now. Shona wanted me to buy high heels but I put my foot down at that. "But ye'll look like a garage mechanic if ye wear these boots." She looks a bit annoyed. I stand firm. No-one is ever going to persuade me to wear high heels.

Linda Dunsire is coming with us. I have become quite friendly with her since the Mr Wolf incident and Shona is not the kind of person to bear grudges, though she does have a bit of a go at her while we sit at the dresser putting on our make up. "You can be a right bitch sometimes," she says. Linda puts her head in her hands despondently. "It's true," I add. "I can't believe you told that poor old lady she was fat." Linda looks at me and says, "I felt terrible about that. That's why I went to the office. I just sat in there crying." - "You should have come and said sorry," I tell her. "It would have made all the difference - the poor old thing was really upset." - "God," says Linda. "I've got to get a grip haven't I?" - "Aye ye do," says Shona. "If yer gonna pal about wi' us. We don't want you scaring the men off." We all laugh and the subject is closed.

Linda looks around our hotel room. She says it's pretty much like the nurses home rooms. "Except we have to share a bathroom with a stripper," I say. "I'll bet you guys didn't have to do that?" - "Aye," says Shona, "I had a sequin stuck to my arse when I got out the bath this morning."

Linda was living in the nurses home when it went on fire, but she wasn't in it at the time. She tells us about the girl that jumped and died. "Why did they have to jump?" I ask. "Why could they not use the fire escape?" - "They were all blocked up - to stop us getting men in," Linda says. "That's terrible! It's outrageous!" I can hardly believe what I'm hearing. Shona doesn't say anything; it doesn't seem to surprise her at all." It's true though," Linda continues. "We would have had men up there if they hadn't done that."

"So where were you when it went on fire?" Shona asks Linda. "I was on nights." She puts her head in her hands again. "We watched the whole thing. It was terrible. It was so fast - and they were all screaming and throwing their mattresses out the window and jumping. It was kind of unreal you know - just standing there watching. Everyone that could went to help, but some of us had to stay on the wards. It was horrible."

"Come on," says Shona, throwing Linda's lipstick into her lap. "Get yer face sorted. We're going out, and I'm going to find myself a matlo." - "What's a matlo?" I ask. "A sailor!" She is incredulous at my ignorance. "Haven't you ever been with a sailor?" - "No - not yet." We all laugh. "Matlo's are the best," Shona tells me, very matter of fact. "Ye cannae beat them." - "Are you going to bathe them gently in the healing lymph of your effluence?" I ask. "Aye, ah am. A'm going to have full mystic knowledge of their suave loins of darkness." Shona and I have been learning by heart the smutty bits of *Women in Love* for weeks. "C'mon lets get a drink downstairs before the club." She picks her bag up, throws in some makeup and perfume, checks how much money she has in her purse and smiles - "Let's get doubles."

We wait in a long queue to get into Jackie O's, standing in the freezing wind. The club is across the road from the sea front. I can feel sea spray on my face. People are coming off buses from Edinburgh, Glasgow, Livingston and Falkirk.

Quite a lot of them have no coats; some of the girls are even bare shouldered. There's a lot of flirting going on. Some people peel off there and then, thinking they can have a good enough time without spending money on the entrance fee to a night club.

When we get to the door we have to show ID to prove we are eighteen. I feel quite nervous about that. I will soon be nineteen but I know I look younger. The bouncer looks at my NHS badge doubtfully. He looks at my feet. I kind of hope he's going to say I can't come in because of my monkey boots. Shona sidles up to him. "C'mon - we're nurses. We're not allowed to start training 'til we're eighteen - honest. I could give ye a bed bath tae prove it." - "All right then," says the bouncer. "Don't mind if you do." He reaches out to take her by the arm. A voice shouts out from further down the queue - "They're eighteen okay?" It's Shona's cousin; we were talking to him earlier. He's quite a bit older than us, tall and well built. "All right," says the bouncer with a sigh. "In ye go." He grins at Shona, "I'll see ye later on the dance floor kiddo." He points his finger at me - "You keep your nose clean."

I hate Jackie O's even more than I imagined I would. I hate the extreme loudness of the music, and I feel very self conscious dancing. I think I would feel more at home on the moon. I manage about three dances then leave Shona and Linda to it, head to the toilets to kill some time. The loos are full of women doing their faces. I look at mine, it looks okay. I stick on a bit more lipstick, then rub most of it off with my finger.

On the right of the ladies there is a corridor that seems more like a tunnel. There are flashing lights spiralling all around it. It looks like it goes on and on and on. I imagine it extending out, crossing the road - under the sea to Gullane. I wander down it as if in a dream. Then BANG! Pain sears through me. I have walked right into the mirror at the end of the corridor. I raise my hands to my face - feel warm, slippery blood on my fingers.

A man comes up to me and puts his hand on my shoulder, guides me back to the ladies. He catches a woman by her arm as she passes. "Katie will you get this kid cleaned up please. She's come a cropper in the tunnel of love." The woman pulls me back in to the loos and over to a sink. She tells me that the guy who brought me to her is one of the bar staff; he is her fiance. "You're a right wee daftie aren't you? Did ye not see your own reflection at the end of the tunnel?" I shake my head - "I don't usually dress like this. I didn't recognise myself." I look down at my jumpsuit and a blob of blood drips down onto the legs of it. Katie tips my head back. She is laughing - "What a case." She washes most of the blood away, dabs the spots off my jumpsuit, leaving big wet patches all over it. She gives me a wad of tissues and tells me to sit at the bar for a while - pinch my nose and hold my head back.

The bar is very quiet. There's lots of empty glasses around, like everyone got up and left in a hurry. I think there's some kind of competition going on in the dance room - Jackie O's Heart-Throb '82 - where they vote for the best looking man and woman. I heard people talking about it in the queue earlier. I sit on a high stool pinching my nose. The barman, Katie's fiance, is called Kenny. He has given me a coke to drink. He's busy collecting and washing glasses but he looks over every now and again to see how I'm doing. There's a girl a few stools away whose eye make up has run all down her face. I guess she must have been crying. Her sequinned boob tube has slipped down to her waist and her large breasts are hanging out. "Maybe you should pull your top up love?" Kenny says. She gives him the V sign, scowling. He carries on with his work, looks over at me and winks.

I'm just about to leave when Shona comes through - "C'mon we're going to a party." - "No, I can't." I shake my head. "Look at the state of me." - "Ye look fine. C'mon. We're going." She drags me out to the foyer where Linda, her cousin, and his friends are all waiting. "What happened to you?" her cousin asks. I explain about the tunnel. He shakes his head, but he looks kind of sorry for me. As we are leaving the bouncer stops me, looking at the blood stained tissue I am still dabbing my face with. "I thought I told you to keep your nose clean?" Everyone laughs. As we are walking up the road Shona's cousin whispers to me - "It happened to me my first night too, exact same thing."

We walk towards Beveridge Park. The party is in one of the big houses there. It's an engagement party and its going full swing when we arrive. There are people everywhere - dancing, drinking, smoking and snogging. It's really warm so I take my coat off. I'm embarrassed about the brown stains on my jumpsuit which are quite visible in the bright light of the kitchen. There's an argument going on between a Tory guy and a Socialist Worker. They are arguing about coal mining. The Tory guy is saying that the unions are holding the country to ransom. He says coal is a dying industry and the pits need to close. The Socialist Worker is getting really wound up. His voice gets louder and higher in pitch. He starts pointing and wagging his finger. The Tory guy stays calm and composed. He looks like he's listening, and he doesn't look unsympathetic, but he keeps on with his argument, his voice strong and firm - authoritative. People start to wander off, shaking their heads and tutting. I want to defend the Socialist Worker, who looks depressed and defeated, but I don't know enough about the subject. I go over to the stove and help myself to a large mug of punch from a big old jelly pan. As I turn to leave the Socialist Worker says - "Do you work in a garage or something?"

We leave about midnight; Linda, Shona and me - start making our way down to the hotel. Shona stops, swaying a little - "I'm going into the woods for a pee." She is pointing at the front garden of a great big old house with three trees on the front lawn. Linda and I sit on the kerb and wait as Shona staggers off up the drive. A car comes by, head lamps blazing. It stops and two policemen get out, one very tall and the other a bit shorter - but broad like a bouncer. "Hello ladies," the broader one says. "Everything okay?" I nod. "We're just waiting for a friend." As I'm talking the other policeman shines his torch into the garden that Shona disappeared into. He shines it right onto her bum. She turns round, waves, then falls over. Linda and I start laughing, but we stop abruptly when the policemen walk over towards our friend. She is rolling around on the grass giggling, trying to pull her tights and knickers up. "Come on then, make yourself decent," the tall policeman says. "Are you a matlo?" Shona asks politely, as she gets to her feet and finishes pulling her clothes into place. "I'm looking for a matlo." A light goes on in the big house.

The policemen take hold of Shona and steer her towards the car, their arms looped beneath her arms. They are walking too fast and she can't keep pace; her feet kick around in the air. She starts shouting - "What have a done? A was just having a pee in the woods!" One of her shoes falls off onto the grass. "Ma shoe!" she shouts. "A just bought them. A spent half ma pay on them!" - "We're arresting you for being drunk and disorderly - and indecent exposure," the shorter policeman says sternly. They push her into the back seat of the car. The taller guy goes back to fetch her shoe and hands it to her. "Thanks pet," Shona says. "Have you ever read Women in Love?" The policeman shakes his head as he slams the door shut.

Linda and I sit on the kerb looking at each other for a while, then stagger back to the hotel. Linda sleeps in Shona's bed. We are woken by her just a few hours later at six thirty. "Wakey wakey girls! I've brought ye some butteries. Fresh baked." She drops a white paper bag down on the dresser, then shivers, blows warm air into her cupped hands. "I'll make some tea," I say, jumping out of bed. "Aw yer a pal."

Shona grins, kicking off her new high heels and jumping into bed beside Linda. I load the tea with sugar and milk - that's how we all like it. "What happened?" Linda is looking at Shona with concern. "Och it was fine." Shona munches her buttery and drinks the hot tea - "Aw man that's great!" She takes another gulp. "Once we got to the station they put me in a cell and told me to behave. I recited some of yer DH Lawrence smut. That had them in pieces a can tell ye. Then a went off tae sleep. They woke me up when it started tae get light. Told me a wasn't tae go peeing in posh folks gardens again."

I've been home for a few days and I have a present for Mr Golinski. It's an apple cake that my mum made for him. Apple cake is one of the things that he sometimes asks for. I'm on a late shift and I've arrived early, so I go straight to his room. He isn't there. I go to the office. Sister is writing in the Kardex. "Excuse me Sister." She keeps on writing, as if she hasn't heard me. Just when I think it might be best to leave she says - "WHAT?" I shuffle about a bit, feeling the colour rise in my cheeks. I wish I had waited to ask Nurse Mayes. "Em...I was wondering where's Mr Golinski is?" - "He's dead," she says. She doesn't look up.

Victoria Hospital
Ward 3 Surgical - Gynaecology
1983 January to March

Enid, who is the eldest of us living at the hotel and almost finished her training has warned us about Sister Tooje. "Keep your heads down and do exactly what you are told," she says. "If you find yourselves waiting on the lift with her you must let her go in. DO NOT GO IN WITH HER. You have to wait until the next lift. If you see her in the canteen, acknowledge her with a nod, but NEVER sit at the same table as her."

She sits at her desk writing in the Kardex ignoring us. I wonder if I could do that - ignore people as if they weren't there. I think I'll try it sometime, find out what it feels like. She's quite young for a Sister; twenty six Enid says. She looks up and I'm surprised to see that she is wearing red lipstick and rouge. She looks like Glinda the Good Witch of the North, from the Wizard of Oz. She must work hard to control her abundance of hair. It's pulled back from her narrow face in a painful looking way, even so, little golden curls escape here and there.

The morning routine is the same as Ward 2: name; age; diagnosis; big bath/bed bath/shower. The only difference is that some of these patients will go to surgery today, so sometimes there is *nil by mouth* and *pre-med* tagged on to the names on our lists. We troop out the door in total silence. My new room mate, Jess, and I are on bed baths with Enrolled Nurse Forrest; a short, plump woman with iron grey hair. "Come on then lets get moving," she says. "We haven't got all day." Her bottom sticks out when she walks. Jess sticks hers out in the same way as we trot along after her, flashing me a cheeky grin.

First she shows us round the ward. There is a special toilet for women recovering from surgery. It shoots jets of warm water from the front and the back of the pan and follows it up with blasts of warm air. "This is an essential piece of medical equipment for gynaecological wound care," says Enrolled Nurse Forrest. "ONLY to be used by patients." She raises an eye brow sternly then turns back to the ward. I prod Jess in the small of her back as we leave and she snorts with laughter. Nurse Forrest turns and glares at us.

The patients look tired and drained of colour, most of them are recovering from surgery. They are slow and uncertain in their movements. One of them is waddling towards the special toilet. She can barely walk. She must be in terrible pain. At the last minute she puts her hand between her legs and breaks into a little run.

Nurse Forrest pulls the curtains round our first patient; a dark, Italian looking woman in her fifties who has had a total hysterectomy. On our bed bath trolley we have: a basin of warm water; clean towels; clinical waste bags; razors, and a tray full of sanitary pads. "And how are we feeling today Mrs Regazoni?" Nurse Forrest asks. She doesn't wait for an answer. She lifts the blankets back and pushes the woman's knees apart, pulls out a bloody sanitary towel, examines it and drops it in the waste bag. Mrs Regazoni watches her curiously then gives me a small embarrassed smile. She drags herself up the bed slowly and says, "Can I really not put my knickers on?" - "No underwear," says Nurse Forrest. "Your body needs air to heal. The girls will help you wash then we'll get you some breakfast."

She leaves us to bathe our patient, but Mrs Regazoni takes the cloth from us and starts washing herself. "Sit down girls," she says. "Take the weight off your feet." - "We're not allowed," I tell her. "Infection control." - "Good God," says Mrs Regazoni. "What a lot of nonsense. And how we are meant to get to the toilet with no knickers on and a sanitary towel between our legs I don't know." Jess laughs loudly, sitting on the end of the bed swinging her legs.

When we've finished the bed baths we have to wash down the mattresses of the patients who have been discharged and re-make the beds for new admissions. There are three beds to be made up and only two pillow slips. Jess goes down to the laundry to get some more but they've run out. Enrolled Nurse Forrest comes over to inspect our work. She asks us why there is a pillow with no slip on it. "There's none in the cupboard and none in the laundry," I tell her. She raises her eyebrows and makes a face. "What am I meant to do?" She raises her eyebrows again, tucks her chin in and sort of snickers then walks off with her bottom sticking out like a shelf.

I go into the treatment room to re-stock the bed bath trolley with sanitary pads and towels. Sister Tooje comes in and says, "YOU. COME HERE. NOW." We stand facing the row of empty beds all ready for the new admissions. The women on the other side of the bay stop talking and look at one another anxiously. I feel my self getting hotter, hold my hands together to stop them shaking. "WHAT'S THIS?" She points at the pillow with no slip on it. "There are no pillow slips in the cupboard or the..." She puts a hand up to silence me. "WHAT WERE YOU ASKED TO DO?" I don't say anything. She says it again, really slowly this time - "WHAT WERE YOU ASKED TO DO?" - "Make the beds Sister." - "AND IS THIS BED MADE?" I think it is actually, but I know that's not what she wants to hear. "No Sister, but..." - "DON'T BACK CHAT ME. IF YOU WANT TO WORK IN MY WARD. IF YOU WANT TO CONTINUE WITH YOUR TRAINING - GET THIS BED MADE PROPERLY NOW!"

I walk as fast as I can out of the ward and into the corridor, my heart pounding. I run up the stairs to Ward 2, and head for the office. Nurse Mayes comes out just before I get there. "You're in the wrong ward," she laughs. "Did you forget?" Then she sees my face. "What's wrong? Has something happened?" I tell her about the pillow slips, hurriedly, as if it's an emergency situation. She looks at me sympathetically. "Did you get hauled over the coals by Tooje?" I nod and feel my face turn hot and red as I try not to cry. "Well I'm sorry but we haven't got any spare pillow slips either." I start over breathing. I think - Oh God I'm having a panic attack about pillow slips, and I think - *I'm going mad* - which makes the panic even worse.

Nurse Mayes puts an arm round my waist, guides me into an empty side room. The bed has been made up for the next admission. She takes the pillow slip from the bottom pillow and folds it. "Take this, Sister Jardine will never notice. And for God's sake remember the opening must always face the window." - My panic subsides. "Yes, I remembered that - thank you." She gives me a little hug. "You'll get through it. You'll be fine."

I run back to Ward 3 clutching the pillow slip to my body like a thief and quickly put it on the uncovered pillow. "Where did you find it?" one of the patients calls over to me. "Did they have some in the laundry after all?" I go over to talk to her. She peers at me then turns to the women in the beds to her left. "She's been crying, for heaven's sake." She holds her hand out to me. "That woman's a nasty piece of work. You shouldn't be wasting your tears on the likes of her." The other patients nod in agreement. "I'd be ashamed if any of my daughters behaved like that," one of them says, shaking her head. "C'mon lass," says the first lady. "C'mon over here." She leans forwards in her bed and puts her arms around me. I sink into her shoulder and the tears start afresh. "Never you mind that miserable creature. You'll be fine. Here, have a sweetie." She holds out a box of Black Magic chocolates. "Take a few," she says.

I am admitting a new patient – a sixteen year old. She's wailing and writhing about, holding her tummy. I don't know anything about her yet. I was just told to take her details and do her obs. I'm trying to take her blood pressure. I've managed to wrap the cuff round her arm, and I've pumped it up, but I can't hear anything through the stethoscope because of all her shouting. Dr Tiwari pushes his way through the curtains. "Sonia McLeod?" I nod. He looks down at her frowning. "Sonia," he shouts, to be heard above her wailing. "Sonia, my name is Dr Tiwari and I'm going to examine you. Let's see if we can find out what's causing all this pain."

I detach the blood pressure cuff from Sonia's arm and stand back to allow the doctor to complete his examination. He pulls back the covers, gently pushes her hospital gown up above her waist. There is blood on the sheet below her. "Sonia, is it possible that you could be pregnant?" She stops wailing for a minute and looks at him as if he's mad. "Sonia, I need you to be honest with us," he says. "We need to know if you've had intercourse and could be pregnant. Nobody will be angry with you. It's not necessary to inform your parents. It's completely confidential." I hope that Sonia doesn't realise all the other patients in this bay and probably the next will be hearing this conversation loud and clear. She looks at me and wails - "What's he talking about?" I lean closer to her - "Sonia, have you ever done it with a boy?" She stops her noise and eyes me suspiciously. I lean in and talk with a low, quiet voice. "Have you ever had sex with a boy?" She looks at me blankly. "You know? Have you ever let a boy put his penis inside you?" - "HIS WHAT?" She looks horrified. "His penis. You know - his thing." I point at Dr

Tiwali's groin. He seems a bit surprised. I feel my own face burning red. "Oh that!" She's not wailing now. She smiles, "Aye, I done that at the church Christmas party."

Her smile fades. Her face pales. She gives a long, low moan. I wince as she squeezes my hand hard. "There it is," says Dr Tiwari under his breath. I look down and see the tiny fetus lying on the sheet, cold and lifeless. I can't believe how perfect it's little arms and legs are. "About ten weeks," says Dr Tiwali. Sonia tries to sit up but he gently pushes her back. "Just lie still now my dear," he says, patting her hand. "Have a rest, the worst is over."

We leave with the baby she never knew she was having in a covered cardboard bowl. "Thank you," Dr Tiwari says to me. "Will you explain to her what happened? How to stop it happening again? You are much better at communicating with her than I am." - "Yes, of course." He nods and thanks me once more.

I am standing in the treatment room, waiting for a staff nurse to check the fetus with me, thinking about how to tell Sonia what's happened, when Sister comes in. "Well, is all present and correct?" - "I think so." - "Think so isn't good enough. I want a yes or no." - "Yes." - "How many weeks?" - "Ten," I say, confidently, since Dr Tiwari told me. She stands looking at me and I feel like I should say something more. "She doesn't know anything about it. She doesn't seem to understand the connection between intercourse and pregnancy. Dr Tiwari asked me to explain things to her. How to avoid getting pregnant again." She turns her attention back to the fetus, looking it over coolly. "That's none of your concern. I'll tell her what she needs to know."

Path house
Kirkcaldy
February 1983

I've left the hotel and moved in to a nurses' home called Path House which is meant to be for trained staff only. When Shona left to do her placement in Lynebank Hospital Jess requested to be my room mate. She didn't ask me, she just did it, and I didn't feel I could object. Jess drives me up the wall because she talks all the time. Shona talks a lot, but not all the time - and she's funny, we make each other laugh. Jess is quite funny as well I suppose, but she keeps going on about being Suzie Quatro's daughter; she is adopted and this is what she believes to be the truth. She does look very like Suzie Quatro, but there's no evidence for her theory beyond that and I find her obsession with it a bit depressing. Also - there was an incident; someone went round all the hotel rooms and stole our knickers from our drawers. There's a lot of talk about ghosts, but I have a feeling that Jess had something to do with it - her and the bar man who she is having a fling with, even though he's married and about three times her age. Anyway, I requested a transfer and I was very lucky to get in here - being a student. To be honest I think they've only let me in because Sister Bonnyface told my tutors that my mum is ill.

It's a big old house at the top of a hill that leads from Kirkcaldy into Dysart. It has three floors and I'm on the third with five other nurses. We share a kitchen and bathroom but we all have our own bedrooms. My room has a view over the

Firth of Forth and a deep window sill that I like to sit on. It's more expensive than the hotel and will leave me with only £180 a month salary, but I think I can manage.

The girl in the room next to me is lovely; her name is Angela and she's a Mormon. She doesn't drink alcohol or coffee or even cocoa and she never swears - but she's very nice. The other nurses that live on my floor are pretty horrible. When I go into the kitchen they stop talking. They don't smile or make any effort to be friendly. They are the kind of girls that have engagement rings hanging from their fob watches when they are on duty. They are just dying for someone to say, "Oh are you engaged then?" Some of the patients fall for it, but usually only once.

I feel them watching me every time I go in there to do anything - then everything seems to go wrong. Pans get scorched, glasses are broken. One day the handle of a mug just comes away in my hand and my coffee spills all over the floor. Honestly, you would think by the way they look at one another they suspect me of witchcraft. I used the twin tub to do my washing the other night and it broke down before I could rinse and spin. I had to finish it off by hand and wring it out. I'm not so good at wringing things out - so it all hung dripping on the clothes horse. They snorted and tutted and looked at each other in disbelief. I've decided not to go in there any more. I'll stick to my room, keep myself to myself.

I'm sitting on the window sill looking out to sea. My bedroom at home has a sea view too. Seaview – that's the name of our house. I wish I was there now, reading poetry in my plum coloured bedroom with its matching wallpaper and curtains. I peer through the glass as if I might catch sight of myself across the water, but all I can see is darkness and rain and a pale reflection of myself here, in this room now. It's late, but I don't want to go to sleep because recently I've been having terrible nightmares. It's the same horrible dream every time - my mum lying dead, me screaming and flaying my head about, vomiting - foul black vomit.

I am hungry but I have no food. I haven't eaten at all today. I smoke a cigarette, then I feel guilty and throw the pack out the window. Five minutes later I creep down to retrieve it from the street below. I hope that none of the other nurses are watching. I find the packet lying in the gutter, it's dirty and wet but the cigarettes inside are fine, all clean and fresh in their bed of silver and white - coffin nails, in their little paper coffin. I creep back up to my room and sit on the sill, light another one, wave to my parents - *I was much further out than you thought, and not waving, but drowning.*

Last night I dyed my hair. It says *Cool Nordic Blonde* on the pack, but it's bright yellow - the colour of a newly hatched chicken. "You look very colourful this morning," Tooje says, one perfect eyebrow raised. I bow my head in shame. We are short staffed and I am not paired up with anyone today. I'm on bed baths again which is always easy on this ward because most of the women prefer to wash themselves. They give me advice on my hair. "You did it very well despite the colour," says one woman. "It's very even, you haven't missed a strand." - "Buy yourself some toner," a voice calls out. "Cut it short," Mrs Anderson says as she hobbles towards the special toilet.

Mrs Regazoni's husband has brought binoculars in and I show her and the others in her bay where my house is in Gullane. It's easy to see because it's on the seafront at the bottom of the hill, and it's pink. Mrs Regazoni turns to me, "When you go home this weekend you can wave to us." - "Okay. What time?" We agree 11am on Saturday morning. "I'll stand in the front garden so you can see me." - "Well we're not going to miss you with that hair." Everyone laughs, even me.

I help someone off the commode and take the pan away, measuring her urine before pouring it down the sluice. I forget to go back and record it on her chart. I move on down the ward, thinking how nice it is that the women support one another through their various trials. I help another patient on and off the commode. "You'll need to get yourself better quick so you can use the fancy loo," I tell her as I lift her legs up into the bed. "I tried it before the op," she says. "It's a marvellous invention." We laugh a bit at that and I take her urine away to measure, remembering that I'd forgotten to record the last measurement.

The curtains are closed and I can hear the doctors and Sister talking to the patient. They have all her charts. They are telling her that she needs a catheter. "But I peed," she protests. "About half an hour ago. The nurse took the pan away - the girl with the yellow hair." Sister comes out and sees me standing. "Is this true?" She says it in the coldest of voices. "This patient passed urine and you failed to record it?" - "I forgot," I stammer. "I was just coming back…" - "DON'T EVEN BOTHER TRYING TO EXPLAIN." She goes back in and I hear the consultant grumbling with impatience. He comes out from behind the curtain and looks at me with utter contempt. I apologise to the patient. She says, "Och, I didn't want to get you into trouble. But they were going to put a tube into me. I had no choice. But I didn't want all this unpleasantness."

I carry on my shift miserably, aware of the other nurses looks. Even Dr Tiwali is quiet with me. At lunch in the canteen I sit with Angela, the Mormon girl who lives in the room next to me. "They might chuck you out you know," she says, looking grave. I push my food away, head out for a smoke. When I get back to the ward Sister has me sit in her office and draw the female reproductive system. She leaves me to it and I find myself becoming engrossed. When she returns she picks it up and looks surprised. She barks out a few questions which I answer without hesitation. "Well you seem to know your stuff," she says. "And it's a very good drawing. But you know that was a very serious incident this morning. If it happens again you will be off the course. Is that understood?"

The next day on my way back to Gullane I stop at a

hairdressers in Edinburgh and ask them to cut my hair short. "Shorter," I keep saying, until it is just below my ears. It doesn't look like my hair anyway I think, as I step over the long yellow cuttings that litter the floor around me. When I get home Mum's face falls. "My God! What have you done?" She is angry. She doesn't talk to me again for the rest of the day. I sit on my bed that evening looking at my reflection in the long mirror that stands in the corner. The colour of my hair is better since the toner was put in it, but the girl in the mirror doesn't look like me. I look around the room - my dolls, arranged neatly on top of my wardrobe, my pictures and books, the big sweetie jar filled with shells and sea glass. Everything the same - except for me.

I stand on the grass at 11am the next morning, waving to my patients. Waving to the women who are kind to one another because they are all losing their most precious things - ovaries - wombs - blood - babies. I stand and wave, and I feel like I've lost something too - but I'm not quite sure what.

🚲 🚲 🚲

Samira's husband is on nights and she wants to go to a club. We decided on Bentleys because I prefer it to Jackie O's; it feels classier. We go into the loos first to check our hair and make up - we've been standing outside in the wind and rain for twenty minutes waiting to get in. There are light bulbs round all the mirrors and doors. It feels very glamorous. Samira has never been before. She seems to like it.

There's a girl in a halter neck top standing to our right. She's the one that was sitting in the bar at Jackie O's on the night of the nose bleed. She's holding her breasts in her hands this time - they are very big. "ALL THEY SEE ARE THESE," she screams to her pal. She is crying again. When she wipes her face with her hands, her thick black eye liner gets pushed up, making black wing like marks at the side of her eyes - it looks quite good, I think I might try it sometime. She leans back, lighting a cigarette and then jumps - "THOSE FUCKING LIGHTBULBS GET ME EVERY TIME." Finishing her fag, muttering and swearing, she turns to leave. There are a row of circular burns all down her back.

I feel very self conscious so we have a couple of drinks before we go out onto the dance floor. They are playing *Thriller*. There's a guy who seems to have learned all of Michael Jackson's moves. The other dancers move away to make space for him. He's really pretty good. Everyone starts clapping in time to the music. "This is better than I thought," says Samira. "I don't understand why you don't like these places."

We dance a while, me very half heartedly, feeling a bit strange in my stripey cotton trousers that I only wear to night clubs. Samira is wearing tight black satin jeans and a boxy blue jacket with the sleeves rolled up. The guy that was dancing to Thriller comes over and asks me to dance. I think it must be some kind of joke. I can't imagine how I would match his moves. I tell him I have to go to the ladies - "Why not dance with my friend?" I gesture to Samira. She smiles at him. "She's the wrong colour," he says. He walks back into the dance floor to find another partner.

Samira marches straight for the cloakroom and I run after her. She has a temper I know, but I have never seen her this angry. "C'mon," I say. "Let's get out of here. Let's go to the Path Tavern." I steer her through the wind and rain down to the pub. When we get inside it is mercifully quiet in comparison to Bentleys.

It's full of men about my dads age or older. They scowl up at us from their pints. It's like we've been through some kind of time slip and landed in the 1950's. The barman is a sullen, sour faced man. "He probably doesn't like Paki's either," Samira says. "Well, I don't know," I stare long and hard at him - "He's always grumpy. I can't be bothered walking any further in this weather though - can you?"

We sit in an overly bright corner sipping rum and coke, trying to ignore the men around us. "I'm angry at myself really," says Samira. "For still getting upset even after all these years. Anyway HAS HE NOT NOTICED THAT MICHAEL JACKSON IS BLACK FOR FUCK'S SAKE? Jesus! Why am I surprised? All through school I got it - *Get back to your own country*. And you know, my family couldn't even live in Pakistan after partition." - "What's partition?" I ask. She rolls her eyes.

The men seem to get used to our presence; they stop staring at us anyway. Samira tells me about partition. She tells me the story of her family coming to live in Scotland; how her father was an engineer but ended up running a shop because the racist abuse at work was so relentless. He thought it would be better to be his own boss. She tells me that she met Donald after someone smashed their shop window. He was a very junior policeman then, kind and sympathetic, keen to help.

"But you're right," she says. "I am too young to be married. I thought it would be different with a white guy, but it isn't. I have to do everything for him. He won't even make his own pack lunch. And he's desperate for me to have babies. He doesn't want me to do my nurse training - the only thing he likes about that is the uniform. He'd be far happier if I stayed home dusting and polishing and looking after him and his babies. But I want to have a good time. I want to be independent. I want to be like you." - "ME?" I can hardly believe what I'm hearing. "You want to be like ME?" - "Yes. I do. Look at you. You have a great life. You're out all the time. Lots of friends. You dress a bit funny - but you make people laugh." - "But you hate my jokes." - "No I don't. I just said that to be mean because you'd said I was too young to be married. I don't even mind the way you dress. I mean, sometimes it's a bit weird, but I like the way you put unmatching things together. You're kind of arty aren't you? Did you never think of going to art school like your brother?"

I tell her that I don't try to put unmatching things together; I'm just not very good at matching. I tell her that I thought about getting married too, before I started my training. I had been with my boyfriend for two years and I honestly thought I would stay with him for the rest of my life. I couldn't imagine wanting to be with anyone else. It occurs to me now, as I tell her this, that it was when we started talking about marriage that I became doubtful about our relationship. Then I went on holiday with my parents to Achmelvich in Sutherland, where we always went - but that summer was different from usual. I made friends with a group of young people from Germany that were only a year or so older than me, travelling around Europe, and I got a strong sense of another kind of life.

My father really encouraged me to try for art school and I did consider it, because I do love making things. In fifth year our art teacher took a few of us on a trip to Duncan of Jordanstone in Dundee, where my brother was doing sculpture. "All my brother's friends came and sat with me in the canteen at lunchtime, and they were very funny, and really nice to me," I told Samira. "But every time one of them got up from the table the others would all talk about how crap his work was. I couldn't handle that kind of thing - that kind of competitiveness. I'd be a wreck." - "Were you in school uniform when you went to there?" Samira asks. "Yes." - "Yeah - that's why they were so nice to you. Artists. Men are men. They're all the same and that's the truth of it."

She goes up to the bar to order some more drinks. I sit thinking about the art students. I do actually remember one of them commenting on my uniform. I think about the Germans from Achmelvich - would they be like that about uniforms? I doubt it. I wonder where they all are now. I think about my friends at university too - all enjoying themselves, learning loads of interesting stuff and going to parties, sharing flats with people they actually like. They don't have to work almost every weekend cleaning up people's shit and watching them die. I can't believe that Samira thinks I have a great life. Hers must be really bad.

When she comes back she asks for a cigarette. She seems to be quite used to smoking. "I sometimes nick one of Donald's when he's in bed," she tells me. "If he caught me he'd be furious. My parents love him of course. They weren't happy at first, with him being white. But now I think they like him better than me. They think it's marvellous that he's a policeman. They think I should spend my life supporting him in his career. They'd kill me if I left him." She stubs her fag out and reaches for another. "You know," she says, waving her unlit cigarette around. "We were crossing the Forth Road Bridge the other day, going to see my mum and dad, and Donald said, 'What if it fell down?' and you know - I thought - I wouldn't care. I really wouldn't give a damn if it all fell down and I was dead at the bottom of the sea. In fact - that would suit me fine."

The women cry so hard when they lose their babies that I find it very difficult not to cuddle them. I think about Dr Chowdhury and what he told me: I should stay on the outside of their pain; I shouldn't intrude on their grief; I should ask myself - what can I do to ease this person's suffering? Well I know a hug helps most people when they are suffering, but if Sister catches me doing that I'll be finished. "My poor wee baby. My poor wee baby. So far away from home," Mrs Moncrieff cries. I take her hand in mine. It feels cruel not to hug her. I close the curtains and take a chance. She wraps her arms round my neck like a child holding on to its mother. "I want my husband," she wails. I sit on the bed holding her, praying that Sister won't catch us.

The curtains open and my heart skips a beat, but it's only Jess. "What's going on?" She points at me sitting on the bed. "You'll be for it if you're caught." Mrs Moncrieff starts wailing afresh. "My baby. My poor wee baby." Jess leans over and hugs her from the other side of the bed. Our patient takes an arm from around my neck and puts it round Jess's. We are like a sea monster - an octopus - all arms and wet, salty tears and runny noses. I can't help it; I start laughing. Mrs Moncrieff starts laughing too. I get up to find the tissues and pass them round. "Thanks girls," she says, wiping her eyes and blowing her nose. "I miss my husband. He's a big bear of a man. Some people say he's fat, but he's my big cuddly teddy bear and I love him. If he were here he would give me the biggest hug. You'll see - when he comes. You'll see what I mean. I'm going to get him to give us all a really big hug." She starts crying again and Jess, who is still sitting on the bed, holds her tight.

The curtains open and it's Tooje. With the golden curls popping out from around her frilly hat and the sweet little puffy sleeves of her sister's uniform, she really does look like Glinda the Good Witch. But there's nothing good about Tooje right now. When I look at her it's like her face is getting paler and paler and her eyes are getting bigger and darker. I think she might bring out her wand and melt Jess into a sizzling heap of ashes. "Get off that bed," she hisses. "And in to my office now."

Everyone is asking me what happened because Jess has disappeared. I tell them I don't know. The next morning she is in the office before me. She looks okay; wiggles her eyebrows at me, gives me a cheeky smile. Sister Tooje is reading from the Kardex, head bowed. We stand with our notebooks waiting for our orders. Finally she looks up - "You, you, you, bed baths. You and you…" She is pointing at Jess and I - "big baths." - "NAH," Jess replies loudly. "I don't think so. I don't think I want to do big baths today. In fact – BUGGER THIS." She turns and leaves. Sister's eyes widen just a fraction, two rosy spots appear on her high, sculpted cheekbones. "YOU CAN ALL LEAVE NOW," she says loudly, lowering her head as if she has work to do. "ALL OF YOU."

Jess has been through the ward and waved goodbye to the patients. We are just in time to see her whip off her cardboard cap and throw it in the air. She stops in the corridor; wriggles out of her uniform; kicks off her smelly white shoes; peels her tights off and drops them in a small heap; flourishes and bows - Prince Charming style, then disappears into the locker room.

Jess wants to go to a Country and Western night at the Harbour Bar before she leaves Kirkcaldy. We are meeting one of my class mates there. She's an older woman called Maggie. I don't see her often, but I like her a lot. She's been a nursing assistant for years; decided to do her staff nurse training after the last of her children left home. She must have been looking out for us because she waves excitedly as we come through the door. She is wearing a cowboy hat and a yellow and brown chequered shirt with a silky golden fringe across the front. Her husband, Jake, who is an ambulance driver, sits next to her dressed like Elvis. I've seen him around the hospital. He isn't exactly dressed up; he always looks like Elvis - as far as his uniform allows. They are delighted that we have joined them. Jake buys us all a drink. "Make them doubles," he shouts to the barman. Everyone is dressed up. Jess and I have checked shirts and jeans on. Jess is wishing she had a hat. Jake takes his off and plops it on her head. She looks great - better than Suzie Quatro ever looked.

Everyone is either singing along to the music or up dancing. A tall, good looking guy comes over and asks me to dance. I get up and start shifting around in my usual half hearted, uncoordinated way. He takes hold of me and starts waltzing and twirling me around. He is big and very strong. He has total charge of me - it's really good fun. We dance for ages then flop onto the high stools at the bar exhausted. "Jesus this place is crazy," he says, laughing. His hair is long and dark and his eyes are very blue against his brown skin. He holds a hand out for me to shake. "Andy," he says, turning my hand round roughly. I think he's going to kiss it, but he opens his mouth wide and bites gently down, then winks and laughs. Jess comes over and flirts with him. He flirts back, but after a bit he reaches for my hand and drags me back on to the dance floor. We dance for another half hour or so then go back to sit with Maggie, Jake and Jess. Andy orders another round of doubles and brings them over from the bar singing along to Johnny Cash - *Because you're mine , I walk the Line…*

"C'mon," he says in my ear, "let's get a breath of air." We slip off out the door. He pulls me round the side of the pub and up a wee close where it's dark and no one can see us. I'm shivering with cold. I wish I'd put my coat on, but he puts both arms around me and all at once I am warm. He kisses hard and I like it. Then he takes his right arm from around my back and lifts his hand up under my chin, his thumb pressing into my throat. "Start screaming and you'll really be in trouble." I kind of laugh, thinking he is fooling about, but I see in his eyes that this is not a joke. He grabs the flesh on the inside of my thigh with his left hand, squeezes it so hard I yelp in pain. The pub door opens and I hear Jess laughing.

"You're so big," she says. "Are you big all over?" - "That's for me to know and you to find out." She's with Jake. They come stumbling up the close towards us. Andy presses my throat, forcing my head back against the the bumpy surface of the wall. "Seems like it's your lucky night after all." He squeezes my thigh again, twists the flesh. "My God, you've enough meat on you to start a butcher's shop."

He leaves. Jess stops snogging Jake and shouts, "Bye then gorgeous, don't be a stranger." - "Oh I won't," he shouts back with a wave, not even bothering to turn around. I stand for a minute leaning against the wall, then make my way past Jess and Jake, back to the pub, my heart thundering, my legs trembling. Maggie is watching the door as I come in. "Is Jake out there with Jess?" I nod and her eyes fill. I slump into the seat beside her, wincing because my thigh hurts, grab a drink from the table - it's not mine. I don't even know what it is. Maggie picks hers up too and we crash our glasses together. "FUCK THEM" I say, my voice sounds weak and croaky. "FUCK THEM" Maggie replies. We swallow our drinks down in one. Reach for the next.

I'm on admissions today. I've been told to prepare a side room. I'm scrubbing the mattress when two guys from the works department come in. "We've to remove the mirrors," they tell me. "You're getting a nun in."

Tooje comes in to inspect the room. She looks at me in her cool, disdainful manner. "You can talk to her but don't expect an answer," she says. For a moment I think she's talking about herself. I must look confused. She sighs heavily, rolls her eyes. "The nun has taken a vow of silence." She says it slowly so that even an idiot like me will understand. "Oh. Right." I turn to wipe the locker down, though I've already cleaned it. I've done everything I'm meant to, but I don't know if I'm allowed to leave the room when Tooje is there. She leaves with another sigh and I turn and look out the window.

There's a ledge just below me with a pigeon lying flat on its back, it's wings flapping madly. A crow has pinned it down with one claw and is pecking a hole its chest. The pigeon is looking right at me, like it expects me to do something. I bang on the window but the glass is too thick and there isn't much of a noise made. The crow carries on unperturbed. I find myself hoping that the pigeon heard me knocking - knows at least I tried. "Sorry," I say quietly. A small oval of condensation appears on the glass. A chain of ambulances come blaring along the road towards casualty. The crow looks up for a moment, then continues it's meal, the pigeon still flapping wildly. I wonder how I am going to do the nun's admission if she doesn't speak.

I just give her the admission form and a pen; she fills out her own details. All the other questions she answers with a nod or a shake of her head. Her skin is pale and tissue like, though she is only in her forties. She is wearing a wimple and a long, plain white nightgown. It seems a bit sad to me that the living nuns' clothes should be so plain when the shrouds that they provide for catholic patients who have died are so beautifully embroidered.

Her name is Sister Mary and she is in for a hysterectomy. I

wonder if she has ever been with a man. I wonder what it would be like to never have to deal with them at all. I raise my hand to the bruise on my throat, the torn and tender skin on the back of my head - testing for pain. I consider, briefly, telling her what happened and how confused and lonely I feel. But I know I can't do that, and anyway, it seems, from the way she looks at me, that she might already know.

Sister has asked me to report to her following the admission. I knock on the office door before entering. "How is she?" She asks, rather politely. "It's a bit hard to tell when she can't speak, but she seems quite calm. She was praying when I left her." - "We have to look after her," Sister says. Enid has told me that Tooje is Catholic. I wonder if she ever thought of becoming a nun herself. I wonder what her husband is like - if she's as cold with him as she is with the rest of us.

When I go back Sister Mary has left her room and is walking round the ward shaking hands with all the women, smiling and nodding. Everyone seems quite moved by the gesture and they clutch her hand eagerly, smiling broadly, blinking back tears. Sister comes out of her office and watches. It's the first time I've ever seen her smile, except when she's with the doctors, and even then, those are kind of frosty smiles.

I take Sister Mary down to theatre the next morning. She is dopey from her pre-med drugs, but aware enough to look embarrassed when I take her wimple off. Her head has been shaved very badly. It's like she's been brutalised - maybe she did it herself. My throat tightens with anxiety as I leave her, though I know she will be fine. Patients come and go all day from theatre, they are almost always fine.

The operation goes well and without complications. She won't be staying with us long; the other nuns will nurse her back at the convent. They are jolly when they come to fetch her. One of them is allowed to speak. She goes round the ward chatting to the patients, giving little gifts; strange, embroidered things - gaudy colours with bits of nylon lace and gold braid. At first I thought they were pin cushions, then I realise they are of no practical use at all. Still, when Sister Mary presses one into my hand as she leaves it feels like I've been given something precious. I slip it in to my pocket. When I touch it I find it strangely comforting.

☩ ☩ ☩

It's my first week of nights. I'll be working four on, four off. This is my first night off. I wanted to go home to Gullane, but I have to wait until the bruise on my neck disappears; besides Samira wants to try Jackie O's and I don't feel like I can say no. Shona has come along with us. I leave the two of them to dance, sit at the bar watching.

There's a guy sitting next to me watching too. He is wearing an old man's cap, a *gone and dunnit bunnet*, as my grandpa would call it. "Don't you like dancing?" He sounds like a Yorkshire man. I shake my head, "I'm a terrible dancer." - "Me n'all," he says, poking his index finger into his chest. "But it dun't really matter does it? I mean - if you like a thing you should do it shouldn't you? Dun't really matter if your good or bad at it. There's no harm in it is there? Dancing?" - "Well I don't really like it," I tell him. This is actually a lie; if I think no-one is watching, I love to dance. "Where are you from?" I ask. "Pudsey," he says. I laugh, just a wee bit. "What?" He grins at me. "What's so funny?" - "You just look like a man from Pudsey, that's all." - "Have you ever been to Pudsey?" - "No." - "Well 'ow do you know what a man from Pudsey looks like?" - "I think it's your hat." - "Nowt wrong wi' my 'at," he says, taking it off and looking at it. "Me mam give me this 'at and I like it." - "I like it too," I tell him. "I think it's cute."

He buys me a drink and we chat for a while. He works at Mossmoran oil and gas refinery. He doesn't mind it, his dad and his uncle work there too. They stay in digs when they are working and travel back to Yorkshire for their days off. I find myself telling him about Ward 3; how much I hate it and how I can't wait to retire. He laughs at that - "I should say you'd best leave the job then. Just leave it if you 'ate it that much. No point in wishing your life away, a young lass like you. You need to find something you like to do." Shona and Samira come bouncing over. "C'mon, there's a party," Shona says. "Yer man can come too if he wants?" - "Oh no," he says. "I canna. I'm on an early tomorra. I've to be up at five. I'll be off home very shortly." He turns to me, "Shall I meet you next week? I'll meet you in the Penny Farthing next Sunday night, seven?"

We leave for the party. It's Shona's cousin's birthday and I like her cousin; besides I'm more than happy to get out of Jackie O's and the threat of being dragged up on to the dance floor. It's not far from the last party I went to with Shona - quite a lot of the same people are there. Her cousin makes a great fuss of us as we come in, steers us into the kitchen and pours us all a huge glass of punch. It feels very deja vu. Even the Tory guy is there - and he's still arguing, except this time he's arguing in defence of the miners. "Thatcher doesn't care about community," he shouts. "She doesn't care about the miners. She doesn't care about the working class. They don't vote for her so why should she? She's out to break the NUM. She's out to break all the unions, because they've got too much power for her liking. They give ordinary working people power - and Tories don't like that. She's decimating the steel industry and coal will be next. And the police will help her. Thatcher's Army that's what they are - Thatcher's fucking army."

People start to wander off. He turns to me - "Easy on that punch kid. It's got all sorts in it." I think he's got a bit of a cheek calling me kid since he doesn't look much older than me. "I thought you were a Tory?" - "I was," he says. "I changed my mind. Ended up joining the SWP - the Socialist Workers Party." - "I know what the SWP is," I tell him, aware that I'm sounding a bit grumpy. He doesn't seem to have noticed. "Do you? Good. You should join. It's fantastic. I love it. It's completely changed my outlook – it's changed my life. I'm a different person"

His name is Norrie and he seems to want to be friends.

"Have you ever been to Paris?" He ladles some more punch into my glass, despite his own warning. "I'll take you to Paris if you like?" I think he must be joking, but he seems to be talking in earnest. "I don't even know you," I say, trying not to look horrified by his suggestion. "That doesn't matter. We can get to know each other in Paris. What's that on your neck?" - "A love bite." That seems to put him off. He wanders out of the kitchen towards the lounge and I leave - out into the night, back to my room at the top of the hill.

It's three in the morning by the time I get in, but I'm wide awake. I take off my clothes, stand looking at myself in the mirror under the bright central light. There is a big ugly bruise at the top of my leg where Andy grabbed it. My body looks lumpy. *Small women don't carry fat well* - I read that in a woman's magazine. I know that I'm technically thin, I can see my ribs and my hip bones, but there are fat bits on my skinny body. "You've enough meat on you to start a butcher's shop." I say it out loud. He's right, I think, pulling the fat bits, nodding at my mirror self - they have to go.

I think about the Pudsey man, over the next few days. I quite liked him, but I don't think I want to go out with him, and I didn't like his hat, it wasn't cute - I just said that to be nice. I don't want to stand him up, but I haven't got a phone number to ring and make an excuse, so I'm going to have to meet him. Shona is back for a while, staying with her grandparents. I ask her and Linda to go to the pub before me and sit on the other side of the bar beside the loos. They seem a bit surprised by my request. I don't even really know

why I'm asking them, but I know I want them there.
He's sitting at the bar with his old man's hat on reading the Daily Record. I sit next to him, clear my throat to attract his attention. He looks up and sees me looking at his paper. "It was here when I came in," he says. "You look different." I look down, wondering why he would say that, then remember he's only seen me in my club clothes. I'm wearing a long green pinafore and an amber necklace. "Is that plastic?" He peers at it curiously. "It's amber," I tell him. "Look, it's got flies in it - fossils." We chat awkwardly. I tell him about the book I've been reading. I'm still on DH Lawrence - he's never heard of him. "He was a miner's son," I tell him. "He was one of the first working class people to become a famous writer. It was after the introduction of free education for children in the 1870's." - "Well I wouldn't know anything about that," he says, looking into his pint. "I'm not an educated man. I 'ated school."

Apart from hating school it seems like we have nothing in common. I see Shona's funny wee face across the bar and I really wish I was just with her and Linda. I look at the man from Pudsey. He seems pretty miserable too. "Excuse me." I jump off my stool. "I'm just going to the ladies." He nods, pulls the newspaper towards him again. He doesn't seem to notice me picking up my coat and bag. Shona is watching as I walk towards her. "Run," I say, in a low, urgent voice, then bolt out the door and off down the high street. I duck into a shop doorway and peek out. Shona and Linda are running towards me, as if they are escaping the man from Pudsey too. "So ye didnae like him then?" Shona shouts, running past me in her high heels. "And him with his best bunnet on too?" We head for the Wheatsheaf, "And then the Harbour Bar?" Linda says. "No," I say. "Not the Harbour Bar." I don't tell them why.

It's 10pm and the last medicine round of the day is finished. We sit at the nurses station quietly waiting for the orchestra of farts. In Gynae almost everyone gets Codis and Pep after surgery - Codeine for pain and peppermint oil for post-operative wind - even the older nurses chuckle from time to time. I am studying. We have exams after every placement. You have to pass each exam to progress on to the next ward. I generally do fine. I don't struggle like I did at school. I do have to work, it doesn't come easy, but I don't mind. I want to know about my patients; what is happening to them and their bodies - it interests me. The staff nurse I am working with sits beside me knitting. The clicking of her needles reminds me of home. We hear the soft swish of the ward doors opening and jump to our feet, smoothing down our uniforms, straightening our hats; but it isn't Matron - it's the man from Pudsey. He stands swaying, pointing his finger in my direction. "YOU!" He shouts, then belches. The smell of alcohol fills the air.

"I THOUGHT YOU WERE A NICE GIRL. BUT YOU'RE NOT. YOU'RE 'ORRIBLE. I WAS GOING TO INTRODUCE YOU TO MY MAM. SHE WOULD 'AVE LOVED YOU, MY MAM. SHE WOULD 'AVE THOUGHT

YOU WERE RIGHT CLASSY. I REALLY LIKED YOU. YOU 'AD ME PROPER FOOLED, WITH YOUR BEAUTIFUL DRESS AND YOUR NECKLACE WITH INSECTS IN IT. I THOUGHT YOU WERE LOVELY. BUT YOU'RE NOT. AND YOU'RE NOT CLASSY. YOU'RE BADLY BROUGHT UP – BADLY BROUGHT UP. AND BY THE WAY THE NEWSPAPER WAS MINE AND THAT'S WHAT I LIKE TO READ. SO YOU CAN KEEP YOUR BOOKS ABOUT MINERS AND THE WORKING CLASS AND ALL THAT CRAP. YOU THINK YOU'RE SOMETHING DON'T YOU? READING ALL ABOUT THE WORKING CLASS. BUT YOU DON'T HAVE A CLUE. YOU WERE BAD TO ME – ROTTEN- RUNNING AWAY WITH YOUR PALS LIKE THAT. YOU DON'T CARE A DAMN ABOUT MEN LIKE ME. DO YOU?"

He turns and staggers back down the corridor, we hear him belching as he leaves. "You did the right thing there kiddo," shouts one of the women from her bed. A quiet chorus of agreements follow - seems like quite a few of the patients have been sitting up watching. Everyone settles down again, the staff nurse picks up her knitting. After a while she looks at me quizzically, "Have you really got a necklace with insects in it?"

Victoria Hospital
Accident and Emergency
1983 May - July

Medical mishaps from dawn 'til dusk and all through the night. Fingernails and toenails, swollen and black; we drive hot sterile needles through them and wait for the blood to ooze or spurt. Needles in feet - X-rayed, dug out and removed. Foreign bodies in eyes, lit up with fluorescent drops then washed away with cool sterile water - the pain stops almost immediately. Scratched eyes, usually self inflicted when trying to remove foreign bodies - the pain may last for days. Lots and lots of cuts and gashes, mostly children. I am amazed how brave children can be for a tuppeny lolly. Fractured tibs and fibs; dislocated shoulders; concussion; overdose (para-suicide); overdose (accidental). Old ladies come in after having fainted in shops and make miraculous recoveries when we remove their clothing: hats; coats; scarves; jumpers; blouses; petticoats; vests; girdles and corsets. They sit back on their trolleys, heady with relief as their bodies cool and their lungs fill and empty, fill and empty, like new borns breathing God's good air at last. "I haven't had my clothes off for years," one of them tells me.

A young man comes in after being in a motor cycle accident. He lies on the trolley groaning, tries to sit up, wants to see the damage. "Let me look first," I say. He nods. I lift the sheet from his leg. Someone has already cut his clothes away. His leg is a total mess of blood and bone. I feel my own blood drain from my head to my feet, feel sick, hold on to the sides of the trolley to stop myself from swaying. "Is it bad?" He looks at me, pale face, big dark terrified eyes. "You'll be fine," I tell him in a wavery voice, watch his panic rise, hold a bag to his mouth and remind him to breathe. The man he crashed into is dead.

We are bit part actors in an endless stream of low budget disaster movies that we will never see the end of.

A woman comes in unconscious with alcoholic poisoning. She was found lying in the street outside a pub. Her hair is black. Her skin is yellow. She lies on the trolley like a corpse, but she has a pulse. A drip is set up and a catheter inserted. "She won't stay anyway," says Sister Bartholomew. "Just wait with her until she wakens." - "Shall I do her obs?" - "If you want." I feel silly just standing about, so I do the obs, record them neatly in a brand new chart. She comes round surprisingly quickly, opens her eyes. I feel my own open wide in alarm. The whites of her eyes are bright golden yellow. She looks like an un-bandaged mummy, or an alien. She pulls her drip out, looks down at the catheter tube in fury. I think she might pull that out too, "NO!" I shout and run for help. Sister comes back with me. "You going then?" The golden lady nods but says nothing. "Take it out," Sister tells me and leaves without further instruction.

Gently I deflate the balloon of the catheter and slide the tube out - "You should stay until you've passed urine." She pushes me aside with a growl and leaves. "Where will she go?" I ask Sister who stands watching with me as the yellow lady staggers towards the hospital gates. "Back to the pub," says Sister with a sigh.

A middle aged lady comes in who has swallowed a spoon. She is calm and composed. Her husband is crying. I walk her up to X-ray, watching slyly, trying not to stare. She has blonde hair, dry and greying at the temples, one eye is blue and the other brown. She doesn't speak. She has no facial expression at all; like she's done her bit and it's no concern of hers now, what happens to her body. The X-rays come back and the nurses gather round to see. In the dark space of her tummy - the spoon, a ring, the top half of a broken fork and a cigarette lighter - one of those cheap, transparent plastic ones. It still has gas in it.

A policeman comes in with constipation. I think this seems like a funny kind of ailment to come to hospital with until the doctor asks him when he last moved his bowels. "I can't remember. About three weeks ago - maybe longer," he says meekly. His wife groans and covers her eyes with embarrassment; as if she is responsible for the inner workings of her husband's digestive system. The doctor shows me the x-ray. "Look," he says, pointing; the faeces snake through our patient's body as if they've been told to form an orderly cue. "This policeman is full of shit," says the doctor, with a wink. He is admitted for observation and a series of enemas.

A couple come in with a baby, about a year old - their first child. He had a fall yesterday and may have banged his head.

He seems quite happy. I sit jiggling him on my knee. He is heavy and warm and pink, full of smiles for me. Sister and the doctor don't seem to have much time for this; they've run all the tests and everything seems fine. "But it won't last," says the baby's mum, her eyes full of anxiety. The father paces nearby, running his hands through his hair. "Come and get me if there's any change," says Sister.

I sit with the baby and his parents in the resuscitation room because there are no cubicles free. "You're very good with him," says the mum. I find myself telling her about my little brother and my cousins and the children I have babysat over the years. I feel happy talking about the children. The baby is happy too, laughing and trying to put his fingers into my mouth. All at once his colour drains, his little body feels floppy in my arms, his eyes glaze over and he isn't warm any more. I press the call bell three times. A small army of nurses and doctors come crashing through the double doors.

There is mayhem as they lay the baby onto a trolley, start pulling out drawers of drugs, opening vials and syringes. "WE NEED A PAEDIATRICIAN," someone shouts. "THERE IS NO PAEDIATRICIAN." Sister shouts back fiercely. The baby comes to. His colour returns. He looks at the doctor and howls. They listen to his heart again. They look at all the X-rays again. They study once more the long strips of paper: the electrocardiogram; the electroencephalogram - peering at the inky peaks and spikes, shaking their heads - perplexed and hopeless. The doctor shines his torch in the baby's eyes once more. Sister pricks his tiny heels, squeezes out a blob of blood. He doesn't like that. He cries, loud and strong - then his wailing trails to a whimper, his colour drains and he flops in his father's arms.

He comes and goes; warm then cold; pink then grey, over the next hour or so. He is to be transferred to the Sick Children's Hospital in Edinburgh by helicopter. His mum clutches my arm - "Will you come with us?" Sister stops and looks at me. "You can go if you like? There will be a doctor with you." I look at her in horror. "Maybe not then. We'll send a staff nurse." The baby leaves in a pink and healthy state, his parents grey with worry. I don't suppose I'll ever know what was wrong with him.

Every now and then there is a lull - an hour or so when all is quiet and no-one is injuring themselves in this cheerless town that sits by the sea but has no seaside. Casualty stops to catch it's breath; cupboards are cleaned, medicines counted, trolleys stacked. We sneak in twos to the sluice to smoke short cigarettes because there isn't time for long ones. I stand with an enrolled nurse who is about to retire. She's worked as a nurse for over forty years. Her eyes are tired but she's always the first to spring into action when there's an emergency. We tip our heads back and fill our lungs with nicotine.

The door flies open and a Nursing Officer stands before us; a small man, with dark hair and a dark beard. "WHAT THE HELL DO YOU THINK YOU ARE DOING?" He screams - red face, temples throbbing - I think - I might be imagining that. "THIS IS NOT ACCEPTABLE" he roars. A junior houseman passes and looks at us in alarm; he was in there smoking just a few minutes before us. I've met men like this nursing officer before - little Rumplestiltskin men. He's a grade above a Sister in rank, but he has none of their imperious authority. If he did we might not have chanced it; after all - nobody smokes in Tooje's sluice. "GET BACK TO WORK NOW." He yells at me. As I scurry off he turns to the enrolled nurse - "WHAT KIND OF EXAMPLE IS THIS TO SET TO STUDENTS? A WOMAN OF YOUR AGE. YOU SHOULD BE ASHAMED OF YOURSELF. INTO MY OFFICE NOW."

Back in the cubicles a little girl, just six years old has been brought in with vaginal wounds. Her mother is dead. She lives with her father. "She fell on a sewing machine," he says. "Do you do a lot of sewing?" I ask. I've never met a man that sews before. The doctor looks at me a little quzzically. He says the child will need to go to theatre to be stitched. "Just a few. Then we will put her in Ward 3 - to be on the safe side." The girl's father slumps in his seat, holds his head in his hands. Ward 3 - Tooje's ward, I think, with a shiver. But even though I hate her, I know that Tooje will be kind to this child. I think how nice it would be if she really was Glinda the Good Witch, the most powerful sorceress in the land of Oz; silver and rose like the fairy from the top of a Christmas tree. She could raise her sparkling wand and wish all the wicked things away.

Patients come in with self inflicted wounds, usually young

women. Waste of time patients some of the nurses call them; their wounds are superficial - rarely requiring stitches. One girl, about my age has placed a twelve inch ruler on her forearm and cut round it with a Stanley knife. "Why did you do it?" I ask, as I wind the soft net bandage round her palm, her thumb, the pale, tender skin of her wrist. She should be dabbing perfume here, I think - fastening bracelets - not cutting round a ruler with a Stanley knife. "Why a ruler?" I persist. She looks at me long and hard and I see something there in her eyes that stops my babble - makes me feel a little sick. I think I am beginning to understand the true depth of these superficial wounds.

Forth Park Maternity Hospital
1983 September - December

Antenatal

Some of the women are even younger than me, past their due dates, hoping their babies will be born before they are induced. Some of them are praying for caesareans. They pace the corridors in their fluffy slippers and long floral dressing gowns or cluster in the day room gossiping. Almost everyone is smoking. I follow Matron in to the day room. She strides across the floor, opens all the windows. "SMOKERS HAVE SMALLER BABIES," she shouts, hands on hips, looking around with sharp blue eyes, pink rosebud lips pursed. She is big and solid and stern looking - both feet in Scotland, my mum would say; a damn handsome woman, my father would say. Her sternness is a front. In truth she is warm and kind, reassuring - like all the midwives I have met. There are no Tooje's here, and although the atmosphere is tense, it's a good kind of tension - like Christmas eve.

"That's what I want," one of the younger girls pipes up. "A nice little baby that'll be easy to squeeze out." Her new found friends giggle and nod. "Nonsense," says Matron. "You want your baby big and strong and don't deny it. And who in this room is wearing a corset?" To my astonishment some of them put their hands up. I've seen adverts for corsets and girdles but I've never actually met anyone younger than my gran who wears one. "Really! Young girls like you! Take them off this minute!" Matron, shakes her head. "Put them in a bag for your hubbies to collect - or better still, throw them in the bin where they belong. We do not need corsets. Eat good healthy food, and nothing between meals. When you walk hold your tummy muscles in, it will strengthen your abdomen and your back."

They've heard it all before, the mums to be, but Matron cuts an imposing figure - and, although she's big, and probably in her fifties, she is in good shape herself, there's no denying it. The women fumble about below their dressing gowns. Half a dozen overstretched corsets are pulled off and brandished in the air. Women's lib I think - almost.

Labour

It's our first morning in Labour, though we've visited before, when we were in college. We were shown the Entinox, some of us were given a small blast of it. One of the girls went back for more then had to be taken away for a lie down. She laughed about it with the other students in college the next day. I envied their easy cheerfulness. I hadn't really taken any of the Entinox in; I was too inhibited, mistrusting of my situation. If I had taken too much Entinox, I would not have been able to laugh about it with the others the next day.

I'm here with another student, Neil - one of three men in our class who are training to be psychiatric nurses. They have to do three months of Maternity so they will understand about bonding. Matron is showing us the delivery equipment again, it's not really her job, but all the other midwives are busy. "Nothing on telly nine months ago today then," they had joked earlier as yet another woman was wheeled in puffing and gasping.

Our patient today sits bolt upright on the bed, completely silent. Neil and I say hello. She acknowledges us with a small flicker of her eyes. "Mrs Leong is Chinese," says Sister, smiling warmly at our patient. "She doesn't speak any English at all. Mind you - who needs chit chat? Mrs Leong is concentrating. Aren't you Dear?" Mrs Leong gives a slight nod. Matron continues, "She knows what she's doing, this is her fifth." Matron has taken hold of Mrs Leong's hand and is nodding at her as she talks, as if the two of them have reached some kind of private agreement. "She's a while yet to go," Matron tells us, patting the bed affectionately as she turns to leave. "Just you stay here and keep her company."

We stand hugging the radiator below the window, chatting. Rain batters against the huge glass panes, the old metal window frames give off an icy chill. "I hate this," Neil says quietly. "I just feel like I shouldn't be here. It doesn't seem right at all. I mean – what do I have to offer these women?" He gestures in Mrs Leong's direction. I wonder if she is listening to us. "Every day I just want to phone in sick." - "I like Maternity," I tell him. "It's the first thing I've liked since Geriatrics." He looks thoughtful - "So you like beginnings and endings?" I'm not sure what to say about that. I ask him how he's finding his psychiatric training, but he stops me short with his horrified expression. Our patient has pulled her covers off and is sitting open legged, peering down as the top of her baby's head appears. She is completely silent but her face and fists are scrunched in pain.

"Ring three bells!" I shout to Neil and he does, but nobody comes. "DELIVERY PACK," Neil yells. I turn to the trolley behind me. There are half a dozen different packs, none of them seem to have a name. "ANY FUCKING PACK," he shouts. I grab the nearest and throw it at him. He opens it, exactly as we have been shown how to and spreads a green sterile surgeon's apron on to the bed for the baby to be born onto. We ring three bells again and a few moments later, though it feels like ages, Matron appears. "Goodness," she says, quickly assessing the situation. "I thought you'd rung the bells by accident."

The baby's upper body is out and the mum leans back and gives a long, hard, last squeeze. A bottom and two little legs slither out. "BRAVO!" Matron shouts, wrapping a sterile apron round herself. "WELL DONE!" She lifts the baby up, small and slippery and squirming, perfectly formed. "A GIRL! A BEAUTIFUL LITTLE GIRL!" I put my hands to my face, realise that I'm crying, but I'm laughing too. I am filled with an incredible sense of well being. "That was fucking brilliant," Neil says. We stand there looking at each other, grinning, then we remember our patient, look to see how she is faring, but she has closed her eyes, turned her face from us, and her child - daughter number five.

Baby was meant to be born at home but the community midwife feared complications and called an ambulance. This is their first child and the father-to-be has come in with his wife. He is running alongside her trolley holding a video camera. The midwives stand at the nurses station frowning. "He has the consultant's permission," one of the porters shouts, rolling his eyes skywards. "Come on then," Edith, the most senior mid-wife on duty today says to me with a sigh, then turns to her colleagues - "You best call Matron."

Our patient's cervix is almost fully dilated. "Not long to go now then," Edith declares breezily. She pats our patient's hand reassuringly. "Looks like you could do with some Entinox?" - "NO DRUGS," Dad shouts from behind his camera. Edith helps our patient to sit up, holds the mask to her face while she drinks the gas deep into her lungs, then lies back in relief. "Better?" Mum nods with a grateful smile. "You just keep hold of that then," Edith says, moving down the bed to see how baby is progressing.

She elbows the father out of the way without even looking at him, but he isn't to be deterred - everything will be on film. I stand by his wife trying not to look gormless. I've never seen a video camera before. I'm surprised how small and light it looks, not at all like the great big things you see on Top of the Pops or Tomorrow's World. I wonder what I will look like on film; imagine the child watching in years to come, thinking - *Who is that gormless looking girl in the background?* Mum is gritting her teeth, bearing down. "PUSH. PUSH," shouts Edith. "Now nice little breaths. Maybe your husband would like to help you with the breathing?" He doesn't move an inch, not even when Matron comes in, adopts her most intimidating stance and glares at him for a good long while.

It's a quick labour, with no complications despite the community midwife's fears. They have a boy, 8lbs 4oz and full marks on the Apgar Score. "MAXIMUS!" His father shouts triumphantly as the boy child appears into the world. "Poor little sod," say the mid-wives later, sipping their tea at the nurses station.

It's 9am, school will have started, the second bell will have rung, but this school girl won't be in today. She was taking too long in the bathroom, making funny noises, not responding to her parent's questions. Her father kicked the door open. She was in labour, they didn't even know she was pregnant.

"She mustn't see the baby," Matron says. "It's to be adopted. - it will be easier on them both if they just don't see each other." We are standing at the nurses station. There will be no students at this birth, Matron and Sister are handling things. The girl's father, the grandfather, paces up and down the corridor wringing his hands. "She says she didn't even know she was pregnant," Edith mutters to one of the other mid-wives. "Aye right," her colleague says, "I've heard that one before."

I wonder if it's unusual to have sex when you are still at school. I didn't think it was, but now I'm feeling less certain. The midwives have lots of stories of under age and unmarried mothers. They are strangely unsympathetic - as if they never have sex themselves, though I'm sure they must. Someone tells me about a Sister who had a baby and left it under a hedge in the park. "The child was almost dead," my colleague says in disgust. "What happened to the Sister?" - "Who knows. She certainly isn't a Sister any more."

I wonder how they can be so sure it won't happen to them. I wish I felt so confident. I feel myself growing uncomfortably warm as Neil passes by with a cheeky smile. I spent last night in his room, woke up feeling happy, but now I feel a new anxiety blooming. I took a chance last night - what if I'm the next one making funny noises in the bathroom? What if I'm the one that ends up hiding her baby under a hedge in the park?

Postnatal

This morning we were shown how to bathe the newborns. Now we are supposed to teach the mums. Neil is terrified of dropping someone's baby. The midwife who is supervising us sees his discomfort and takes pity. "I'll leave you both to get on with it," she says with a wink, trots off in the direction of the office. Neil sits down and lets me do the bathing. The women poke fun at him. "You'll be a daddy one day, you might as well learn now." We don't look at one another but I guess he's squirming like me.

Most of the women prefer to bottle feed; they line up waiting to have their breasts bound to stop the flow of their milk. Great lengths of bandages are wrapped round their upper bodies. It feels ancient and wrong; mummifying their breasts; staunching their milk - their precious life force, while their babies lie crying in the nursery. There's something good about it too though - women caring for women. I like that feeling a lot.

The ward is quiet and Neil and I stand at the window chatting. A double decker bus pulls up right below us outside the hospital entrance. Two passengers and the driver jump out, bustling round a heavily pregnant woman. Her knees buckle. We hear her cry of pain. Two nurses run out with a wheel chair. The pregnant woman sits in the chair and the bus driver loops her shopping onto the handles behind her. She manages to turn and wave to the passengers in the bus. We hear a cheer as she is wheeled off by the nurses. The driver stands watching for a moment then jumps back in to his seat, toots the horn twice, then off he goes, back to his normal workaday route.

We turn back towards our own new mums. Matron is watching as one of them kisses her baby - slipping her tongue right into his mouth. She has twins, a boy and a girl, the baby girl lies crying in her crib. "What are you doing?" Matron isn't looking very impressed. "I'm kissing him," says Mum. She looks to me like a woman in love. I walk over and pick up her girl, hold her close, kiss the top of her fuzzy little head, then remember Matron; we aren't really meant to kiss the babies. Matron isn't worried about that though; she is watching Mum, her brow furrowed, her mouth downturned. She seems to shiver, despite the heat of the ward.

The mums and babies stay with us for a week - the mums on the ward, the babies in the nursery. The babies wear little white hospital robes while they are here, but on the day they go home they are dressed in proper clothes by a nurse. New fathers hover nervously while their wives dress themselves in the big bathroom - putting on make up, wrapping corsets round their swollen bellies, cramming puffy feet into tight high heeled shoes.

I love dressing the babies more than anything else I've done in my training. I love carrying them down to the main entrance, standing on the top step having my photo taken with them. The mums get emotional, the dads too sometimes - shaking our hands vigorously, squeezing just a little too hard. They slide the brand new carry cots into the back seats of their washed and polished cars. Everything feels good and right in the world, standing there smiling in my bright white uniform, my cardboard hat with two blue stripes, my hair newly dyed and bobbed, cradling other women's babies against my own flat, empty tummy.

Springfield Woods
1983 November

Neil has brought me to his house by the river Eden. He shares with a couple from Hull called Rod and Celia, and a great big guy that they call Pie - Celia says his real name is Fergus. Rod studied Philosophy with Neil at St Andrews and he's now working on his Phd. Celia is a nurse in the little cottage hospital in Cupar, but she studied at St Andrews too - English Literature. Pie was doing Economics, but he dropped out half way through his second year. He isn't really meant to live in the house; he came to visit several months ago and never left. He calls me child. He stares at me a lot, and calls across the room - "Come to me child." When I go over to him he just keeps looking at me, like he's in a trance. Neil says I should just ignore him. Celia has put a padlock on the fridge to stop him eating all the food. She told me the combination and Neil thinks Pie is going to try and wheedle it out of me.

On the kitchen table there is a giant bowl of punch that has magic mushrooms floating in it. Celia says we should eat lunch before we even think of having any of that. She has made some very thick pasta soup and really delicious bread with olives baked into it. After that we each have a mug of punch, then Celia, Rod, Neil and I get ready to go out for a walk to the pub in the village. Pie stays put, sitting in a big old rocking chair by the window. Celia locks the fridge and tells him not to put anything else in the punch and not to take any more of it. When we get outside she says, "He'll have the lot, just you wait and see."

We trek through the woods and along the riverside. Rod points out different types of fungi, tells us their names, the ones that are edible and the ones that would kill you. We stop for a smoke in the ruins of an old cottage. A small group of people appear quite suddenly before us; none of us had heard their approach. They look like a family; a mother; a father and three pale and very tired looking children. The father asks us if we know the way to the sugar beet factory. Rod turns and points behind us in the general direction of the house. "It's over that way, but I don't think you'll get to it from here. You could try walking along the river, but I'm not sure it's possible." - "We're looking for work," the father explains. "I don't think it's open," says Rod. "I think it closed a few years ago." The parents stand staring at Rod, as if they are willing him to be wrong. Then the wife nods and smiles, kind of subserviently. They thank us politely and carry on walking. We stand for a while, until they have passed the house and we hear the clank of the farm gates beyond. "That was weird," says Rod. "I'm pretty sure that sugar beet factory's been closed for years."

We talk about them as we make our way up a muddy road and on towards the railway crossing; how they just seemed to appear from nowhere; how poor they looked; their strange accent which none of us could place. "Those poor kids," Celia says. "Well they might be all right," Neil argues. "They probably get lots of exercise and maybe not such a bad diet - maybe like a wartime diet. Very healthy you know, war time diets." Celia looks at me sideways and we exchange a little smile.

There are cows in the fields on either side of us, some of them are frolicking around. Rod says that means there's a storm coming. We stop to look at them. They start wandering towards us, steam coming out of their nostrils in the cold air. They stand at the fence regarding us with their huge black eyes that look like planets. Celia leans on the fence beside me. I turn to speak to her and it seems to me that her eyes have grown really big and dark too, and her eyelashes seem to be getting longer. I start laughing and it's hard to stop, but I manage to tell her what's happening. She stares into the cows eyes, then at me. "Oh my God," she says. "Yeah – you've got cow's eyes too!" We all stand staring at the cows and the cows stare back. "I will never eat you again," I say to one of them. Celia nods in silent agreement; her and Rod are vegetarian like me, but I've been slipping a bit recently, eating black pudding rolls in the canteen. I never ate black pudding before, there's no way I would have eaten it as a child, but lately I positively crave it. "Is black pudding made from cows?" - "Shhh!" Celia covers my mouth with her mittened hand. "You'll make them sad." They do look sad. It's hard to imagine how these beautiful creatures could become black pudding. I wonder how many of them I have eaten in my life - ten, fifteen, twenty? I imagine all the eaten cows standing in front of me staring with their planetary eyes.

There are sheep in a little paddock by the pub and they run

over to be petted by us. We sink our hands into their bouncy woollen coats in amazement. "They are magic sheep," says Celia. We lean across the fence, making soft, baaing noises, our noses almost touching theirs. I smell my hand and it honestly smells like roast lamb flavoured crisps. The others copy me and everything is impossibly funny.

We are the only people in the pub. The bar man eyes us suspiciously. All the lights are on and it feels cold and unfriendly. The barman's neck is long and thin. He has a very big Adam's apple, when he talks it goes up and down like an animal trying to get out. Rod stands next to me as we wait for our drinks and I wonder if he can see this throaty phenomenon too, but when I look at him he seems preoccupied by the hairs on the back of his hand.

A guy comes in wearing a black leather jacket, a torn tartan shirt and jeans with beermat patches. Rod buys him a lager and he comes over to sit with us. He has a leather thong round his neck with a Celtic cross. His name is Irish - though he doesn't seem to be Irish. He has long straggly blonde hair, small, very dark eyes and pale, delicate looking skin. He looks at us curiously and Neil tells him about the mushrooms - he laughs at that, nods knowingly. Rod tells him about the family we met and asks about the sugar beet factory. "Gypsies," Irish says. "They camp in the grounds of the hospital every year, but you're right, the sugar beet factory closed ages ago - 1970 I think."

Walking back through the woods in the dimming light it

feels like a fairy tale forest; all deep and dark and green. I can't believe we met gypsies in the woods. Everything feels strange and unreal. Nothing is normal here, today. Even the most ordinary things - the more you stare at them, the more incredible they become. *Incredible* - I think about the meaning of that word and it is the perfect word for what's happening to me now. When I look down to the ground I think I can see little creatures wriggling around my feet. That feels a bit too freaky, so I focus on the leaves which are falling as we walk, flip flopping in the air, as if they are floating down to greet us. Some still hang on to their branches, like curls of precious metal - gold and copper and bronze spinning in the dusk. The moon is slowly appearing, big, like a harvest moon, but paler, colder.

We find the body of a fox, it looks like someone has chopped its head off with a knife. Rod and Neil and Irish, who is coming back with us, examine it closely. I have to look away because it seems to me that there are little creatures writhing about there too - in the gaping wound where the head should be. "That wasn't done by an animal," Irish says. "Well not a four legged one," Neil adds. "It'll be the farmer," Rod says. "He'll have hung it up as a warning to other foxes." - "But why would he chop it's head off?" I hear my own voice, high and childish in the quiet of the wood. "Maybe he thought it would be more scary to the other foxes," Rod says. We stand for a moment, thinking about foxes being scared - well that's what I'm thinking about. Then I think - I could never marry a farmer. Tories, policemen, butchers, farmers - that's my list of who not to marry - so far. "Well something took it down again," says Celia. "Maybe Mrs Fox," I say. Neil gives a little snort.

It seems like we've been away for hours, days even - but when we get back to the house it's not even tea time, not that anyone wants anything to eat. Celia was right, it was best to eat food before the mushrooms. Pie has had more punch but there's still some left and we all have another cup full. We sit by the fireside drinking and smoking and laughing for no sensible reason. Rain lashes against the window and wind whooshes in the chimney. Irish looks wild, like he's just come in from a storm this minute. I think he probably always looks like that. I don't think his hair has ever seen a comb, but he really seems to be quite nice - quiet and gentle. Pie sits at the window staring. Neil says he's sleeping with his eyes open. Celia puts a blanket over him.

We decide that, as it is nearly December, we should put some fairy lights about the place. Celia takes me upstairs to her and Rod's room. It's a beautiful room with a sloping roof and deep window sills. There is a long speckled mirror, a colourful patchwork bedspread, and silk scarves about the place, but it is cold and our breath streams out of our mouths in long stringy puffs. I sit on the window sill as Celia rummages about under the bed then pulls out a box of Christmas decorations. "Oh they are so lovely!" I say, rushing over and falling upon them as if upon a trunk full of treasure. I bury my face in a bundle of tinsel. It smells like Christmas. I pull out a fluffy silver strand and wrap it round Celia's head, tie it at the back and weave it through her thick dark hair.

We go back downstairs. The warmth and the smell of the smoke and the cheer of the fire feels wonderful. We hang lights along the mantle piece and around the window frames. Pie seems to come out of his stupor and laughs as I wind red tinsel round his head like a ruby crown, reciting scraps of primary school poetry.

"What would you Fergus, King of the proud Red Branch kings?
Be no more a king, but learn the dreaming wisdom that is yours.
A king is but a foolish labourer who wastes his blood to be another's dream
And so I laid the crown upon his head to cast away my sorrow..."

Pie reaches out to pull me onto his lap and I let him, hugging him for a moment; it seems to me that he is a sad and lonely man, and really could be Fergus the King of Scotland who gave up his crown to become a wandering poet.

The next day Celia and I are up first. We wash all the dishes and glasses, empty the ashtrays, throw out the bottles and cans, clean out the fireplace and set a new fire - while the men lie sleeping upstairs. I don't mind. I love being alone with Celia. She has read all the same books as me and many more. We both like George Eliot and some Thomas Hardy. She is less keen on D H Lawrence, though she seems to enjoy my dramatic recitations of the steamy bits. She hasn't read Sunset Song but she's always meant to. I can't wait to lend her it and talk about it with her.

We can't eat yet, we have no appetite, but we drink lots of coffee, sitting on the lumpy old sofa in front of the fire with a tartan rug over our knees. Celia rolls a joint and she asks me how I'm enjoying my maternity placement. I tell her that it's my favourite placement so far because I like working with women and I love babies, though I don't want one myself for a very long time. I tell her about the school girl mum. She tells me that she had a baby when she was fifteen, with a boy the same age who she was in love with. "We could have been okay. We might not have stayed together forever, but we really loved each other and we would have loved our child. But our parents said we were too young - the baby was to be adopted. We didn't have any say in the matter at all."

She is wiping her face on the sleeve of her jumper. I reach into my bag for some tissues. She blows her nose loudly. "I can feel him wanting me all the time. I can still hear his cry - and I want him so much. Sometimes I feel so bad I think about killing myself. But I can't do that because one day he might try and find me. He might need me. I have to stay in the world for him." She starts moaning loudly and bashing her hands against her head. I reach out and stop her, put my arms around her. We sit like that for a while, rocking gently. It feels a little like we are on a boat, lost at sea, but the fire crackles and snaps and draws us back to the present. Celia sits up and looks at me. It's like her soul is sitting right behind her eyes. I think that hers is a soul that will always be in pain.

We stoke up the fire, make some more coffee and snuggle

down under the blanket. I tell her that I fell in love when I was fifteen too, with a boy from school, a couple of years older than me. As I'm telling her I realise that he had pain there in his eyes, all the time, like Celia - even when he was laughing or smiling. I think I thought his sadness was because of something I had done, but now I'm starting to realise it wasn't anything to do with me. I don't know what caused it, but I don't think it was me. I've been thinking about him a lot recently, because of the things I saw in casualty and because I want to feel the way I felt about him again, and I'm beginning to think I never will.

I had wanted be with him for ages before we became a couple, and that first year together was like being in heaven. I had never dreamed I could be so happy. But after a couple of years something changed, and we began to row. He became increasingly more moody and possessive, not wanting to go out and be with other people. I started drinking heavily, smoking cigarettes - behaving in every way I knew he hated. I behaved horribly. Then one night, after I'd said I felt we were too young to get married, he took an overdose. My brother found him, lying on our living room floor. He was meant to be sleeping on the sofa, but instead he had eaten the contents of my parent's medicine box: Paracetamol; Aspirin; Warfarin; Digoxin - even some of my mother's birth control pills. We were told at the hospital that, if he hadn't washed everything down with whisky and vomited some of it back up again, he would have been dead. "Whisky saved him," Dad said in the car as he drove me home later. "Uisge Beath - water of life."

I tell Celia how unhappy I am living in Kirkcaldy, and how I don't really feel like a nurse. I tell her about Rab and Andy and Tooje and my mum, who we thought was doing well, but is now being investigated for lumps in her throat. I tell her about the woman who had faeces coming out of her mouth before she died - the nightmares I've had ever since. She takes my hand and looks at me very seriously. "Don't give up till you've done your psychiatric placement. I think you'll find you fit in better up there."

Path House
Kirkcaldy
1983 December

It's my last weekend in Kirkcaldy, my last night in this nurses' home. I am in the kitchen gathering my things; some small pots and pans that I have never used because I hate going in there. A few of the nurses are sitting round the table. I nodded politely when I came in, but we didn't talk. I can feel them watching me as I rake about in the cupboard below the sink. "You off out tonight then?" Someone calls out and I realise, because no one else answers, that she must be talking to me. I turn round and see they are all watching me. "If you are going out you can relax in the morning. Peggy and Jean are both off." Peggy and Jean are the cleaners, they seem quite nice when you meet them, but they will tell on you if you step out of line, they are famous for it. "Thanks," I say, wondering why they are taking an interest in me now, guessing its because I'm leaving.

I trawl through my clothes looking for something to wear. We are going to Jackie O's - I can't really wear a long dress there. I pull out the stripey cotton trousers that I bought with Shona, and a short white fluffy jumper. The trousers will be too cold and the jumper will be too hot, but I don't care. It's my last night in Kirkcaldy. In the morning I will be going home for Christmas and in the new year I will start my psychiatric placement. If I like psychiatry then I'll switch to that. If I hate it, I'm going to give the whole thing up. I haven't told anyone yet, but I've decided that I'm never going back to the Victoria hospital again.

Shona and Samira are dressed in super short, tight dresses. Samira's is split in two with a small metal chain holding the top and bottom half together at the front. "I know," she says. "I look like a right little tart. I've heard it all from Donald and I don't give a damn." - "You look amazing!" She really does; she is so tall and slender and her brown skin looks gorgeous against the white and gold of the dress. "No wonder he's worried." She bites her lower lip, frowning. "Maybe I was a bit hard on him. Maybe he's just feeling insecure - and I told him to go to hell." - "He'll be fine," Shona says. "It's good to make them jealous every now and again. Keep them on their toes." Samira looks at me, neither of us are convinced. She sits on Shona's bed and lights a fag, takes a swig of the pineapple liqueur that Linda brought back from her holiday in Toremolinos.

Jackie O's is mobbed; everyone seems to be even drunker than usual, so I don't feel too self conscious dancing. I'm excited about Christmas, and I quite like the music, though I would never buy it - Don't You Want Me Baby, Tainted Love, Do You Believe in Love… Shona is going crazy because there's a crowd of Navy boys in from Rosyth - matlos as she calls them. They like her too and they really like Samira, who is very drunk and flirting like mad. I've never really met anyone from the forces and I have no idea what their life must be like. I get talking to a quiet guy called Harry; he is a bit older than the others - they call him Harry Belafonti. "Who is Harry Belafonti?" He laughs, "Oh just an old git like me." - "You're not old," I tell him. He's very good looking; lean faced; kind blue eyes; short, reddish hair and a light tan, despite the time of year - but he has a moustache, as if he is actually trying to look older. We leave the dance bar for the quiet bar next door; the one I sat in after I bashed my nose. It isn't quiet at this bar tonight though; the whole place is heaving. "Aren't you hot?" He pinches the sleeve of my fluffy jumper. "I'm roasting," I tell him. "And I hate this place." - "Likewise," he says. "Is there anywhere better round here?"

We buy chips from a van on the promenade; stand at the sea wall eating, looking across the water. I point out my village. We wave and shout goodnight to my mum and dad and my little brother. It's a very still night, not especially cold for the season, but my legs are freezing in the thin cotton trousers that stop quite a bit above my ankle. My jacket isn't very warm either. I start to shiver. He puts his arm around me, offers to walk me home. "I have some beers in my room," I tell him. "Excellent," he says.

We sit up for ages talking. He tells me about the Falklands. He tells me that they were given capsules to swallow if they were captured; suicide pills, so that they wouldn't give information to the enemy if they were interrogated under torture. I tell him that I'm a pacifist. He laughs and says, "Well so am I" - "But how can you be?" - "You think I want war? Especially now - it's just a job you know. It's good money and it keeps the wife happy." I must look horrified because he laughs. "Ex-wife," he says. "And not exactly happy. It's been a long time since I made her happy." He seems low in his mood now, broody. He misses his children, shows me a picture - a girl about five with her arms round a younger boy - her baby brother. "Will you see them for Christmas?" He shrugs, "Maybe for an hour or so."

We talk some more about the military and war and what he could do if he left the Navy; he seems to be considering it. It's very late and we are quite drunk because he had whisky in his pocket and we've been drinking that too. At about 3am he says he's going to sleep in his car, which is parked down by the sea wall. "You can stay here if you like?" I tell him, remembering that the cleaners are off tomorrow. "It's too cold to sleep in a car." We get into bed and he curls round me, saying, "You're just a kid, we'll just cuddle."

I wake up fully dressed, Harry's body still curled around mine. He's sleeping soundly. I'm starving, so I slip out of bed, pull the duvet up around him and put my boots and coat on. The home is quiet; the early shift nurses will have left already; the lates will still be fast asleep. I nip down to the bakers on the corner and buy some fresh baked doughnuts, eat one as I wander back, warming my hands on the brown paper bag. The doughnuts are light and greasy and delicious. I lick the sugar from my fingers, think about Harry; how much I like him, even if he is a bit older and in the armed forces. I think about Shona and her obsession with matlos. Thinking of Shona makes me smile.

I guess as soon as I hear the screams, and sure enough when I get to the top of the stairs I see Peggy's big behind. She is screaming hysterically. Harry is behind her saying, "What's the matter? What's the problem?" He is looking around as if a bunch of enemy soldiers might come leaping through the walls, but the only enemies are Peggy and Jean. They stand together like a pair of armed forces in themselves. Peggy turns to me, her face twisted with rage - "YOU'VE DONE IT NOW MADAM. YOU'RE OUT ON YOUR EAR NOW. I'LL SEE TO THAT." - "Jesus," says Harry. "What's the problem?" - "THERE'S NO MEN ALLOWED IN HERE" Peggy roars. "AND FINE SHE KNOWS IT. THE LITTLE TART."

Harry straightens himself up. "That's enough," he says, in a cold, commanding voice that seems to take them by surprise. "Go on. Piss off. Both of you. It's her room. She pays the rent. You should never have come in here without her permission." He pushes them gently down the corridor, pulls me through the door and slams it shut. "Jesus," he says, sitting on the bed. "Where were you? What a bloody fright I got. I was fast asleep and all I heard was screaming. I thought I was dreaming, but, when I opened my eyes that big one had her face right next to mine. I thought - Jesus Harry, what have you done? Were you really that drunk?" We both start laughing, though I know I shouldn't. I know that I'm in big trouble. "I was definitely told that they were on holiday," I say to him. "Oh yeah? By who? Your friends in the kitchen?" I sit down, still clutching the doughnuts, remember the conversation the day before, and groan out loud because I know he's right.

He brings his car to the front door and piles my stuff into it. Two of the nurses are standing at the doorway watching. He waves politely, then flicks the V's as we leave. He drives me all the way to Gullane. When we get there we sit in the car for a while, parked in front of my house. We look at the sea and Kirkcaldy beyond it. "I'm never going back there," I say. He squeezes my knee. "Do you want to come in and meet my parents?" He laughs. "Yeah sure - they would love that - an ancient old git like me that's probably just got their daughter thrown off her course." - "You aren't even forty," I say, my voice high and indignant. "And you aren't even twenty," he says. "I will be next week," I remind him. I had thought it seemed quite old, twenty, but the look on his face is telling me otherwise.

I don't tell anyone in my family what has happened. I know in my head that I haven't done anything particularly shameful. I have done some bad things in my life and this isn't one of them - but I feel ashamed. I feel as if I have done something so terrible that it mustn't ever be talked about. I don't tell them that I'm planning to give up my general training either.

A letter from the College of Nursing arrives on the day of my birthday and I read it at the breakfast table with my parents watching. I read it quickly and stuff it in my dressing gown pocket as if it's nothing. "What does it say?" Mum is looking a little concerned. "It's just about my next placement - the psychiatric hospital. It's just the details for the nurse's home."

I ring Neil that afternoon when my parents are out. He seems pleased to hear from me, until I tell him what happened, then he is very quiet. "Nothing happened," I tell him. "I mean, with him and me. He just needed somewhere to sleep." I tell him that I have been told to report to the head of the college on Monday 10th January - the day I'm meant to start my placement. He says I need to give him time to think.

He rings me on the 5th January. Mum answers the phone and I have to talk to him in the kitchen with her there, chopping vegetables, trying to act like she isn't listening. She seems to know that something is wrong. It should have been a really happy Christmas, with her having been given the all clear for cancer; but I'm not very good at hiding my anxiety. I've been smoking a lot - she's really angry about that.

Neil tells me that he's arranged for our union rep to accompany me to the meeting on the tenth. He says I'm entitled. He says, "They are Born Again Christians. You won't stand a chance without help from the union." - "What about us?" I ask him. "Is it over?" - "I don't know. You tell me." There is an awkward silence and I realise that I actually want it to be over. "There's your answer then eh?" He puts the phone down without saying goodbye. Mum turns and looks at me, but I ignore her.

The union rep phones me the next day; luckily Dad is at work and Mum is out shopping - I can talk to him properly. He works at the psychiatric hospital so I haven't ever met him. He's Irish and his name is Colm; he pronounces it like Colin with an M at the end. I tell him my sorry tale, find myself trying to convince him that nothing happened between Harry and I, that we didn't even take our clothes off. "I don't need to know," he says. "And neither do they. Just keep your mouth shut. Let me do the talking. You say NOTHING. Got that?" I start crying and he becomes a little kinder. "We'll get this sorted," he says. "Over my dead body will they end your training over this."

The Director of Nursing is unavailable due to a family emergency, so his assistant, Miss Gillhoolie, is to interview me. I arrive early and sit in the corridor outside her office. She struts out and asks me to come on in. "I'm waiting for my union rep," I tell her. She stands looking at me very frostily. Colm arrives, looking impatient, as if he'd rather be doing anything than this. He doesn't shake my hand. He says, "Come on then, let's get this over with."

We sit looking at Miss Gilhoolie across the desk. Nobody says anything. She heaves a big sigh then leans back in her chair looking at me down her long nose. "What have you got to say for yourself then? You know full well there are no men allowed in any of our nurses' homes. Our domestic staff were very distressed by this incident. They felt unsafe and intimidated by your... friend's behaviour towards them. You put everyone in that house at risk." She is staring at me, expecting an answer. It's hard not to speak. I look at Colm, but he doesn't look like he's about to say anything either. Miss Gilhooly continues - "The question is - should someone who behaves in this manner be allowed to continue their training?"

Colm leans forward in his seat - "Am I to understand that you are considering ending this girl's training?" She turns her haughty gaze in his direction. "That's exactly what we are considering." - "So what's to happen to all the male nurses who were caught with girls in their rooms last year? Seven male nurses - SEVEN have told me they were caught and nothing happened. Not one word about their training being discontinued was there? And what about that party in the male nurses home last September? Lots of girls there that night eh? And a sink pulled off the wall I believe? Quite a lot of water damage, the room out of use for several months as I understand it. Quite a lot of damage all in all. Must have cost a bit. Nobody's training was under question following that incident was it? And no complaints from the domestic staff either, they took that in their stride didn't they?"

Miss Gilhooly's face turns white with anger. "There are obvious differences in terms of risk and gender which I don't think even you can deny. This - girl - brought a stranger into our property. A military man I believe - and left him, free to roam the building as he pleased." When she says *military man* her nostrils flare and her bottom lip quivers in a way that makes me want to laugh so I have to look down at my lap.

"Anyway, if we keep her on, where is she to stay when she comes back from her psychiatric placement? Our domestic staff have made it quite clear they don't want her back at Path House." - "I'm not coming back," I butt in. "I'm not coming back to General. I want to swap to Psychiatry - please." Miss Gilhooley's shoulders drop a bit, as if with relief. She throws her pen on to the desk in front of her. "Well that puts a rather different complexion on things I suppose. I shall leave this mess for my psychiatric colleagues to resolve. But make no mistake," she leans forward in her seat and hisses at me - "One more episode like this and you are out."

Stratheden Psychiatric Hospital
1984 January

I've been given a temporary room in the nurses home. It's a large, mixed sex home that sits within the hospital grounds. I haven't brought much with me: my coffee pot and cups; my Dansette; a few records, some books and a small suitcase of clothes. I've bought some food from the hospital shop. I take it along to the big old kitchen. Three female nurses are in there, sitting at the table smoking. I feel their eyes upon me. Everyone seems to know what happened at Path House. At first I thought it was just in my head, but Neil laughed at that. "No, it's not just in your head. Everyone knows." He has a new, rather cold tone when he speaks to me now. I stuff my food in the fridge and leave the kitchen without saying anything. I'm not going to eat it anyway.

College starts the next day. In the morning, not long after we have started our first lecture, Mr Williamson, the Director of Psychiatric Nursing Studies comes into our classroom and asks me to come to his office. I follow him along the corridor, wondering if I'm going to get chucked off the course, wondering if Colm should be with me. *Mr William Williamson* it says on his door. I think that seems a very practical, informative name, unless his father was called Bob or something. I would like to ask him, but of course I won't.

Mr Williamson isn't like Miss Gilhooly at all. He is very polite and he looks kind, and sad. There is a hostess trolley in the corner of the room with a kettle, teapot and mugs. He asks if I would like a cup of tea. I watch as he fusses around making it. I have an uncle called Maurice and a cousin, his son, called Maurice and they are known as Big Maurice and Wee Maurice, though nowadays my cousin is quite a bit taller than my uncle. I wonder if Mr Williamson is called Wee Willie by his parents. Or maybe his father is dead and he has his own son now, so he would be Big Willie. What would happen if there were three generations of Willies living at once? When does Big Willie become Auld Willie and Wee Willie become Big Willie? I wonder if they have some kind of ceremony. I can't believe I'm thinking these ridiculous thoughts when something really bad might be about to happen to me.

He sits down at his desk, sipping his tea and says, "So you are from Gullane then?" We have a little chat about Gullane; the beautiful beach, the four golf courses. His wife is a fan of a writer that lives there - "Nigel Tranter - perhaps you know of him?" - "Yes I do." I sit up in my chair, feeling very surprised at this pleasant and unexpected conversation. "His grand daughter is a good friend of mine. I've met him at her house a few times, and I often see him running along Gullane beach." - "Really? Perhaps you could get a book signed for me?" - "Of course. I'd be happy to sort that out." Surely he wouldn't be asking me to do that if he was about to throw me off the course. He sits back in his chair looking at me wistfully. I look back at him, trying not to think about the Big Willie/Wee Willie thing. I think about Nigel Tranter running on the beach in very small underpants. I think - I'll have to take a pen with me as well as the book.

Mr Williamson seems to waken from his reverie. He tilts his head and smiles, then he says that he has been told he must take action to protect the other nurses. He says he has no choice. He's sorry, but I am to leave the Stratheden nurse's home and live in the old nurse's home above the Adamson Hospital in Cupar. It hasn't been used for years. I will be the only person living there.

I have to go into the Adamson Hospital to get the key to my room. It's a convalescent hospital and most of the patients are old. They don't really look like they are convalescing - they mostly look like they are about to die. A little lady with a very sweet smile waves to me. I wave back. She seems to think she knows me. "That's Isa," says the Sister, smiling. "She's a wee darling." I wonder if the Sister knows my story. If she does, she doesn't seem to care; she is cheerful and pleasant. "I'll give you the key to the biggest room," she says. "The cleaners have been up, so it's all ready, and you'll certainly be warm enough. Miss Gilhooley told me I was to keep the key here. You're meant to collect and return it every time you go out, but I don't see any need for that nonsense. You just keep it and do as you please. I'll give you a back door one too, so you can get to your room without traipsing through the whole building."

I love my room. It feels kind of melancholy, in a good way; tranquil, with 1930's utility furniture and a sage green carpet that has a pattern of squares and little brown flowers. One window looks out onto the long, curved hospital drive with meadows and the old sugar beet factory in the distance. The other looks on to some woods and the entrance to the mortuary. The main body of the mortuary seems to be beneath my room.

There's a small kitchen with a tiny fridge that's really meant for keeping medicines in, a two ring Baby Belling stove, a twin tub washing machine and an overhead pulley. The sitting room is big with a large bookcase and a table by the window - no television. There are lots of old paperbacks, mostly Mills and Boon but some by Victoria Holt, Barbara Cartland, Catherine Cookson and two Nigel Tranters. I wonder if William Williamson's wife ever lived here. Nurses often marry other nurses; maybe he thought he'd send me to a place that he had fond memories of. Not that he would ever have visited her here I don't suppose; that would be against the rules. There's a bible, a medical dictionary, hundreds of old copies of Nursing Times, and the British Journal of Nursing - also a huge pile of Scots Magazines dating back to 1962. Amongst it all I find an old edition of Vanity Fair. *A Novel without a Hero* it says on the heavily decorated frontispiece. I take it to my room to read.

The bathroom is huge with no shower, just one bath, deep and long with chipped enamel and orange stains below each tap. I put all my things about the place; my dressing gown and toiletries, as if it was my own house - but I lock the door before I undress, just in case. The rusty brown water gushes out with incredible force. I've put bubble bath in and I have to scoop some of the bubbles out into the sink so they don't overflow onto the floor. I lie floating on my back watching the steam rise up towards the lemon coloured ceiling, then flip over on to my tummy and kick my legs in the hot, foamy, rose scented water.

Tucked up cosy in my bed later I start reading Vanity Fair. I wonder who read it before me - maybe William Williamson's wife, maybe someone older. Perhaps it hasn't been read for decades. It might have been a gift, from a man to his sweetheart, before he went off to war - they're probably dead now. I think of the bodies lying quietly below me and I feel completely at peace.

Stratheden Psychiatric Hospital
Ward 4 Men's Long Stay
1984 January - March

All the men under sixty go off each morning to work in the hospital farm, or the gardens, or the cement works, where they make concrete slabs which the hospital sells. A few work in the laundry or the auto-clave unit, putting things in little bags which will then be sterilised, but it's mostly women that do that lighter kind of work.

I wonder who buys the slabs. I ask the patient I am sitting next to. His name is Raymond. He usually works in the gardens but he's off just now on account of his nerves and his eczema. He scratches his hand rather viciously as he tells me that. "I suppose it's garden centres," he says. "For people's patios and that. I think they are quite nice slabs you know - not like pavement slabs." An older man, small and fragile looking, sits next to him nodding. "This is Charlie," says Raymond. "He's retired. Aren't you Charlie? You're too old to work now aren't you?" Charlie nods some more. He sits very close to Raymond. "Charlie is my friend," Raymond says putting his hand over Charlie's and rubbing it affectionately. "I'm knitting him a scarf." He holds a ropey looking yellow rectangle up for me to see, lots of dropped stitches. "Do you like the colour? I got it from OT. They have a big box of wool that they sometimes let me choose from. Charlie likes this colour, don't you Charlie?" Charlie nods in agreement, gives me a polite little smile.

"So if any of us ever need slabs for our patios we'll know where to get them," Raymond says. We all laugh. I think it's interesting that Raymond recognises the fact that I am just as far away as he and Charlie are from ever having to worry about slabs for a patio - well, almost as far. "It must be hard work down there at the cement works?" Raymond nods in agreement. "Very hard work. Only the stronger men work there. They come back filthy, all covered in horrible white dust. They must be breathing that in, poor things. I couldn't do it because I get asthma, and I'm hardly big and strong am I?" It's true. He is very thin, vulnerable looking in his oversize brown industrial style dungarees. "Do you always wear your dungarees?" He tips his head to the side. "Mostly. I like the colour. I think it suits me, don't you?" - "Do the men that make slabs get paid more than the ones that work in Autoclave?" - "No. We all get paid the same," says Raymond. "£2.50 a week - therapeutic earnings. Apparently it's good for us."

On Friday after tea there are three long queues to be managed instead of just the usual two: one for medication; one for cigarettes; one for wages. As each patient opens his pay packet he takes out the £2.50 and gives it to a staff nurse who marks beside each man's name - £1 towards his funeral, £1.00 for tobacco and fifty pence for the patient to spend as he chooses.

🎆 🎆 🎆

This morning I have to take the older men to OT -

Occupational Therapy. It's a big, bright room, much sunnier and cheerier than the Ward 4 day room. There is a huge bucket of buttons that we have to sort into matching sets. We are there for two hours with a fifteen minute tea break in the middle. The tea comes out of the pot with milk and sugar already added. Raymond has joined me because he's still not well enough for work but he's getting bored sitting around on the ward - and he wants to be with Charlie. Charlie sits in silence as Raymond and I chat. The occupational therapist tries to persuade him to sort some buttons, but he just smiles and ignores her. "You're a rebel aren't you Charlie?" Raymond jokes, when the OT is safely out of earshot. Then he turns to me - "He won't be told to do anything."

Raymond tells me about his mum who died when he was fifteen. She taught him to knit and how to cook too. "Not that I need to worry about cooking now," he says, raising his eyebrows. "She taught me how to make the things my father likes; stew and dumplings; tripe in white sauce; shepherd's pie - all those kind of things. She knew she was dying, but she never let on, not one word. She just wanted to make sure I would be able to look after him. Give him all his favourite things. Everything my father wanted he got." When Raymond talks about his dad it seems to me that his face, his whole demeanour, becomes slightly distorted. It's a very slight thing- fractional. It's more like I sense it than see it. It's as if there's something inside him trying to get out; something bad, something very very angry. Then Charlie touches his arm and Raymond comes back to us, with his round, brown, friendly guy eyes and his cheerful chatter. "My mum taught me how to knit, but she never showed me how to follow a pattern. Do you know how to follow a pattern?"

At the end of the session the OT goes round the tables and sweeps all the buttons back into the big bucket. I look at her in astonishment but the men don't seem at all surprised. "That's what they always do," says Raymond. "They've been sorting those buttons for years."

On the days that the older men are not sorting buttons at OT they have to go to Recreational Therapy - RT, which, I'm told is a branch of OT. The therapist, Maxwell Greenlow, has been to our college to tell us about his work. He looks like he could be about seventy. He's been working here for over forty years but he loves his job far too much to retire. "RETIREMENT IS BAD FOR YOUR HEALTH!" he shouts, though there are only six of us in a pretty small room. He can name every muscle in the human body. He calls Neil out to the front of the class to prove it. At first we struggle not to laugh, but when it comes to Maximus Gluteus and he smacks Neil's skinny backside with his long wooden poker we laugh out loud and realise that is exactly what he's been waiting for. It seems Max loves an audience.

The old men sit in a large circle exercising every muscle in their body twice a week on Mondays and Thursdays. After the exercises Max gets a ball and throws it out randomly - 'to keep the men alert.' Perhaps it's their medication, or maybe it's dormitory living, or the leucotomies, or just plain boredom, but very few of the men could be described as alert. Some of them are actually sleeping. Some just sit, stuporous, letting the ball bounce off their body, fall to the floor and roll away to towards the exit doors, as if even it is too bored to stick around. In fact, it seems to me, that the men move less in Max's sessions than they do anywhere else.

None of the men ever seem to relax. If they are not rummaging around trying to find bits of things to augment their tobacco - fluff, or dried up grass, or old crumbs from the side of the sofa, they are pacing up and down the corridors muttering to themselves, shaking their heads, wringing their hands. Most of the older ones have tardive dyskinesia; they grind their teeth; push their bottom lips and tongues in and out; twist their heads around for no apparent reason. "It's their medication," Jim, the only nice staff nurse in the ward tells me. He doles out some more of it, crushed up and mixed into a spoonful of jam, to a shuffling, shaky, grimacing old man. "It more or less gives them Parkinson's Disease."

"If they've had leucotomies how come they need medication too?" I ask Jim. "Because they do," he shrugs. "Ours is not to reason why." - "You mean - theirs not to reason why." He looks at me quizzically. "Theirs not to reason why, Theirs but to do and die." When I say the lines I gesture into the day room at the twitching men milling around. "Charge of the Light Brigade, Alfred Lord Tennyson: Theirs not to make reply, Theirs not to reason why, Theirs but to do and die. Into the valley of death rode the six hundred." - "Let's just give out the meds eh?" Says Jim, shaking his head in mock dismay. Well I think it's mock.

I usually sit next to Jackie Lowe when we are in RT because he tends to get a bit upset by the whole experience. I wonder if he would have charged unquestioningly towards twenty five thousand enemy soldiers; it's a fight to get him to do anything at all. I have to clasp him with both arms to walk him down the corridor to the RT hall. He shouts and protests the whole way. When we get there he settles down quite quickly, but as soon as he sits down he wants to go to sleep and he gets very grumpy if anyone wakes him up. When Maxwell throws the ball at him he throws it back in furious indignation, shaking his fists and shouting, "I'M GIVING YOU ONE LAST WARNING."

When Maxwell is off on holiday the students take his place, sitting in the middle of the circle of old men, reading from the exercise script. Neil usually does it because he likes reading out the Latin names of the muscles, which Max has typed below each exercise. We aren't supposed to call out the muscle names, they are for reference only, but Neil does it anyway, with a good dose of comic effect. Some of the men find it very funny, they laugh and turn quite pink and rub the tears from their eyes. We don't bother if the men don't do their exercises. We let them doze if they want, and we never throw the ball at them because, actually, although we like Max, that exercise just seems mean to us.

In General hospitals the Kardex is updated at the end of every shift. In Ward 4 it is updated once a year. We sit in the dining room writing - three students; me, Neil and Colin, who is also in our class. We have fifty entries to make - *No change to this patient's condition or treatment plan.* It's like writing lines at school.

The Charge Nurse, Bobby McGloan comes in to see how we are doing. He's a stockily built man, not fat - muscular, like a rugby player. He's quite good looking I suppose, with black hair and blue eyes, a very straight nose. He looks like a Roman Centurian - I can easily imagine him in a leather tunic, and I suppose he could command a hundred men if he needed to. He has his ways.

"Where are the treatment plans?" Colin asks politely. Bobby shrugs. "In the medical notes I suppose" - "May we see them?" - "That's a good idea," says Neil. "I'd really like to see the notes." Bobby raises an eyebrow but says nothing, walks away, his white coat flapping in an important, doctorly kind of way. When he isn't wearing his white coat he walks with his hands in his pockets so that his trousers stretch tight across his bottom. Five minutes later he comes back carrying a huge stack of medical notes. They must weigh a ton. He dumps them on to the tables in front of us and says, "That do you for now?" - "Yes thanks," says Neil. We smirk a little as he leaves, clapping his dusty hands together loudly.

The files are fat so we know that there was a time when people were interested enough to write about our patients.

Some of the entries are from the 1940's. Handwritten or typed on tissue thin paper; lofty recordings by learned men:

```
Robert Dodds 12 Aug 1942:
This rather highly strung young man, with a
history of Endogenous Depression threatened
a police officer with a garden implement
following an altercation with his boss's
wife. The lady is said to have found him
in her kitchen wearing certain items of
gender inappropriate clothing which she
recognized as her own. .

Alan Murray 31 Jan 1943:
A strange individual, never popular at
school. Informed his parents on 23rd
December 1942 that he is not in fact a man,
but a jar of Gentlemen's Relish. Since that
date he has refused to leave the family
dinner table even to urinate or defecate
which, rather he chose to do in a Minton
and Boyle soup tureen which he knew to be
treasured by his mother and her mother
before her. ..
```

And so their psychiatric histories began: Legal detention; Hydrotherapy; Insulin Shock Therapy; Modified Insulin Therapy; Electroconvulsive therapy; Industrial Therapy; Lobotomy/Leucotomy; Behavioural Modification; Minor tranquillizers; Major tranquillizers; Voluntary detention...

None of the men seemed to have had Art Therapy or Cognitive Behavioural Therapy or Rational Emotive Therapy or Transactional Analysis, even though we have been told all about them in college as if they were common practice. "Those are psychological therapies," Neil says. "Maybe there are separate notes for psychology." Everyone looks doubtful.

As the notes progress in time the writing becomes less legible and the entries less frequent. After the first year or so there are very few references to the actual men; it's just their therapies and the odd violent incident that are recorded.

```
12 treatments Bilateral ECT to commence
1st May 1952

Nil by mouth from midnight 31st April.

50mg Chlorpromazine IM administered
following violent altercation over potato
rationing for reducing diet. Condition
currently stable. Further 50mg prn may be
administered if volatility in mood
continues.

Daily insulin commences: 21st May 1955, 25
units Insulin, patient response
satisfactory

22nd May 1952, 35 units Insulin, patient
response satisfactory
```

Only two or three of the men in our ward are detained under the Mental Health Act, the rest are all voluntary and, technically, could leave at any time. Where would they go? How would they live? There is very little in the notes of their lives before their admission, nothing really indicating that they are part of a family or social group. In fact there is hardly any information at all, beyond the odd chest X-ray, after they have been admitted to Ward 4. I have never seen a psychiatrist, a psychologist or a social worker on the ward. I have never seen a visitor either, and none of the men ever go home for visits. There is no patients' telephone. Nobody receives cards or letters. Apart from us, our patients are completely isolated from humanity. They don't even talk to one another, though perhaps there are other couples, like Raymond and George, that I don't know about. It seems to me that the Long Stay men are one hundred percent dependent on the nursing staff for every aspect of their survival.

Colin and Neil and I talk about this for a while: whether seeing a psychiatrist is a good thing or not; whether psychology has anything to offer people with psychotic disorders; how many of the men are actually psychotic; whether asylum is a good thing or not; whether we should write treatment plans for each patient. "What's the point?" says Neil. "No-one's ever going to look at them." So we just keep on writing: *No change to this patient's condition or treatment plan.* "Stop a minute," Colin says to me about half way through. "That guy's actually dead." - "Oops," I say, scribbling out my note, sticking his Kardex back on the pile.

✉ ✉ ✉

His name is Joseph Capaldi. I have never heard him talk, not one word in the two months that I have been here. His notes say that he was admitted two years ago with: *Reactive Depression following multiple bereavements* and *Generalized Anxiety Disorder*. Bobby says he's only here to hide from the Kirkcaldy mafia. I ask Jim, the nice staff nurse, if that's true. He looks uncertain. "Could be," he says. "He does look pretty terrified doesn't he?"

He does look terrified. He never smiles and rarely makes eye contact. He is different from the other men - he wears his own clothes; a navy cardigan with gold buttons; a wide, royal blue satin tie. He wears a wedding ring and a signet ring with his initials and a small ruby embedded in it. I wonder who the multiple bereavements were - if one of them was his wife. I wonder if he has any children. I think this is a strange kind of hiding place. Surely, if he really was just hiding out he could have found somewhere better than this. I try to talk to him, but he doesn't even turn his head to look at me. His eyebrows are very high up, so he always looks a bit shocked. His face is a pink, waxy oval. He has a very small mouth. He looks like Humpty Dumpty. "I hope you are talking Italian," Bobby shouts over, shaking his head - at the futility of my efforts or my stupidity, I don't know which.

I try to imagine Joseph Capaldi as a child. That's what I do when I find it hard to like a patient. I find it helps me to feel empathy for them; this was someone's little boy and they would want me to help him - but I find I just can't manage it this time. Joseph's large, fleshy hands are trembling and beads of sweat appear on his bald head. I can see my presence is distressing him so I move to another part of the day room.

The day room is huge - about forty feet long and twenty feet high, blank walls, wipeable vinyl chairs in neutral colours all round the sides, and a television in the corner that is never on. The men pace back and forth twitching and twisting in the centre of the room, wringing their hands and muttering to the voices in their heads. One man stands at the television arguing loudly with an imaginary barman, sipping his imaginary pints, throwing back invisible whisky chasers.

Neil and I talked about it after we'd had a smoke recently and decided it's like The Veldt - the short story by Ray Bradbury. It catches the *telepathic emanations* of our patient's minds and creates a life more suited to their needs and desires. The men think tobacco and there is tobacco - in the cracks between the sofa cushions, though it looks like fluff to us. The men think alcohol and the telly becomes a bar. They think love and there is love, from a dead mouse in their pocket, from an elderly man who sleeps in the next bed and hasn't said a word since he was leucotomised thirty years ago.

When I'm in the day room I usually sit next to Raymond and Charlie or Davie Ross. Davie Ross lives in the Independent Living Flat and he is my favourite patient in the ward. He's very tall and strong, from working in the gardens.

He looks quite scary when he's chasing people with a hoe, but he likes me because I managed to fix his radio twice. It was pure fluke and good luck, but he thinks I'm a genius now. He makes me presents from his old Airfix model boxes - once a necklace that was an actual plane, a WWII Spitfire, strung with fine red thread. He hung it round my neck and stood back admiring with a tear in his eye. It seems I'm his ideal woman, though he is never inappropriate and always a gentleman.

Bobby calls me over. He is holding a pile of clean linen. He says, "Stop pissing about and go up and change the beds in the Independent Living Flat." Two other patients live in the Independent Living Flat with Davie Ross - Adam Sinclair and Dougie Short. These three are the strongest and fittest men in the ward. They really only sleep in the flat, coming down to the dining room for all their meals and spending most of their spare time outside in the courtyard or in the day room. Dougie and Adam work full time making slabs. You always know when Dougie has come in from work because you can hear him singing…

When the golden sun sinks in the hills
And the toil of a long day is o'er
Though the road may be long in the lilt of a song
I forget I was weary before
Far ahead where the blue shadows fall
I shall come to contentment and rest
And the toils of the day will be all charmed away
In my little gray home in the west...

Adam Sinclair never sings. He doesn't talk either, except when he screams in my face: "STOP GIVING ME SEXUAL IMAGES." He's tall and lean and broad in the shoulders. He has a wild look in his eyes - pure rage, almost all the time. I'm terrified of Adam.

The flat is right at the top of the building, three floors up, with no alarms - no bell that you only have to ring three times and a small army of nurses and doctors will come running. My heart races, my palms sweat, standing there in the corridor looking at Bobby with his pile of linen. I can see Davie Ross outside, sitting on the step smoking his pipe. I can hear Dougie singing in the day room. If anything happens to me I can't look to them for help. "Shouldn't they change their own beds?" I try to sound casual, as if it's no big deal and I'm only concerned that we are creating dependency. Bobby glares at me, his top lip curled in contempt. He shoves the bundle of linen at me. Slowly I turn to climb the stairs. "What's the matter?" Bobby's voice is low and mean - "Scared of getting raped?"

When I was home for the weekend a few weeks ago I told my brother in law about the way Adam Sinclair screams at me. He's a social worker and always interested in how I'm getting on. "Just ask him to stop," he said. "His behaviour is completely out of order. Tell him it has to stop." I don't really think this suggestion is feasible. Adam is like a rumbling volcano. He even looks like he's on fire inside, his skin is so pink; rubbed raw from excessive scrubbing. When he isn't at work he paces round the courtyard reading a tattered copy of Moby Dick. Every now and again he stops abruptly as if some radical new idea has leapt off the page and presented itself to him. I sometimes think he'll get so hot and bothered that smoke will start coming out of his ears.

"None of the men in the Independent Living Flat do anything for themselves really," I told my brother in law. Mum must have been listening to us because she said as she passed by, "If any of those men actually achieve independence be sure to let me know because I'd really like to meet him." She stomped up the stairs with her own bundle of freshly laundered boxer shorts and shirts.

Now here I am standing outside Adam's room, three floors up so no-one that might help could ever hear anything. My brother-in-law's idea is laughable - though I don't feel much like laughing now. I knock politely on Adam's door. There's no reply. I push it gently, let it swing open, crane my neck to see round the corner to his bed. It's a mess, but it's empty; he isn't in. I get to work stripping the rumpled sheets and blankets off as fast as I can, thinking furiously that I can't remember a time when either of the two male students were asked to change any beds. I'll bet that they are in the office now, doing *Spot the Ball* or the Daily Record crossword. As I throw the bedding into the laundry skip something heavy falls out. It's his book - Moby-Dick. It must have been lying in the folds of the covers. Curiosity gets the better of me; I sit down, hold the book in both hands and let it fall open where it may.

He has underlined a passage:

...his special lunacy stormed his general sanity, and carried it, and turned all its concentrated cannon upon it's own mad mark; so that far from having lost his strength, Ahab, to that one end, did now possess a thousand fold more potency than ever he had sanely brought to bear upon any one reasonable object.

He must have climbed the stairs so quietly that I couldn't hear him - either that or I was too absorbed in Moby-Dick. He stands in the doorway staring. The sun shining through the circular window behind him throws an orangey glow round his chestnut hair. "I've never read it," I say, holding his book up. He smiles and walks across the room, perches himself on the chest of drawers, head inclined towards me. I've never seen him smile before. He looks handsome in an ordinary kind of way. If he was a friend of mine; if he wasn't ill; if whatever terrible thing that happened to him hadn't happened; if he wasn't a patient and I wasn't a nurse - we would chat about parties and mutual friends. We would find a dark, smoky bar and drink cold frothy beer from thick glasses with handles, discussing Moby Dick and other books we've read. Maybe I would ask him who it is in this book that he identifies with. What drives him to read it over and over?

Here we are though - patient and nurse. I'm the strong one who should ease his suffering. That notion doesn't seem to figure much in this ward. My mouth is dry and I sit on my hands to stop them shaking. He looks like he doesn't know what to say so I start. "I get really scared when you shout at me." My voice is thin and wavery. "I wish you would stop doing it because I am not trying to upset you in any way." His face turns deepest pink. His right ear which he has tucked his long hair behind, is astonishingly red. "I'm sorry," he mumbles, lowering his head, looking at me from below his thick dark brows. "I didn't mean to scare you. I didn't know." We are silent for a moment. I'm trying not to cry. I take a handkerchief from the pocket of my uniform and dab my eyes before blowing my nose, then hold the book up. "I've heard a bit about it, but I've never read it. It looks really interesting. I'll look for it next time I'm in the library."

I stand up and finish making his bed, fast and efficient, pull everything tight and leave it that way; there's not much danger of him suffering from foot drop. He leans on the chest of drawers silently watching. I pull the laundry skip towards the door, turn to say goodbye before I leave and see him take a little run at the bed. He flops on to it, stretches his long body, and raises his arms up behind his head like Huckleberry Finn on the sun warmed banks of the Mississippi river. "Thank you," he says with a grin. I think - he's not Captain Ahab, driven mad by a crazed and tortured whale. He's just somebody's boy - and maybe I have eased his suffering, just a wee bit. I'll make his bed again next week and I'll do it gladly.

Heading back downstairs I hear Dougie coming up to his room.

There are hands that will welcome me in

There are lips I am burning to kiss
There are two eyes that shine just because they are mine
And a thousand things other men miss
It's a corner of heaven itself
Though it's only a tumble down nest
But with love brooding there, why no place can compare
To my little gray home in the west.

It's Saturday and we are doing the pools. Jim picks my numbers because I don't really understand how it works. Some of the staff put bets on horses too. I sometimes do, depending on my money situation. I don't really understand how that works either - the odds and all that stuff. I just pick a horse with a name I like.

Jim goes into Cupar to put the bets on and brings back cakes from the local baker - Fisher and Donaldson. They really are the best cakes you could ever taste. Cakes and gambling on a Saturday afternoon is a Ward 4 tradition. "If I had a race horse I'd call it Fisher and Donaldson." I say, sticking a small spoon into the cream of my Coffee Tower. Jim laughs. Bobby snorts - "Never you mind horses, just you get that cake down you. You look like you haven't eaten a meal in a month." He doesn't say it in a nice way. "You can't fatten a thoroughbred," says Sheila the domestic, winking at me. "Not if they're on drugs," says Bobby, staring at me hard. Neil shifts about uncomfortably in the seat next to me. I just keep on eating my cake.

Sheila's husband is the head gardener for the hospital and they live in a cottage on the grounds. I ask her about the gypsies. "Oh they haven't come for years my love. Not since the murder. There was a fight - when was it again Jim? Back about 1970 wasn't it?" - "Aye, that's right. The same year the sugar beet closed down - I remember that anyway. Aye, two men at each other with a knife. One of them got killed, though it was accidental really I think." Sheila nods, and looks thoughtful then turns to me. "Crime passionel," she says, winking again. "It was over a woman. That was the last we saw of them wasn't it Jim?" - "Aye," says Jim. "All those years they had come and stayed, and never a problem. The doctor would go down and check them all over, give them any medicine they needed. They were never a problem. The night of the fight two of them came running up for help. But it was too late. The lad was dead. Women. They've got a lot to answer for."

Bobby throws his Daily Record into the middle of the table, lights a fag, gets up and wanders over to the window that looks out onto the courtyard. He opens the window, leans out, his trousers tight across his bum, puts his hand to his mouth for added volume and shouts - "HOOF." Several of the men jump in alarm. Bobby laughs loud, slaps his muscular thigh. He thinks it's hilarious. I guess that's why he does it at least three times a day.

£ £

There are only big baths on this ward. There's a shower in the Independent Living Flat, but it's used for storage. Nobody gets a bed bath unless they are dying. We, the students, are sent round the ward with the bath book to round up our patients for their weekly wash. They do not have a choice. If their name is in the book they are having a bath.

There are three baths, side by side, deep and long like the one in the Adamson Hospital nurses home, but these ones have huge plugholes so that they can be drained very quickly if someone is having a fit or has tried to drown themselves. Quite a few men have drowned themselves in the past, it seems. They are not allowed in the bathroom unsupervised now.

The men undress without embarrassment. Even Adam will casually shove his dirty clothes into my arms and step eagerly into the steamy rust stained water. It seems to me that everything here in this hospital is tinged with red. Even the squirrels are red. Adam will scrub his body red raw if you allow him. You have to really shout at him to stop and he always gets out the bath in a temper because of it.

We have to empty the pockets of each man as he discards his clothes for washing. Sometimes they object, especially if you find an animal. Quite a lot of the men collect animals to stroke and whisper to. I suppose they must find them dead or else how would they catch them? Then again - you don't tend to see lots of dead mice or birds lying around. I've never seen any of those animals alive anyway. Willie

Somerled always has one in his pocket, along with the remains of a piece of old cake or a biscuit, which suggests it was alive in there at some point. You have to watch Willie when you turn out his pockets because he's liable to punch you for taking his little friends away. He did that to Brenda - one of the female staff nurses that fancies Bobby and he likes to flirt with. Bobby jumped on him and pinned him to the ground. "HIT A WOMAN WOULD YOU?" He screamed in Willie's face. I thought he would punch him because he raised his fist, but he didn't. I think it was just an automatic thing. He didn't hit him. He just held him down while Brenda ran off to get an injection from the cupboard. They injected him right there on the bathroom floor. He slept for two days after that. He looked strangely resigned throughout the injection bit of that episode. I wonder if, on some level, it's what he had wanted.

Most of the men wear the same clothes all the time; black woollen suits with narrow lapels on the jackets; narrow trousers; thin black ties; white, small collared shirts and Doctor Marten shoes. Accidental fashionistas all of them; wearing what's been in the clothing cupboard for the last forty years. Students aren't allowed in the clothing cupboard. Only Jimmy the ward orderly is allowed in there. He guards it like it's his own personal treasure trove. No one gets anything new until their old stuff is in tatters. Summer and winter the men wear the same black woollen suits. Nobody owns a coat because they only have to walk short distances, from one part of the hospital to another.

Willie Somerled's jacket is always particularly grubby. From time to time he starts scratching and itching like crazy. If Jimmy, the ward orderly, sees him doing that, he will tear the jacket off his back and jump up and down on it. "It kills the beasties," he explains to Neil and me the first time we witness it. "Doesn't it Willie?" Willie nods agreeably, puts his jacket back on, with all Jimmy's dusty footprints on it. He walks off, not itching at all. "Folie a Deux," says Neil under his breath. "The poor wee mice," I say, understanding now why they are always dead.

Neil and Rod are coming to have dinner at the Adamson. Celia and I are cooking a big pot of vegetarian chilli in the hospital kitchen downstairs. The hospital cook is very interested in what we are doing. "You're the only vegetarians I've ever met. What else do you eat besides this?" Sister comes in for a nosey too. "It looks very healthy," she says. "I'll bet that's why you girls are so nice and slim. I never thought of being a vegetarian. Maybe we should try it for our patients that are on reducing diets." She looks at Cook who shakes her head energetically. I don't think it's going to happen while she's around.

We sit round the table in the living room upstairs. I've put candles in the centre. I found some old, hand embroidered napkins in the kitchen which I've folded and curled into our wine glasses. Rod brought me a bunch of daffodils from the woods that I've put in a big earthenware jug I found under the sink in the bathroom. I think the place feels very cosy. "It's a gorgeous jug," Celia says. "I wonder what they used it for?" - "Washing their hair?" I suggest. "Or pissing in," says Neil. Rod and I laugh. Celia tuts - "Who would piss in a jug?" "Me," says Neil. Rod and I laugh again. "He would too," Celia says, looking at me. She doesn't seem to find it funny. I wonder if they've had a falling out.

Celia comes to visit me before or after most of her shifts, so this place is nothing new to her. Rod comes up to collect her in the car sometimes and if he's early he pops in for a coffee - so he knows the place too. Neil has never been before. He roams about looking at everything in fascination. He picks up the old brown Bakelite phone in the hall. "Has it ever rung?" I laugh. "I would shit myself if it rang." - "And yet you're happy to sleep above the corpses?" He stands looking at me in a slightly hostile way. "I like the corpses," I tell him, taking a swig of Black Tower wine. "They keep themselves to themselves. Very quiet and peaceful. Good listeners too. I can always rely on them." - "Well I think it's absolutely shameful you being here," says Celia. "However nice you've made it. I think it's disgusting - so unfair. Doesn't it make you angry?" - "Not really," I tell her. "Because I like it so much. But I don't really understand why I'm here. I mean, it seems to me it's like musical beds up there in the Stratheden home and no-one gets chucked out."

"It's because you are openly promiscuous," says Neil. "I heard the tutors talking about it in college one day." Rod and Celia exchange an embarrassed glance. I feel my face flush crimson. "You mean the tutors think she is promiscuous," Celia says. "The tutors, who just happen to all be men or Born Again Christians?" She looks furious. Neil tips his head to the side as if he doesn't much care about the technicalities. "FUCK 'EM," says Rod pouring more wine into our glasses, raising his - "FUCK MEN!" I think that Neil is about to say something smart, but Celia glares at him in warning. He lowers his head, starts rolling one of his tiny prison style cigarettes.

Later I lie in my bed above the corpses wondering what kind of people they were. They would have been better than me; wiser; more thoughtful - chaste. I wonder if I'll ever be loved by a man again - if the dead people downstairs were loved. Little Isa is down there now. She died yesterday. Celia was very upset about it. Little Isa, with her wonderful smile. I'll bet she was loved and would know how to love back. I don't think I'm very good at loving people. Mind you, I'm glad I didn't fall in love with Neil; he has an underlying coldness. I didn't see it at first, but I see it now. "So I'm not getting everything wrong," I say aloud to my dead friends below, as if they are the ones making judgements upon me.

Jackie Lowe is dying. They brought a bed down from the dormitory and put it in a wee room near the day room. There doesn't seem to be anybody to phone; no family or friends to spend a last hour at his side. Bobby asks me to sit with him, which surprises me and makes me think he considers it women's work. "He's asking you because you're good with him," Jim says. I wonder if it's obvious how much I hate Bobby. I am genuinely astonished that they think I'm good with Jackie. He's only ever looked at me in absolute terror. "You can get him to do things, - go down to RT and all that," Jim says. "Not voluntarily," I say. "I have to practically drag him." - "Yeah well it's more than anyone else ever managed."

A terrible feeling comes over me; a horrible suspicion that I've been set up. All those weeks being told to take Jackie for a walk, or over to OT, or down to RT. They probably didn't think I had a chance in hell. "OUT THERE?" Jackie would scream. "YOU MUST BE MAD. LOOK AT WHAT'S HAPPENED TO THOSE POOR DEVILS!" He would point at the men lying around the courtyard or on the grassy banks. "They're just resting," I told him, again and again - because they were. When they are tired they just lie down like dogs in the sun, the men from Ward 4 - wherever they happen to be. Jackie just looked at me in disbelief.

He is stuck in some long ago world, a world of death and terror, and I dragged him out there, back to the trenches. I could have left him sitting safely in the day room. I could have just said - "He won't do it. He won't go." I feel like all the warmth has been sucked from my body, like any goodness I thought I had was nothing more than a delusion. I'm just as bad as the nurses I've been silently loathing ever since I came to this place. It was all for my own good - my need to please Bobby and the others. My need to do well - get another tick in my assessment book. It wasn't for Jackie's benefit at all. Jackie looks at me with the fear that never seems to leave him. "Are you scared Jackie?" His eyes widen. I wish I hadn't asked him, because I don't know what to do to make him not scared. I cover his hand with both of mine, sit nearer him, kiss his knuckles, making no effort to hide my tears. His hands are like my father's hands - strong, workworn - capable. Where is this man's family? He had children. He's probably a grandfather. Would the fear have left him if someone had put a child on his knee.

Jim comes through and stands watching. "He's Cheyne-Stoking. Can you hear it?" I nod and sniff and he leans down and peers at me. "Aw you've grown fond of him haven't you?" He puts his big warm hand on my shoulder. "We'll give him some Diamorph." He pats my back. His kindness is like medicine to me, though I don't believe I deserve it. He leaves and I sit staring at Jackie. Jackie lies staring at the ceiling, his pale eyes filled with anguish - then not.

I can never get used to people dying. It's like they've just slipped out of their body to fetch something and they'll be back in a minute. One second there's a man with all his long history: childhood; love; marriage; fatherhood; war; madness; hospital - a moment later he's gone and there's nothing - a body, a shell, a lump of meat. How can a person just disappear like that? I get up and open the window and, even though I don't believe in souls that live on in some heavenly afterlife, I stand back to let his out.

I've been painting horses quite a lot recently. Not from life - though there are horses in a meadow not far from here. I would be too self conscious to go out there and paint in public. I hide in my room, looking at books I've found in the library. There's a guy that I keep seeing in the library who seems quite nice; quiet, but friendly. I saw him looking surprised as I was getting my books stamped. I guess I don't look the horsey type.

I used to go to riding lessons as a child. It wasn't through choice. It was my sister that wanted to go, and for some reason our dad enrolled all of us. He must have thought it would be good for us - or else he got a bulk deal. I hated it. So did my brother. I remember looking at him as we were being shown how to groom. I knew we were thinking the same thing - brush your own horrid smelly horse. We were scared of their power and unpredictability. One day my brother was bitten and that was the end of it, he refused to go back and so did I. Our sister had to go it alone. She didn't seem to mind. She had all the equipment; the hat; the trousers; the whip - everything except the horse. She begged and pleaded but our parents resisted. My brother and I silently rejoiced.

I like the way they look though - horses. I like their thick veined, quivering coats, their nervy elegance. I think I understand why people would want to conquer them. But conquering has never been my thing. I'm trying to draw my horses wild, standing atop purple mountains with the wind in their manes.

There's a knock at my door. I jump, making a squiggle which I suppose can be turned into a bush, or a tree. It must be Celia, though I am sure this is her day off. I open the door and there's a man about my age standing there; short in height, dyed blonde hair, pale blue eyes, boxes piled up at his feet. "Hello Mon Petit Cheri. I'm Crawford - your new neighbour." He motions at the room behind him. The door is open and there are more boxes on the floor inside it. I open my own door a bit wider and he strolls right in. "Uh - huh," he says, as if it's everything he expected it to be. He wanders over to the window, "Is that the mortuary? Tres macabre." He turns and looks at the pictures I have pinned to the wall. "I guess you like horses then. Is this your poem?" He reads it out - loud and very camp.

The Song of the Mad Prince

Who said, 'Peacock Pie'?
The old King to the sparrow:
Who said, 'Crops are ripe'?
Rust to the harrow:
Who said, 'Where sleeps she now?
Where rests she now her head,
Bathed in eve's loveliness'?
That's what I said.

Who said, 'Ay, mum's the word':
Sexton to willow:
Who said, 'Green dusk for dreams,
Moss for a pillow'?

Who said, 'All time's delighted Hath she for narrow bed:
Life's troubled bubble broken'?
That's what I said

"Did YOU say that?" He looks at me, wide eyed, full of admiration. "No." I can't help laughing at his expression. "Walter De La Mare said that."- "WHO HE? I want to meet? NOW DARLING. NOW!" - "He's long dead. He's as dead as the folk in the mortuary down there." - "Oh just my luck. Bloody typical."

"I didn't think anyone else would be coming to stay here," I say. He turns towards me, makes a very serious face. He's wearing white jeans and a tight cap sleeved t-shirt that shows his nipples. He's just a little short of stout. "I'm here for the same reason as you dear." - "A man in your room?" - "EXACTEMENT!" He stretches his eyes wide again then drops down on to my bed with his head in his hands and wails - "I hope yours was worth it because mine certainly wasn't"

I show him the kitchen and the sitting room, the napkins, the earthenware jug, full of tulips now. He clasps his hands in delight, picks up the old bakelite phone in the corridor, "'Ello' Ello 'Ello. Is that Walter De La Mare? Come on up to the Adamson. We are 'aving a party, mon petit amie et moi. Nothing formuel, just a little 'ouse warming. La tenue de soiree n'est pas obligatoire." - "He was English," I tell him, laughing. "Walter De La Mare - he was from Twickenham." He looks at me indignantly, "Twickenham France?"

I show him the bathroom last - thinking he will like it's faded ostentation - he does. I apologise for all my stuff and he says - "Oh don't worry about that. Wait 'til you see all my crap. Honestly darling, you are frugal in your toilet compared to moi." He picks up a bottle of cheap perfume - *Roses Roses* by Yardley and, perhaps because my sisters always tell me how terrible it smells, I feel I have to explain. "When I was wee I used to try and make perfume for my mum. I used to mash rose petals in a jam jar with a stick and give it to her. It smelled a bit like this - right after it was made anyway. It reminds me of summer, warm days in the garden, no school - it makes me feel happy." - He sprays it all over himself then me and stands with his nose in the air, his hands upturned. "Ah! The poetry of roses."

We eat together at the big table in the living room later - instant cheesy pasta, washed down with his favourite cocktail - Vodka, Malibu and Coke. We decide to call it *Peacock Pie*, after the Walter De La Mare book. Later I show him the wee staircase that leads to the roof of the hospital. We sit on a blanket between the chimneys smoking a joint, reciting poems. "*Twilight came: silence came; The planet of Evening's silver flame.*" We tip our heads back, watch as tiny little stars begin to reveal themselves against the darkening sky.

Stratheden Psychiatric Hospital
Ward 5 Women's Long Stay
1984 April - June

It's equal in size to men's long stay; fifty beds; a similar layout; the same, neutral coloured waterproof furniture. The two wards are right next to each other. I can't work out why this one seems so much brighter and cheerier. There are more patients on the ward during the day here. Only a few of them leave; they work in Autoclave and seem to enjoy it. "It's because they get to see their boyfriends there, isn't it Janet?" Sister Jamieson teases. Janet smiles coyly, her cheeks turn the colour of her pastel pink cardigan.

None of the women have their own clothes, they have been here too long for that. Their outfits are chosen for them by the nurses. I like to take my time and pick out the nicest things. If you rake around you can sometimes find something in lamb's wool, or even cashmere. Things that must have been bought by patients themselves before they came to live here. It's strange to think of them out in the world shopping. You can tell which clothes are ward stock because there are lots of them in different sizes and everything is machine washable: nylon twin sets; crimplene skirts; zip fronted tunics; tan stockings and greying elastic garters. Sister doesn't allow tights; she says they are unhygienic.

"Do they really have boyfriends?" I ask Sister, as we stand at the window chatting later. "Oh yes," she says absently, looking down at her slim, bare, legs, twisting them about to check the even-ness of her tan. She's not long back from a holiday in Gran Canaria; I think it's one of those places where it's always sunny. "We've got quite a few of them on the pill." I must look shocked because she laughs. "Well we don't want any little accidents to take care of do we?" I gaze into the ward at the desolate looking women thinking that one or two little accidents might be quite nice - but they wouldn't be allowed to keep them, so it would only be more heartache. I want to ask her if the women know they are on the pill, but I don't, because I know I will be one of the ones dishing it out whatever the answer.

Like the men in the neighbouring ward, some of the women have been here for thirty or forty years. Some of them have had children, mostly illegitimate, sometimes the result of incest. No one has any visitors. "We are their family now," says Sister. "And I love each and every one of them." She is a small, neatly made woman in her thirties with rosy cheeks and bright, mischievous eyes. I believe she does love her patients. She lavishes them with an affection that seems to be infectious. I haven't witnessed any cruelty here, not on this shift anyway. Every nurse I meet is cheerful and kind. Sister wouldn't have it any other way.

The younger nurses encourage the patients to brush their hair and put on some jewellery and make up each morning. The older nurses aren't so particular. As long as the women are clean and comfortable, that's as far as they go with them. Most of the patients have necklaces, brightly coloured plastic beads, nothing of any value - the kind of things we had in our dressing up box when I was a child. A few of the women wear wedding rings. There are pictures of them on their bedside lockers - long faces under lacy veils. Sometimes less formal scenes - young girls smiling in summer dresses, leaning into baggy trousered, undernourished men. When I look at the men I feel a bubble of anger inside me, rising like a toxin, that I know will turn to rage if I let it. I imagine them now, living comfortable lives of freedom with no thought for their brides at all. Then I remind myself that some of these men will be long dead, and those who aren't are survivors of war. I wonder if I will always have to turn men into victims in order to like them.

Perhaps some of the women in here are better off than they would have been out there in the real world. Not many men could manage the unswerving love and devotion that Sister Jamieson bestows upon her charges. Their hair is clean and neatly styled, their finger nails are trimmed and filed, their beds are clean, their chins are shaved. Every birthday is marked with music and dancing and cake, even if they are completely mute, as quite a few are. Even if they sit staring, blank eyed into space responding to nothing except the gentle nudge of a spout or spoon at their lips - nobody's special day goes unacknowledged. I don't remember any birthdays on the men's ward.

There are only two of us on nights. We do the rounds together because we get spooked wandering about on our own. We do one round an hour, shining the torch quickly across the rows of beds to make sure our patients are still breathing. I'm working with a staff nurse called Mary. I like her a lot. She has just finished her training and she's a bit nervous being in charge, but we don't really have to do very much at all.

Mary is from Grangemouth. Her dad works in the refinery. I can tell she doesn't like him. When she talks about him I can see the little girl in her - scared and anxious. It's a bit like Raymond, without the anger. When Mary talks about her father I want to hold her hand - tell her that everything is okay now - but of course I don't.

We chatter so much that we miss a round. Mary gets very anxious and guilty. She takes her time shining the torch on each bed, really making sure everyone is alive and well. She stops at one particular bed for quite a while, though you can clearly see the woman is breathing - in fact she's kind of over breathing. "Is she crying?" I whisper. Mary approaches the bed, torch held high. "Maisie? Maisie are you all right there?" Maisy pops her head up. She looks flushed, but it could just be because the sheets are so white. Mary feels her forehead. "She's roasting," she says to me. She takes Maisie's hand - "Are you all right?" - "Yes nurse," says Maisie. I think she looks a bit embarrassed, but Mary is too busy taking her pulse to notice how she looks. "Tachycardia," Mary says to me, her eyes wide with alarm. Maisie looks terrified. "You sit with her," Mary tells me. "I'm going to ring the duty doctor." Some of the other women are beginning to waken up now. I tell them all to shush and go back to sleep. I sit by Maisie's bed watching her. She lies with the covers up to her chin staring back at me. "Are you not too hot?" I ask her. She shakes her head.

The doctor takes ages and I sit listening to the women snoring and babbling in their sleep. Mary runs up with the sphyg, but says she has to go back down to wait for the doctor. She leaves me to do Maisie's obs. Her blood pressure is fine, so is her pulse. I'm just wondering if I should go and tell Mary when she comes in with the doctor. Maisie sits up in her bed, poker straight, ready to be examined.

The doctor is really grumpy. She's pretty young, a junior houseman probably. When they are on call they have to stay in a special flat in the nurses home. They don't seem to like that. She stands glaring at Maisie. "Pull your nightdress up," she commands. Maisie looks at me in terror so I help her with her nightdress. The doctor sits, lips pursed waiting, then sets the diaphragm against Maisie's chest without warming it at all. Maisie jumps and looks a little tearful. After a bit the doctor puts the stethoscope down with an impatient sigh. "She's absolutely fine." She gets up and starts packing things away, "I can't believe you got me out of bed at 3am for this." - "But her pulse was racing," stutters Mary. "She was roasting hot." Even as she is talking it dawns on me why that might be. I can see it has dawned on Mary too because she has stopped explaining and is now apologizing profusely as the doctor marches down the middle of the ward to the stairs. We hear the back door banging as she leaves.

Mary turns to Maisie, "Ye might have told me!" Maisie glances nervously at me. She looks so funny and sweet in her flowery nightgown that I can't help laughing - then Mary starts, then Maisie too. We laugh so much we have to sit on the bed holding our tummies. Maisie sits between us, laughing her strange girlish laugh.

"I'm awful sorry Maisie," says Mary as we settle down from the hilarity. "I didnae mean tae embarrass ye. Can I get ye a wee cuppy Horlicks or something?" Maisie nods and Mary gives her a quick hug. As we leave I say to Mary, "You write up the Kardex, I'll get her drink." Then I feel bad, because it's not my place to order a staff nurse about, but she doesn't seem to mind, she just says, "Thanks pal," and disappears into the office.

Later when I join her she still hasn't written the Kardex. "I don't know what to write," she says. "What did the doctor write in the notes?" - "Nothing. She didn't do any notes." - "Well maybe that's your answer." She looks at me hard and long, "We could get into trouble you know." We think a while, smoke a few cigarettes, drink strong sugary tea to keep ourselves awake. "Let's just tell Sister," I say. "Do whatever she says?" - "Aye, good idea," says Mary, "that's what we'll do."

She asks me to stay with her while she tells Sister. The story doesn't seem so funny any more; I think we are both imagining it going round the hospital - both of us being ridiculed. Sister Jamieson laughs out loud when we tell her. "Oh priceless!" Mary and I look at each other in shame. "Oh don't worry girls, your secret's safe with me. I can't say I'm sorry for the doctor, she's no friend of mine - but poor wee Maisie! No we'll not bother putting that in her Kardex. Don't worry - this will go no further."

Mary and I stop in at the canteen to have breakfast together after our shift. I tell her about the Adamson and how much I like it there. "Aye," she says. "I've heard about you and the Adamson. I don't think its fair ye know - so I'm glad ye like it. I wonder if they might let me live there?" - "Maybe," I say, sipping my hot, milky coffee. "But you might have to get caught with a man in your room first." I am joking, but she colours a little. "Fat chance of that. No - I'll have to think of some other misdemeanor."

Carstairs State Mental Hospital
1984 June

About twenty five of us are going, not just students - any staff who are interested in knowing more about the state hospital. There is an air of excitement. Anybody would think we were taking a trip to the seaside. People are kneeling on their seats so that they can see one another better. Crisps and sweets are being passed round and the air is thick with smoke. The trained staff at the back are talking loudly about an incident back in the 70's when two patients murdered a nurse and a police man with an axe.

South Lanarkshire is not an area of Scotland that I'm familiar with. I'm not altogether sure where in the country I'm going to. "There's something about you and directions isn't there?" Neil says. "You're absolutely hopeless." I nod sadly, because it's true. I have a very poor sense of direction. All I know about east and west is that the sun rises in one and sets in the other. I doubt I could find my way across a desert based on that knowledge.

Mary has been to Carstairs before - escorting a patient who was being transferred from an Acute ward. "Once is enough. I felt terrible leaving that lassie there. A'm no goin' back if I can help it. No thank you." Mary has finished her training though, so she doesn't have to come - we do. Neil sits beside me telling me all about the *I Ching*. He's quite happy with the trip, thinks it will be interesting. The bus stops for about ten minutes at the gate. Eventually someone comes striding along and lets us in. When we get through the gates the bus slows down to about five miles an hour, "In case someone runs out and throws themselves under it," the nurse behind me explains in an excited whisper.

We are shown round by a red faced, swarthy looking nurse with tightly permed hair. She is very friendly and apparently rather proud of her role and workplace. She shows us the padded cells first, where all patients are put on admission, regardless of their mental state. It has nothing at all inside it, not even a bed or a toilet, just a kind of shallow gutter round the sides, not deep enough for anyone to drown themselves in anything. Next she shows us a padded cell with a mattress that is made from a patchwork of super strong fabric that cannot be ripped. "After three days, all being well, patients will progress to this cell," she explains. "Why are there no blankets?" I ask. "Because they might use them to kill themselves," she replies coolly. "Once a patient has settled in, and it's been established that they are safe to be moved, they can go to an ordinary cell."

The red faced nurse leads us to the next block. On the way we meet a couple of other staff who are escorting a female patient to her psychology appointment. When they say *psychology appointment* the Carstairs nurses smirk a little, and one of our gang says, "Oh well that'll be helpful eh?" Our guide for the day turns and smiles at her broadly - "You said it kid." Then she turns to the patient - "Tell them what you had for your lunch today." The patient looks at us - "Dowps." - "Say it again," commands our guide. "I don't think they heard you." - "DOWPS," says the patient, shuffling her feet, looking ashamed. "And then you were sick I'll bet?" Our guide, stands with her hands on her hips, smiling. The patient nods. "Well just you make sure and tell the psychologist all about it eh?" We wander along, a bunch of our nurses cosying up to the Carstairs nurse now.

We are led through a maze of locked gates and doors until eventually we end up in an 'ordinary cell' with a middle aged man sitting on his bed waiting for us. He puts down his magazine and stands politely while we scrutinize his room. There are photos on the wall, faded polaroids, groups of gap toothed grinning boys that look like they were on a day trip too - happier than ours I hope. His cell is quite cosy compared to the others we've been shown. There's a knitted patchwork blanket on his bed. "Roy knitted this blanket himself," the Carstairs nurse tells us, beaming at her patient proudly. Some of our gang express their surprise. The blanket is beautifully made, but I suspect they are more impressed by the fact that Roy was allowed access to knitting needles than his skill as a knitter.

After the tour we are joined by some Carstairs nursing officers for a sandwich lunch in the canteen. They shake hands vigorously with our nursing officers, slap each other on the back, like uncles at a wedding: "What are you driving these days? What's your handicap? How's the wife?" The Carstairs nurse brings out a book and a pen. "We have several vacancies at present," she tells us. "If you are interested just write your name and address in the book. I can assure you we will be in touch." Eleven nurses stand in a queue to write their details down. Neil looks like he's thinking about it. "You've got to be kidding," I say. He colours a little, "Yeah, I guess not."

Mary has moved in to the Adamson. She didn't have to misbehave; she just told Mr Williamson that she was feeling a bit low and needed to be somewhere quiet and peaceful. Crawford is cooking our dinner. My parents gave me a little two ringed table top stove so that we can cook more than one thing at a time. They think it's strange that the nurse's home is so ill equipped. I haven't told them it's not the proper home, or why I am here. Anyway Crawford is in the kitchen singing in fake French with a mountain of chopped vegetables all around him which he says is going to be curry. I ask him if I can help but he shooes me away.

Mary has the room at the end of the hall, the one with the Bakelite phone outside it, but she's in my room just now, telling me about the nurses' home at Stratheden and how she's always felt out of place there. "Why do you think that might be?" I ask her. "Well you know, I'm not trendy or anything. I don't know anything about music, or how to dress, or how to dance properly. I'm overweight. I just feel like an outsider."

Crawford comes breezing through, "Oh well you're in the right place mon cherie. This is the Outside Inn." He drops down on to the floor and starts lighting up his bong. Mary watches, fascinated. He offers her a smoke but she doesn't take it. "I'll wait and see what happens to you guys. Maybe I'll take some the next time." - "I can't dance properly either," I tell her, as I take hold of the bong. "I'm rubbish at it. I just pogo." - "It's true," says Crawford, his voice weak and croaky from smoking. "She can pogo for ages."

The rain is battering against the window. It feels warm and safe, with the heating raging and music playing and cooking smells beginning to waft through the rooms. Mary is looking at my pictures of horses and some poems that I have pinned to the wall. Crawford says - "She's a poet and I'm a novelist." Mary looks impressed and disbelieving at the same time. "What kind of novels do you write?" - "Tragedies. My current one is called, *The Phone Never Rings*." - "What's it about?" Mary asks politely. " Well I haven't actually written anything yet. It's still in the planning phase. But its going to be about isolation, loneliness, humiliation – all that jazz."- "Well it sounds very interesting," says Mary. "Good luck with writing it." Crawford nods and leaves, looking sad and reflective.

Our dinner is terrible - overcooked vegetables in salty water with chillies floating. We grate some cheese in, but that doesn't help. We add some ketchup - it's so disgusting we can't eat it. Mary goes to her room and fetches a tin of biscuits. "Imagine having a tin of biscuits," says Crawford. "That's so grown up." He sticks two in his mouth. I stick three in mine, try to munch them without letting any of it fall out. Crawford takes a swig of beer and crams another four in - then falls over on to his side laughing. "The pair of ye's are totally nuts," Mary shouts, but she's laughing too. "Ye's are disgusting!" She looks very happy.

We talk and talk and talk; about our parents; school; the boyfriends that none of us have, about college and the wards and how much we all hated the Vic hospital. Every now and again Crawford gets up and puts on some of my jewellery, or a scarf, or some make up. He paints his own toenails, then ours. The rain seems to get even heavier and we can hear the wind above the music. We drink beer and Peacock Pies, eat all the biscuits and smoke until it feels like our lungs are going to burst.

There is a small lull in the conversation and I think I hear a faint ringing. "Is that the phone?" Mary says, looking puzzled. Crawford gets up and turns the volume down on the record player. We all hear the ringing. "What did you say about the phone never rings?" I laugh nervously. Crawford's face turns very pale. I pull myself up, open the door to the hall and look down the corridor at the Bakelite phone. It sits silently in the gloom. "THANK FUCK!" Crawford says. He looks genuinely relieved. We start laughing, but I can still hear ringing, and it's really puzzling me because I've never heard it here before. I go over and open the window. A gust of wind and rain blows in. Crawford and Mary shout out in protest. I lean my head out into the dark and listen. "It's the mortuary," I say, but the wind catches my voice and Mary and Crawford don't hear me - they have started chatting again. I stand there listening to the ringing. I was in there with Celia the other day and there definitely wasn't a phone.

Stratheden Psychiatric Hospital
Ward 5
Women's Long Stay

In this hospital you work either A Shift or B Shift. There are a lot of married couples employed as nurses and if one of them works A Shift and the other B they don't need much in the way of childcare. They will never work the same weekends. They will never both have to be on the ward for 8am or both work until 8pm. The handover period is brief and within school hours. The system is very practical but it means you always work with the same team and each team has it's own Sister or Charge Nurse.

After coming off nights Neil and I have been put on B shift. It's like working at a different hospital because I only really know the A shift nurses. The B shift Sister for Women's Long Stay is Sister Ross and I only ever see Sister Jamieson at handover. I've asked her if I can be swapped back but she says it's unlikely - not until someone else wants to change, and that doesn't happen often. Sister Ross is about the same age as Sister Jamieson but she looks older, maybe because she never looks happy. She doesn't really talk to the women. She just shouts orders at them, swishing about in her blue uniform with her frilly cap, though the women seem blessedly oblivious, locked in their own worlds as most of them are.

I've heard that Sister Ross is having an affair with Bobby McGloan. "Are you a drug addict?" She asks me on our first tea break together, with all the other staff and a few patients milling about. "No," I say. She nods like she's prepared to take my word for it. "Why are you so thin then?" Sister Ross is a sturdy looking woman, her uniforms are very tight. "I just like being thin." She sticks her bottom lip out and bobs her head about like that explanation seems reasonable. She's just eaten three chocolate biscuits. One of the patients who has been hovering around behind her reaches out to take one, maybe thinking she'll have my share, but Sister is too sharp and raps her hard on the back of her hand with a teaspoon.

Sister Ross isn't scary like Tooje, but there's not a lot of love or joy in the ward when she's there. Sometimes she tries to be nice like Sister Jamieson, if it's someone's birthday, or if they are ill or something. I think she wants to be kind, but it embarrasses her, she's clumsy with it. She is very particular about the timing of everything. Her shifts are run with military precision. All patients must be dressed and washed by 9am. Beds changed or made by 10am. Make up and shaving by 11am. Dressings are changed between 2pm and 3pm. Bed covers are folded back, nightdresses laid out and a small plastic tub placed on every woman's locker with one Steradent tablet in it by 7pm. Teeth are gathered and washed at 7.30pm after the bedtime drinks.

She is very strict when it comes to food portions. No one on a reducing diet is allowed anything more than the dietician has prescribed. She stands behind us, hawk like, as we portion out the soggy fare at mealtimes; one scoop for you; two scoops for you; no scoops for you. A lot of food is wasted, scraped into pig bins that are brim full by the end of each meal. I never put bacon or ham in those bins.

Bobby comes in as we are doling out the evening meal. It seems he's changed to B Shift too. He sees me putting a slice of ham in the general waste bin. "THIS ONE," he shouts loudly, like he's the boss of Ward 5, not Sister Ross. "THE VEGETARIAN HERE THINKS THAT WE SHOULDN'T PUT BACON OR HAM IN THE PIG BINS. SHE THINKS THE PIGS MIGHT BE UPSET IF THEY HAPPEN TO EAT THEIR OWN PARENTS." The other nurses stop what they are doing and look at me. Bobby stands with his arms folded shaking his head, smirking. "Is that true?" Sister Ross asks, coming towards me with an empty metal food tray, dumping it into a sink full of hot soapy water. I nod. "How would you like to eat your own mother or father?" She stands there staring at me for a bit, hands on hips, feet apart, like she's actually considering eating her own parents and it might not be such a bad idea. She turns to Bobby - "You must admit, she's got a point. I think she's right. I don't think we should do it." She turns to the other nurses and shouts, "NO MORE BACON OR HAM IN THE PIG BINS OKAY." I'm not sure if she really does agree with me, or she's just trying to get Bobby back for acting like he's the boss here. He leaves swearing under his breath.

We have a new admission in the afternoon. It's the first new admission in several years - a middle aged woman who was a maths teacher before she got married. She has been diagnosed with alcoholism and endogenous depression.

She's been in the Acute ward for eight months following a suicide attempt which was very nearly successful. She is not suicidal now and is being admitted, with a good degree of persuasion it seems, on a voluntary basis. She stands next to her locker holding a flimsy looking dressing gown; a pretty woman with blonde hair, red lipstick, puffy circles under her eyes. I think she's been crying. Her husband sits on the bed looking guilty. I show them both around the ward then do her admission with him looking on. It's just the same admission routine as the general wards, blood pressure, pulse, temperature, respiration, though this woman is not in any way physically ill. They both seem a little bemused.

Sister Ross comes in with the bath book. "Your baths will be Monday and Thursday." She says it quite politely, for her. "What do you mean?" The new lady looks at us quizzically; I don't think they have bath books in Acute. "You will have a bath every Monday and Thursday." Sister says it a little more assertively. "Four o'clock. One of the nurses will remind you." - "But I don't like baths," the woman protests. "I like a shower, in the morning when I get up. Don't I have any say in this matter?" - "No you don't," says Sister Ross. "You'll have a bath, and you'll have it when I tell you to have it." The woman looks at her husband. "Put those things back in my case," she commands. "I'm not staying here with this ridiculous woman." Her husband jumps up and starts packing her things. Sister stands, scarlet faced, looking like she'll either explode or start crying. I'm not sure what to do so I suggest that the couple wait and talk to a doctor. "I don't think so," says the almost patient. She is every bit as imperious as Tooje, she could be her nicer sister. "If they want me to stay in this hospital a minute longer they'll have to section me." She shoots her husband a warning look and he quickly finishes fastening her case, puts her coat round her shoulders and steers her towards the door.

Sister Ross sits in the office smoking. The door is closed but we can see her through the window. Word has gone round and everyone knows what happened. The women who are able enough to work have come in from Autoclave and even they seem to know. Someone defied Sister, openly refused a bath, called her names. Someone made her cry. Bobby arrives with one of the nursing officers and they huddle there in the office for ages while the rest of us pretend not to be interested.

Later she beckons me in. "What did you think?" She says, offering me one of her cigarettes. I consider telling her the truth. I consider saying, "That woman is the sanest person I've met since I arrived in this hospital." But I just say, "Maybe the patients should be allowed to bathe or shower when they want."

I've been seeing a guy called Sam for the last few weeks. He is an engineer on the rigs. I met him at Neil's birthday party. He's an old friend of his from university. We left the party together at 4am on Saturday morning and he stayed with me for the rest of the weekend. He's been back a few times since, took me to dinner one night, but mostly we just stay in my room. Neil is pissed off with me. In the canteen eating scrambled egg rolls on the Monday after the party he says - "You know Irish is really upset with you don't you? You came to the party with him and you left with Sam. It's not on you know. It's pretty shoddy behaviour to be honest. Do you actually enjoy hurting people?" I put my roll down; I'm not really enjoying it anyway - I really wanted black pudding. "Just because I walk to a party with someone doesn't mean that I have to stay with him all night does it?" Neil doesn't even bother answering me. He says, "Sam isn't really interested in you. He was in love with a girl called Cathy at uni and he'll never be interested in anyone but her. They were a great couple. She was so nice, really beautiful - special. She left him for someone else. He's never going to get over it." He pulls a photograph out of his wallet; a picture of Sam smiling broadly, his arm round a very pretty girl with blonde curly hair and a bright, cheerful smile. He must have looked it out just to show me. I pull the picture out of Neil's hand and study it. I like Sam a lot, he's tall and good looking and funny, but I don't think I'm in love with him. I remember that first morning; he was lying in my bed looking at the poems and drawings I have pinned to the wall. I thought he might ask me about them, but he didn't. He just said, "You're a strange fish aren't you?" I don't think it's love for him either.

To be honest I can't stop thinking about the guy I keep seeing in the library. I don't think he works because I see him on weekday mornings when I'm off or on a late shift. "How come you always pick the best books?" He asks me, tilting his head back, smiling. "Did I take the ones you wanted?" He laughs and shakes his head. "No. I'll let you read them first, then you can tell me if they are any good. This one I've read." He is pointing at a book called Birdy by William Wharton. "It's very good. I think you'll enjoy it."

We walk down to the high street together and as we pass a little cafe he asks if I would like a cup of tea. There are hardly any other customers. We sit at a table in the window looking out onto the town square, order a pot of tea and two toasted scones. I think maybe it's going to be awkward, but it isn't. We chat, as if we'd known each other for years. His name is Hamish and he's just finished doing a degree in English Literature at Aberdeen University. He's not sure what to do next. "I'm thinking about youth work," he tells me. "I've been volunteering at the YM - basketball, football, a wee bit of boxing - I really like it." He looks very fit, broad in the shoulders, strong, brown forearms. He doesn't look like an English Literature graduate.

I tell him that I'm a psychiatric nurse and he nods. "I've seen you in the pub with the other nurses. Bit of a bunch of hippies eh? All into the old psychopharmacology I'm guessing? What's that all about?" I have a think about that, watching the Fisher & Donaldson's queue across the road. I wonder if there's ever a time when it doesn't have a queue. "I guess our job attracts the kind of people who are interested in the mind and perception - altered realities. Though not all psychiatric nurses are interested in that of course." - "But you are?" I don't answer him. I'm a little uncomfortable with this conversation. I look around the cafe to check who's there. It occurs to me that he might be a plain clothes policeman. The waitress comes over and we sit quietly while she lays out our tea and scones. After she has gone he says - "I've not got much time for drugs. Something really bad happened to me last year. Someone thought it would be a bit of a laugh to slip a tab of acid into my lunch. I ended up in Kingseat Hospital - been taking medication ever since."

We talk a bit about his hospital experience. "The nurses were really nice," he tells me. "I think I was a bit of a favourite. It was actually okay. Things were pretty shit at home. My step-father and I have never got on, and I was depressed - though I hadn't acknowledged it. My step-father's the same. I think if he went on anti-depressants everyone's life would be a lot easier, but there's no way that's going to happen. That's why I'm in the library all the time. If I'm in the house we just fight. Anyway - I was in hospital for a few months and in the end I didn't want to go home, but they kicked me out and here I am." I think, with a shiver - if he had been admitted to Stratheden, I might have met him in men's long stay.

"Come on, pop up here," I say to Maisie patting the treatment room couch. She sits on the couch and I help her swing her legs up. She gives me a small sideways smile. She looks a bit anxious. "Have you ever given a jag before?" - "No. You're my first." I jiggle the syringe about in the metal tray in mock anxiety. She jumps up staring at me. "I'm kidding," I laugh.

"It's fine. I've done loads - honest." She looks at me suspiciously then lies back down again, lowers the waistband of her skirt, she still looks a bit nervous.

A pupil nurse comes in. If you are training to be a staff nurse they call you a student, if you are training to be an enrolled nurse you are a pupil. Her name is Lara and she never usually talks to me. She stands in the doorway waiting as the needle glides smoothly into the upper outer quadrant of Maisie's backside. "Have you heard about Crawford?" My heart starts to race, but I keep my hand steady as I push the thick yellow anti-psychotic syrup slowly down through the syringe then pull the needle out.

I can tell from the look on Lara's face this isn't going to be good news. Her eyes shine, her cheeks are flushed and she can't help but smile. "They've found drugs in his room - up there at the Adamson." Then she stops, steps back with a theatrical gasp, her fingers to her mouth. "You live there too don't you?" I busy myself helping Maisie up, rearrange her clothes so that she is all neat and tidy again. She smiles at me, takes my hands in hers and lifts them up and down a few times as if we are playing some childhood game. I give her a quick hug, help her off the bed and walk her to the door.

"You really shouldn't be talking about that kind of thing in front of the patients," I say as Maisie makes her way back to the day room. Lara's face flushes. Technically I am her senior, though I can guess what she thinks about that.

"What's happening?" I soften my tone, because I don't feel I'm in a position to be lecturing anyone about anything, besides, I need to know what's happened to Crawford. She turns around, starts fiddling with the sharps bin. "He's been escorted to the gate." She walks over and leans against the bed looking at me slyly - "He's only getting what he deserves as far as I'm concerned. There's no place for junkies in nursing."

Sister Ross is in the office. I wander in and pick up my cigarettes from the windowsill. She looks up from her paper. "Have you heard about your pal?" I nod and sit down. "Lara came in and told me just now." Sister snorts. I don't think anybody likes Lara. "Silly sod," says Sister. "I hope you haven't left anything in your room?" I shake my head and she sits back looking kind of relieved. "They've walked him to the gates. That's it. He's finished. He'll never get to be a nurse now - and all for a wee bit of cannabis." - "Is that all it was?" I try not to shout. "Fuck's sake." Sister Ross raises an eyebrow - "Why? Did you think they might find something else?" - "No," I respond, a little too quickly. She narrows her eyes, "Just you watch yourself."

Maisie appears at the door. She stares at us through the little square window, hopping from foot to foot as if she needs the loo. Her lower jaw is grinding from side to side - tardive dyskinesia. I hadn't noticed it in her before. Sister curls a finger for her to come in and I open the door. "What?" Sister barks. "Can I have a marshmallow?" She nods in the direction of Sister's desk drawer. The two women stare at each other. Maisie would stand there staring for hours if you let her. Eventually Sister purses her lips, trying not to laugh. She feigns confusion - "What marshmallows?" - "The ones you hide our tablets in," Maisie says. Sister looks at me and we burst out laughing. She throws a half eaten bag of marshmallows at Maisie, tells her to scram. She turns to me, offering me a cigarette. "Nothing gets past that one eh?"

Later on that day Mr Williamson comes in to the ward. I've been doing big baths and washing hair. Now I'm putting rollers in, for those that want it. "Just to give it a wee bit of bounce nurse," Janet is telling me. "Just a suggestion?" I ask her. She giggles because that's what Sister Ross says every time Janet holds her plate out for potatoes - "JUST A SUGGESTION OF POTATOES FOR JANET."

Mr Williamson clears his throat behind us. When I turn and see him my heart sinks to my feet. As we walk towards the office I imagine myself being escorted to the gate, see my name on the list that is sent out every year by the Royal College of Nursing - all the nurses that have been struck off, never to be employed by the NHS again. Sister comes in with a tea tray, clears her desk and sets it down. "Do you want me to stay?" She asks quietly as she leans forwards. I shake my head. She looks a bit disappointed. "Well, actually - yes please - if you don't mind?" She doesn't even ask Mr Williamson if it's okay. She just plonks herself down and stares at him, very hostile. I notice there are three cups on the tray.

Mr Williamson tells me that the Adamson nurses' home will close. Mary and I are to leave by Saturday; there will be a room for each of us in the Stratheden nurses home. He doesn't say anything about Crawford and neither do I. He looks kind of sad, but he always looks sad. After he leaves I ask Sister Ross if it would have been him that walked Crawford to the gate. "Him? No. He's far too soft. Nobody would ask him to do it. It's the Director of Nursing Services that does it. He'd have no qualms."

I don't go to the canteen at tea time because I know they will all be talking about Crawford. Neil catches me as I'm getting on my bike to cycle home that night. "Come on," he says. "Let's go'n get pissed." We go back to the Adamson to get Mary first. When she opens her door I see she's been crying, but it seems she's been waiting for me and she's all ready to go out. Other nurses have gathered in the pub - people who like Crawford. We sit like mourners, genuinely sad, but glad it wasn't us it happened to. Hamish comes in and nods. I motion for him to come and sit next to me. Neil throws him a stony look. Hamish seems sorry when he hears what has happened. "I played pool with him once or twice. He seemed like a nice guy. He would have been a good nurse." - "So I guess we're going to need a lift to the nurses home on Saturday," I say to Mary. She looks like she might start crying again. "Maybe not," says Hamish. "I think I know somewhere you two can stay."

Mary and I meet Hamish outside the cottage with his friend John who inherited the farm from his father. "It's a bit unlived in," John shouts. He opens the door and ushers us in. "I've tried to spruce it up a bit." It's cold despite the hot summer sun. There's a strong smell of paint. "It's not a warm house I'm afraid. There's just the fireplace and some electric heaters. Electric blankets on both beds, hot water bottles if you need them - though maybe not with the electric blankets." He makes a funny face when he says that. "You can help yourself to wood from the pile by the back of the farm house." It seems funny to be talking about these things in the middle of June.

The living room is coldest. It's dark and cheerless with heavy brown furniture and a shabby looking colourless carpet that looks like it's been there since the 1940's. The kitchen is huge and the sun streams through the window onto sticky looking orange linoleum. Mary walks over and opens the back door. "Heat!" She shouts. We all bundle out into the scruffy little yard at the back. The cottage looks nicer from this side - bigger, and dryer. We stand chatting for a bit then troop back in to continue the tour. The middle bedroom is fairly big, - white emulsion over 1950's paper, a queen size bed in the corner. Mary sits on it and bounces about a bit. "No bouncing on the beds," says John. "Not in daylight hours anyway." He turns and winks at me. Mary gets up, raising her brows.

The smell of paint gets stronger as we approach the second bedroom. John stops and says, "It'll be £10 a month each okay? And you can use my washing machine and tumble dryer." Mary and I nod, hardly believing our luck. John turns and opens the bedroom door, shouting, "Okay. It was an experiment." - "Fuck me!" Hamish says. "Tractor paint?" John nods sheepishly. The room is bright red. "It's like High Plains Drifter," I say. "Exactly!" John shouts.

Apart from the red paint it's not too bad - a single bed, a wardrobe and big chest of drawers, a nicer carpet than the other rooms. "Which room do you prefer?" I ask Mary. "The white one. I couldnae sleep in here. I'm sorry, but I just couldnae. Ad have nightmares." Hamish walks over and opens the window. "Nobody's sleeping in here tonight anyway. The fumes would kill you."

Stratheden Psychiatric Hospital
Playfield House
Department of Child and Adolescent Psychiatry
1984 July - August

The building is new and purpose built. There is a big cheerful day room, two classrooms, a playroom and a hydrotherapy pool. Children can have their own bedroom, or share if they prefer. There is a bungalow attached to the unit as well; for troubled families to stay in. We have a family here just now: Mum; Dad and three little boys. They use the hydrotherapy pool every day - all of them, though it's a very small pool. They are learning how to be close to one another. It seems to be working because the parents look very happy and proud and the children aren't wetting their beds like they did when they first came in. They were here before me, so I don't know what they were like when they were admitted, but I'm told there was a lot of shouting and hitting going on. It's hard to imagine because there's nothing like that now. Every time I see them they are smiling and hugging one another, as if they have come through some kind of disaster and are amazed to find one another still intact.

We don't wear uniforms here. We wear more practical clothes, because we have to go out and play with the children; Rounders; Tig; British Bulldog; What's the Time Mr Wolf. I like playing with the infants best. We are told to let them get dirty. We are told to let them lose - but not every time. I help them make a shop in the garden and we sell mud pies, using stones for money: three stones for a plain pie; four for one with dandelions; five for a dandelion/daisy mix. You can buy loose flowers and leaves too, even, sometimes a worm, though I'm less keen on that - trying to persuade the children to be kind to animals, insects included.

Some of the children have obsessive compulsive disorder. Quite a few are phobic about dirt, but I don't really have to try too hard to get them to participate in the mud pie shop game; they are all quite excited about it. They treat the stones as if they are real money and grub about in the earth trying to collect as many as possible. If someone finds a pile of them they all dive in trying to gather as many as they can. It's a fine borderline between excitement and aggression and it's hard work trying to stop them kicking and scratching one another.

We have our meals with the children too. We are meant to eat what they eat. We sit round the table like siblings, with a staff nurse playing mum. "I don't eat meat." I tell the staff nurse, Pat, who is just about to put my food down. She lifts my plate into the air. I think she's going to give it to Neil, but the charge nurse, Mr Bevan, who we are meant to call Larry, shouts from behind, "WE DON'T ENTERTAIN FOOD FADS HERE." The staff nurse puts the plate down in front of me. "Sorry love. Go an' just eat it?" I eat the vegetables, trying to avoid the gravy. "You've got to eat it all or you won't get to watch TV," a wee girl called Paula tells me, her tiny eyebrows raised in concern - little dark triangles above big brown eyes.

I smile at her and start to eat because I can see she is worried.

Neil steals the roast beef from my plate, sticks the whole slice into his mouth. His cheeks puff out comically and the children start to giggle. Pat pretends not to see, but she is looking down at her plate smiling. Larry Bevan prowls behind suspiciously. He doesn't seem to include himself in the eat with the children rule.

I fight my case, encouraged by Neil, and some other staff too, surprisingly. "I think it's a matter for the union," Neil says in an off hand way at the beginning of a team meeting - loud enough for everyone to hear. Nurse Bevan talks it over with the consultant and they relent, tell me that I can help in the kitchen washing the pots and pans during mealtimes. "You could still fight that," says Neil. "You're not employed to wash dishes." - "No," I tell him. "Let's not make any more trouble. I like it here."

I do like it, though I go home to the cottage and cry most nights because I can't believe the cruelty that has been inflicted on some of these children. Mary tuts and shakes her head at me. She's done a placement there too, during her training. "You're too soft. You'll soon learn." She clicks and puffs, knitting and smoking, but she looks concerned all the same. She's knitting baby clothes and when I ask her who they are for she just shrugs.

My dad is a social worker. There have always been books

and magazines and research papers lying around our house about the neglect and abuse of children. Last year he wrote the introduction for a book called *Violence in the Family*. I read his introduction, but I didn't read the rest of it. I had a rough and general notion of how things can be for some kids, but I had never read individual stories. I had never associated what was written in those books and magazines with an actual child. Now, reading the notes, the horror stories within them, knowing the things that have happened to the wee souls making mud pies in the garden is almost unbearable.

On Saturdays the children are given pocket money and we go into Cupar to spend it. I am to look after Paula, who for some reason seems to have attached herself to me. She really likes the shop game. I told her one day, that when I was little, I used a toy pastry making kit to make mud pies. We stand in the toy shop looking at one now - a tiny rolling pin and some pastry cutters in the shape of a star, a teddy, and a heart. It's only fifty pence so she has enough money, but it's right at the top of a rotating display stand, too high for me to reach. "Don't touch anything," I tell her, walking over to the counter, hoping the shop keeper will think this beautiful child is mine.

Just as I'm asking him if he can help me get the toy from the stand there is a terrible crash. Paula has pulled the rotating display stand down. She's picking up the pastry making kit from the spill of cheap toys. "NO WAY," shouts the shopkeeper. "NO WAY MY LADY." Paula doesn't seem in the least alarmed. She turns and pulls another rotating stand down - key rings with popular names on them. They crash heavily to the floor and I'm worried that she might get hurt. But she is wild with excitement now, tearing round the shop pulling down anything she can and hurling it to the floor. The shop keeper's face is twisted with rage. "GET THAT CHILD OUT OF MY SHOP!" I pull Paula, kicking and screaming, out the door. She's still holding the pastry making kit.

My heart is pounding when I tell Pat what's happened. She looks at Paula sternly, drops herself down to the child's level and says, "Give me the toy." She says it loud and firm. Paula spits in her face and starts laughing loudly. Some of the other children join in. Pat stands up, wiping her face, pulls the toy from Paula's hand and starts walking towards the shop. "CUNT CUNT CUNT," Paula shouts at the top of her voice over and over. The people of Cupar who are out for a pleasant Saturday afternoon stroll look at us in horror. Neil picks Paula up and bundles her into the minibus, sits down and holds his arm across her while she writhes around squealing. I get the other children in and watch Pat cross the road and open the door of the shop. She pushes it a little, then pulls it closed, comes back towards us at a brisk pace. "He's completely raging," she says as she climbs into the drivers seat. "Here, just take it," she says to Paula, throwing the toy into her lap. Paula stops shouting immediately and looks at me with a smile, holding the little kit up to show me - as if nothing untoward has happened. I sit, looking out the window, shaking.

Later at tea break Pat says, "He looked like a mad man, shouting and swearing. No way I was going in there. Jesus what a mess though eh? How did she do that? And her so tiny!" - "She was like something possessed," I say, laughing now. "And there was me hoping he would think she was mine." - "Oh my God," says Pat. "Heaven help you if you land up with a wee devil like that."

After tea break we bath the children and get them ready for bed. I'm on story telling duty. Paula sits on my knee, snuggling in. She smells so sweet and clean, little ladybird buttons on her dressing gown, perfect pink feet sticking out from soft, fleecy pyjamas. If another child comes too close she will kick them hard.

It's the Cupar gala day and we are having a picnic in the Duffus park. Sam is back on shore and he's been staying with me at the cottage. I feel a bit awkward introducing him to Hamish, though nothing has happened between Hamish and me. I'm not sure if he's really interested in me or not. He's friendly enough to Sam, but he doesn't stick around for long. I'm happy anyway. I like Sam a lot; he's good fun, and he's kind. I can't imagine him ever being unkind.

Neil is chatting up a girl called Dot who's recently started working at Stratheden as a nursing assistant. She's wearing an Iron Maiden T-Shirt, brush denim flared jeans and a leather choker round her neck with a wolf's head pendant. I hear

Neil telling her that he has very catholic taste in music. "What? Like monks and that?" She sees me looking and grins. Neil asks her if she wants to play frisbee and she jumps up excitedly. He looks so pleased and surprised I feel a pang of guilt; he's asked me to play frisbee loads of times and I always say no.

It's lovely weather and the park is full of families and groups of excited teenagers trying to look bored. I wander over to get some ice cream from a van parked under the trees not far from us. A tall woman is standing in the queue in front of me - long limbs, very slim. She turns round and I'm sure I can feel my pupils dilate - she is so beautiful. She smiles down at me with big grey eyes, black hair cut in a dramatic bob. She's wearing a blue and white striped 1950's summer dress. She looks amazing.

The queue is long and we get chatting. Her name is Sylvia. She's just moved here with her husband who works in IT in Glenrothes. They thought Cupar would be a nice place to bring up a family. "How many children do you have?" I ask her. "None yet," she replies, blushing a little. "But hopefully soon. We're not long married. We'd like two at least." There are fine lines round her eyes and mouth; she's quite a bit older than me, maybe about thirty. She's a musician, plays the harp, does a bit of teaching, but she's stopped working for a while. Her husband earns enough for both of them. She's focusing on their new home for now; it's old and it needs a lot doing.

I think it all sounds very romantic and I feel kind of envious. I have a very strong feeling that I will never be anyone's wife. A fleeting image of Sylvia at Stratheden buying slabs for her patio floats to the surface of my mind. I blot it out. I don't want to think of her anywhere near Stratheden. Sylvia is stirring something within me and I'm not sure what it is. It's something about the way she moves and talks - nervy and uncertain, as if she needs protecting. I tell her where I'm working and we talk for a bit about it, her broad forehead creased with concern; she would never have imagined children in a psychiatric hospital. I hear someone call her name. She looks up, her whole face brightening so that she is more beautiful than ever. "Here's my husband now." I turn around and Andy is standing beside me.

My stomach turns over. My legs feel like they are shaking. I rest a palm on my thigh to steady myself. "Hello Hello!" He is as friendly as can be. Sylvia begins to introduce us - "No need sugar babe," he says. "We're old friends aren't we?" He looks down at me, smiling. "Nice to see you again. Are you living here in Cupar now?" I nod. I can't seem to speak. "Well Sylvia could do with a friend and you'll do fine." He's holding my arm, his fingers pressing hard just above my elbow. I try to pull away but he doesn't let go. "I think you and Sylvia will get along very well. You've a lot in common." He relaxes his hold and I pull myself away. "Nice to see you again." My voice wavers a little. For a moment I think Sylvia sees that I'm scared, but he slips his arm around her and starts kissing her neck. She tips her head back in delight - just a pair of newly weds in love.

I go back over to Sam and tell him the queue's too long. I can't be bothered standing all that time just for ice cream. "That's all right pal." He hands me a beer, pulls me down to sit with him. We sit on his leather jacket amongst the huddle of our friends, laughing along with the jokes and silly talk, basking in the heat of the sun. I know I could tell Sam about Andy, but I'm too scared. Sam is a big guy, but he's not a fighter, and he's all good. I couldn't bear to be the one to spoil that.

Neil and Rod say there's no such thing as evil people; there's just people - sometimes we do good things and sometimes we do bad things - for all sorts of reasons. Celia isn't convinced about that; she thinks theirs is a male perspective - blind to the experiences of women. I understand why she thinks that, but I want to agree with Neil and Rod, because it seems to me that theirs is a more constructive way of thinking. I certainly don't think it's right that it says: *This child is a psychopath*, on the first page of little Paula's medical notes. I think it's wrong and unjust to write people off in this way. But when I think of Andy *evil* is the word that comes to mind. It's like an instinctive reaction - a sensor has been switched on and it's flashing red for danger.

Stratheden Psychiatric Hospital
Community Psychiatric Nursing
1984 September - November

I am twinned up with a community psychiatric nurse called Agnese. She is from Latvia, though you wouldn't guess it from her accent which is sort of English with an American twang. She dresses in slightly old fashioned clothes; tan and cream coloured twin sets with pencil skirts or slacks. Her glasses hang round her neck on a heavy gold chain. She smokes John Player Specials with a fancy looking cigarette holder. Apparently the cigarette holder has a special filter that means you are less likely to get lung cancer. I don't know if I believe that, but it looks good anyway, with her long fingers and peach painted nails. She looks very glamorous. We don't talk much, but I feel okay in Agnese's company.

We go to her house in Glenrothes at least twice a day for coffee and to let her dog, Oscar, into the garden for five minutes to do his business. Oscar is a greyhound. He was found in a dump with a broken leg, almost starved to death. Agnese tells me it's not uncommon for racing dogs to be abandoned in this way, if they are injured and less likely to win a race. His leg is healed now and he doesn't even limp. He's big and healthy looking and very happy. He can't be taken off the lead on this estate though. Even with his old leg injury, he can run very fast and if he sees a cat he will chase it and probably kill it. It's hard to imagine Oscar killing anything; he's such soppy creature, lying across my knees on the sofa, looking up at me with huge, dark, loving eyes. It feels like heaven cuddling him. It reminds me of home, we never had a greyhound, but lots of other dogs and all very cuddly.

Agnese never married and has no children. She'll be retiring in a few years and she's going to live in a house by the sea with Oscar, so he can run along the beach whenever he wants. Agnese looks very dreamy when she tells me that. She has very dreamy eyes - pale and thoughtful. It's like she can see something interesting far away in the distance, then, when she turns and looks at me, she seems a bit surprised, as if she'd forgotten I was there and she is happy to see me. That makes me feel kind of special, though I guess she does it with everybody, not just me.

We drive around the county in a little blue mini. We don't wear uniform, to prevent stigma, but there is a huge Fife Health Board logo on each side of the car. If we were dressed like nurses people might think we are going in to help someone who is physically ill, but we aren't, and I'll bet most of our patient's neighbours know fine well what kind of nurses we are. We cover the whole of Fife, so our weeks are mapped out mostly according to geography. Generally we deliver tablets and give depot injections: Modecate; Peraldehyde, or Depixol, if people have a diagnosis of schizophrenia - Lithium for those who are manic depressive. Sometimes we are offered a cup of tea or coffee. I wait for Agnese to say yes or no; she knows the hazards of each household. It's very embarrassing to be given tea and not be able to drink it because the cup is dirty, or you saw someone dribble into it.

I sit in people's living rooms rubbing the tiny glass vials between my palms then breathing on them to warm them up. These drugs are designed to sit like a blob of glue in the patient's muscle and slowly dissolve into their system over three or four weeks. It's almost impossible to draw them up if they are cold. Peraldehyde is the worst; it needs a lot of warming, and it needs to be drawn up into a glass syringe because it reacts with plastic. You have to pull hard to get it into the syringe, then push it hard to inject it into a persons body. Agnese says it is made of the same stuff that is used for embalming. I wonder if that's why people look so stiff and waxy when they are on it.

It's true that the medication stops our patients delusions and the voices that only they can hear - evil voices, for the most part, demeaning and cruel, telling them to do terrible things to themselves. But it stops other things too: energy; curiosity; spontaneity; joy. I wonder if my patients are thinking along the same lines as me, sitting politely watching and waiting, understanding that if they refuse their injection they will be back in hospital by the end of the week.

Most of our patients are poor; living in council estates in the bigger towns, Kirkcaldy, Glenrothes, Cardenden, but even the wealthier villages have people living in abject poverty. We visit a couple in Falkland - Ronald and June, who met when they were both patients in Lynbank hospital; a hospital for people with learning disabilities. They are both profoundly deaf. They speak in sign language and lip read. I wonder how anyone ever knew they were psychotic and how they managed to get out of hospital and marry.

Ronald and June's focus in life seems to be basic survival - food and fuel. They are lean and brown from roaming the woods and beaches for coal and firewood. They cook cheap sausages on the living room fire and drink stewed tea from a pot that rests permanently on the hearth. A dead rabbit lies stretched out on the kitchen table waiting to be skinned. Next to it sits a bowl of wormy looking windblown apples. In the living room there are only two chairs, nothing else. Ronald and June insist we take them when we visit, while they stand, or crouch beside us. There are yellow splatters on the windows from the eggs that are thrown by children as they pass by on their way to and from school. There is one picture in the house, to the left of the fireplace - the Queen on her coronation day.

June takes me upstairs so I can do her injection first. The lumpy looking double bed is surrounded by newspapers and magazines, piled high all around the walls. There doesn't seem to be a theme: Women's Own; National Geographic; Vogue; The Sunday Post. I think they pull some of them out of bins; some, I understand, are given to them by their GP. Agnese says they use them to light the fire, but there is a Scientific American lying open on an upturned box by one side of the bed and a TV Times on the other. I wonder why they would read the TV times when they don't have a telly.

The bed is neatly made and covered with a green candlewick bedspread, that kind of institutional green you see in schools and hospitals - the colour of paper towels. There is no source of heat in the house except for the fire downstairs. June lies down for her jag and little goose bumps appear on her skin as she bares the top of her buttock to be injected. She nods in thanks when it's over, fastening her skirt back up, tucking in her blouse, indicating that I should wait here for Ronald to come up. The whole business is over and done with within ten minutes and we are back in the car, sitting in a Ronald and June like silence all the way to St Andrews.

Our first patient in St Andrews, Mrs Merriman, is a small, very slight, sixty year old Welsh woman with manic depression whose husband died just a few months ago. She has kept fairly well despite her bereavement and having to live alone for the first time in her life. Her 1930's bungalow is extremely neat and tidy, but everything in it seems to date from about the same time as the house was built. She sits in a big Odeon style armchair that is the same milky brown colour as her stockings, looking at me with her fixed, parkinsonian stare, rubbing her hands together nervously, saying absolutely nothing. I find it very hard to imagine her being manic.

Agnese leaves me to do my case study with Mrs Merriman while she visits another patient. I know by now that means she is going to the bookies. The clock on the mantelpiece ticks loudly. The fire is set but unlit. Outside I hear a mother chastising her child: "Oh now look what you've done. You've completely ruined it." The child lets out a wail of despair. Agnese has told me that Mrs Merriman has a history of shop lifting and sexual disinhibition whenever she becomes unwell. I wasn't planning on bringing any of that up since it's all in her notes anyway, but Mrs Merriman seems quite keen to talk now that Agnese has gone. "Usually it starts in the library," she tells me. "You know - propositioning men." It seems to me that she is getting a little excited telling me this and I'm not sure whether I should encourage it. I ask her what she steals, which feels like safer territory. "Lingerie," she says, raising her eyebrows a little as she pulls her sensible tweed skirt up above her knees to show me the black lacy edges of her scarlet bloomers.

"I met a nice man in the library recently," I tell her, as she lets go the hem of her skirt. "Oh yes," she says. "It's a good place to meet men if you are fond of reading. My George was a good husband to me, but he couldn't abide a book. When I was young my mother said, 'Choose a husband that reads books.' So when I met him I said, 'Do you read books?' And he said, 'No, I never read books. I have no interest in them.' But I married him anyway you know, because he was nice and I could see he was going to be a good provider. But you know he never read a book, never in his life. He was too busy. Worked hard. Too busy working to read books, George. But maybe my mother was right because I'm a devil for propositioning men in the library." She smiles and clasps her hands together, prayer like, holding them up to her chin. "It's not just the men though - I love to read. I'm reading a very good book just now. It's called *Last Call for Love*. It's about a woman that gets pregnant out of wedlock and the man doesn't want her to have the baby." - "That's tough," I say, nodding. Mrs Merriman nods too, and sighs, lowers her clasped hands to her lap. "Yes, he wants her to have a termination, but she doesn't want to." - "That sounds like a very sad story." - "Yes it is. But she just goes ahead and has the baby anyway, even if she has to raise it herself - and you know, that was a difficult thing to do in those days." - "It still is - don't you think?" She sits back in her chair staring at me for a few moments. The clock ticks. She seems to have gone into a dwam. I shift in my seat, clear my throat and she leans forwards, rubs her hands together. "Yes I suppose it is," she says and carries on with her story. "He doesn't want her to have the baby, but she just goes ahead and has it and it dies in birth. It's very sad for her - but he's not a bad man and maybe it will all turn out good in the end." She sits back in her seat, spends a few moments studying her tweed skirt, then looks up smiling, "Maybe he'll marry her and they will have a family later." - "Or maybe she's better off without him?" I say. She looks at me with her fixed, unsettling stare than she says - "Well you never know how the story's going to turn out do you? You've got to read the whole book before you know which way the story's going to go don't you?"

She's still staring at me and I look around the room in discomfort. There are no books at all. "Didn't you ever steal books?" She shakes her head. "No. George wouldn't have allowed that. He would have put his foot down at that. I wasn't allowed to read in the house. I just read in the library. He tried to stop that too. Because of the men he said. But it was the books too - he didn't think they were good for me. Mind you, they do gather dust don't they?"

Agnese comes back and says we have to press on, we have three more visits to make. We say our goodbyes then sit in the car smoking. "Did you get what you need for your case study?" - "I think so. We spent most of the time talking about a book she was reading about a woman losing her baby." - "Hmm, yes," Agnese looks at me with narrowed eyes. "Yes, Mrs Merriman had a child but it was taken away from her by social services. Her husband didn't object, seems he felt he had enough on his hands looking after her."

I look out the window, see Mrs Merriman peeking through white net curtains that have sailing ships punched into their lacy design. She gives me a little wave. I wave back, realise that my face is wet with tears, wipe them away roughly. I wonder if she sees me doing that. I don't care if she does. Agnese doesn't seem to have noticed. I stare out the window thinking about what I want to write, there's a story forming in my head, but it's not the kind of thing I could put in a case study.

The next patient is a student, he's only having tablets delivered. "You go in," says Agnese. "There's no need for me to see him." - "But what do I do?" I don't like this idea at all. "Just ask him how he is." She lights another fag, opens her paper at the racing pages. I make my way down the corridor of the halls of residence to my patient's room. His package of tablets is sealed, so I don't know what he's been given, but there's a lot of it. I hear voices as I stand outside his door - loud, authoritative public school accents. They seem to be talking about philosophy, or maybe politics. A particularly loud voice is declaring that someone called Hegel had very disparate ideas, some radical and some more conservative. When he died his followers split into factions and that's where the political concepts of left and right originate. I go back to the car. "He's got company," I say to Agnese as I open the door. "Well that's nice," she says. "I can't go in there if he's got friends round." She rolls her eyes. "He knows we are due today. We are not coming back - we haven't got time. Just give him the tablets, you don't need to say anything. You don't even need to go in."

I make my way back to his room, knock loudly. "COME," his voice booms through the closed door. I open it and stand with the package in my hand. "WELL COME IN THEN FOR GOD'S SAKE." There are loads of students in there, about ten of them, lying and sitting around. I cast my eyes about, trying to guess which one is the Hegel expert. They smile and smirk and exchange snide glances as I step over their outstretched legs to my patient who is in the far corner of the room. "GIVE THEM HERE THEN," he bellows impatiently. "Are you ok?" I ask him. "YES, YES. JUST PUT THE BLOODY TABLETS DOWN." I drop them on to his lap and leave as fast as I can.

As I settle back into the car, Agnese stubs out her fag, folds her paper away, puts the key in the ignition and turns to me - "He's a right little shit isn't he?" I laugh pretty hard at that, then I tell her the stuff about Hegel. "How interesting," she says. "It's amazing what you learn in this job." She turns a corner rather fast and we head for Auchtermuchty. "Chrissie first, then the Laughlin's," Agnese says. "I've saved the best for last."

Chrissie is standing at the window waiting for us and the door swings open as we walk up the path. "Could your skirt not be a bit shorter?" She shouts at Agnese. Agnese says nothing and doesn't seem in the least bit annoyed. I feel indignant. Agnese always looks good - and her skirt isn't even particularly short. The old lady snorts as we come through the door and I think I hear something about tarts, but she holds up a box of cakes so she's maybe talking about them. "I've got ye some Mr Kiplings." She turns to me - "I do love a Mr Kipling - there's nae yin better than another."

We sit in her living room drinking tea and tucking into the cakes. I like the contrast of the soft coloured icing, the moist crumbly sponge and the sticky white goo inside. I have two, Chrissie has three, Agnese doesn't have any, she just smokes. Chrissie's wee dog, Hendry, watches closely, his little head following our every move as we eat. "ROLLOVER!" Chrissie shouts. The wee dog immediately rolls. "PLAY DEAD!" He lies on his back with his feet in the air. Agnese sits chuckling and I clap my hands with delight. He is a Terrier/Corgi mix, reddish brown, with big ears and a long nose. His tufty fur is white under his chin and belly. "He looks a bit like Basil Brush," I say, but Chrissie and Agnese don't seem to know who Basil Brush is. "BEG!" Chrissie shouts and he sits up on his hind quarters squirrel fashion. She rewards him with half of the last cake.

Chrissie has had periods of depression so severe that she becomes catatonic. Her first admission to hospital was in the 1940's just after she had her son. She was diagnosed with post natal depression. When she was discharged a year later her husband had divorced her and married someone else, they were raising her child as their own. Chrissie never saw her son again and has been in and out of hospital ever since. She was discharged from her last admission about six months ago and Agnese visited her weekly, then fortnightly and now only monthly.

"So how have you been since I saw you last Chrissie?" Agnese asks. "Och, no braw hen, but nae sae bad either. A think they new tablets are working okay. But it's the wee dog that helps the most. Isn't it Hendry?" She pulls the dog up onto her lap and presses her face between his big pointy ears. "A'll no be hurtin masel' any more Agnese, ye can rest easy on that one. A've got Hendry to look after now, and a'll thank ye for that, for it was you that telt me tae get a dog. It was your suggestion and a'll no' forget it." Agnese sits back in her chair looking very pleased. I feel like I'm going to cry again, but this time it's with happiness.

We hear children outside. Chrissie jumps up and raps on the window loudly. "I SEE YE THERE SMOKIN' YER REEFERS!" The children look up for a moment, walk a little bit further away from her window, then carry on with what they were doing; they seem to be exchanging things. Chrissie turns to me, "Look at them. Just look at them. They're selling drugs - REEFERS. A ken all about it, av' seen it all on the telly." I get up and walk to the window, open the sliding doors and cross the small patch of lawn towards the children. Hendry comes running after me despite Chrissie's calls.

There are six boys - a bit younger than my wee brother; about nine or ten years old, unkempt and dishevelled looking in black and white uniforms, huge big Adidas bags hanging across their small bodies. They look at me with interest, and when they see Hendry they reach over the fence to pet him. Hendry gets very excited and starts spinning round and round chasing his tail. "PLAY DEAD!" I shout and the wee dog immediately flips onto his back with his feet in the air. "ROLL OVER!" The boys roar with laughter. "PLAY DEAD!" They all start shouting, "ROLL OVER!" The dog runs round the garden, rolling and playing dead and chasing his tail, then digging little holes in the lawn. He is wild with excitement.

"What are you up to boys?" I ask when the laughter subsides. "Football cards," the tallest boy says, holding his cards up to show me. "Is that old lady mad?" - "Och no. She's just not used to children." The smallest one looks at me with big, earnest eyes, "I don't think you get reefers in Muchty." Some of the others look like they're not so sure about that. I try to look like I wouldn't know. "Oh well, maybe she's just watching too much telly." They all nod, it seems like they understand the implications of that problem. "Tell her we like her wee dog," the taller kid says. "It looks like Basil Brush. Tell her we'll walk him if she ever wants us to."

I go back in and Chrissie is standing at the window wringing her hands. "What did they say?" - "They like your dog," I tell her. "They offered to walk him." She looks at me in horror - "JUNKIES WALKING HENDRY?" I'm glad the children have moved on out of earshot. "It was football cards," I tell her. "Oh," she says. "Oh. Well mind you, there's a lot of drug dealing in Muchty. Ye'd be surprised. Ye cannae be too naive aboot these things or more fool ye." She walks over to her dog and says, "What about it Hendry? Are ye going out for a walk wi' the boys?" Hendry looks up at her hopefully, as if he knows exactly what she's saying and he's ready to go right now. "I think he'd like that," she says to me. Agnese gets up, "Well you'd better be a bit nicer to those kids then eh Chrissie?" - "Aye maybe," Chrissie looks thoughtful.

We gather our things to leave and she says to Agnese, "Will ye show me again how to use that video oven?" - "You mean the microwave?" - "Aye, aye, microwave, video, whatever the hell ye ca' it. I cannae fathom it. Can ye no get me ma proper cooker back?" - "I'm afraid not Chrissie. You've had one too many close shaves with the cooker. If you want to stay out of hospital you need to get used to using the microwave." - "Well it's all that bloody ECT thats shot ma memory. An a didnae ask for any of it!" She stands looking furious. "Let's not get into that," says Agnese gently. "You're home now and you want to stay home don't you?"

Chrissie stands muttering as Agnese shows her how to work the microwave. "Look." I point, to a small cork pinboard. "Someone's written out the instructions there." - "Och I cannae make head nor tail o' that," says Chrissie, tears in her eyes. Agnese runs through it once again. As we are leaving Chrissie reaches out and holds me back. "Here," she says, in a confidential whisper. "Do you think they laddies would like Mr Kiplings?"

"Right," says Agnese, revving the engine of the wee blue mini as we leave Chrissie's house and we bounce out in to the middle of the mercifully empty street, "The Laughlins." I've read the notes already so I know that Mrs Laughlin had a short spell of psychosis after coming off Valium without any medical advice. She had been taking the drug for over a decade and decided, on the day of her fiftieth birthday, that she was done with them. She ended up in hospital for six weeks, but she's kept well ever since discharge on no medication at all. "Why was she taking Valium anyway?" I ask Agnese. She shrugs, "Endogenous Depression I think – no particular reason for it." Myself and the other students in my class are very suspicious of the Endogenous Depression diagnosis which seems to be awfully common in Fife, especially amongst middle aged women. "Don't you think there's always a reason for depression?" Agnese doesn't answer. She sits staring out the front window of the car. I follow her gaze, trying to figure out what she's looking at, but it's just an empty street of gloomy looking council houses. I'm about to get out the car when she says, "Yes I do think there's always a reason."

They welcome us in as if we are royalty. Coffee and home baked ginger cake appear on the table in front of the fire. There are pictures all over the place, of their children and grand children, a Sacred Heart of Jesus in a golden frame on top of the telly. Mr Laughlin sees me looking and says - "The telly won't work without the good Lord on top of it. Isn't that right Bridget?" - "That's right," his wife says, nodding. "As God is my witness, that television will not work without the Sacred Heart right there on top of it. I suppose it's the signal - but you never know now do you?" - "It's true," Mr Laughlin continues. "The Lord works in mysterious ways sure enough." He gives me a wink and gestures for me to take a seat.

Agnese and I sink down into the huge green velvet sofa, our hosts perched on matching armchairs either side of us waiting for the good news, which Agnese delivers with an air of victory. This is to be her last visit; Mrs Laughlin has been discharged to the care of her GP. "You mean she's actually sane?" Mr Laughlin shouts jovially. "Can we have a certificate to prove that?" His wife laughs along - "Well it'd be more than you ever had Joe Laughlin." She kicks a slipper clad foot in his direction playfully. "That's for sure," he shouts. "God help me if I'm ever to sit that test."

Mr Laughlin gets up and walks over to the sideboard - "Well now, if ever there was a reason to celebrate." - "Sure there's always a reason to celebrate with our Joe now." Bridget winks at me as she says this. She's a very pretty woman - soft caramel coloured curls and light green eyes. She is smoking a cocktail cigarette, thin and brown with gold and pink bands. She offers me one. I look at Agnese for permission. The two women laugh at my timidity. "Aw now, go on my little darling," Bridget says. "You have one if it pleases you and you're most welcome."

Joe stands over us with a bottle of spirits and four small glasses. "Potcheen," he says, then spells it out: "P-O-I-T-I-N! You'll not be leaving my house today without a drop of it." Agnese protests - "I couldn't possibly. I'm driving - I have to keep this child safe for her mother." - "Oh that's for sure, that's for sure," our host agrees. "Well she can have yours."

I can't say I like the taste of the Poitin, but I drink both glasses all the same, and I feel very strange when I get up to leave half an hour later. It's a little bit like when you've just taken some magic mushrooms, but warmer - fuzzier. My body feels pleasantly heavy, which is an unusual feeling for me.

Just as we are leaving the GP arrives, a quiet, friendly man in his fifties. He looks a little smudgy at the edges I think as he stands shaking my hand. He peers at me in a doctorly way, then turns to Agnese, "Poitin?" Agnese nods, smiles her shrewd little smile and says - "Who needs Valium?" Everyone laughs, except for me; I'm just trying to focus on walking. "Here," shouts Joe, coming towards me with another glass - "Adam's Ale." I look at the clear liquid suspiciously and he laughs. "It's water, that's all, but sure you look like you need it." Safely back in the car I turn to Agnese and say - "Maybe it was Endogenous Depression after all?" - "Hmmf," says Agnese - "You're not Catholic are you?"

It's Mary's twenty second birthday and we are having a party. We've scrubbed the cottage from end to end, though we know it will be a total mess tomorrow. Hamish has set the fire and brought a basket of fresh wood in. I've made punch and Neil's new girlfriend, Dot, has baked a huge chocolate cake. Mary is wandering around in a daze. I get the feeling she's not used to being made such a fuss over.

We go to the pub first. It's taken for granted that anyone there is welcome at the party. Sylvia is there but not Andy; he's in Holland on business. Mary likes Sylvia too and the three of us walk back to the cottage arms linked singing, Danny Boy and Happy Birthday and...

I love a lassie, a bonnie bonnie lassie,
She's as pure as the lily in the dell,
She's as sweet as the heather, the bonnie bloomin' heather,
Mary, my Scots bluebell...

Hamish lights the fire in the living room and Neil makes a sarcastic comment about him making himself at home. I head for the kitchen and the big bowl of punch which has changed colour since this afternoon. God knows what people have been adding to it. Hamish comes through and looks at it suspiciously. "Don't drink it," he says, but I fill my cup when he's not looking. It tastes heavy and fizzy at the same time, and very very sweet.

Sylvia is sitting at the kitchen table with Mary and Celia and a guy called Craig. I don't know Craig very well but I've seen him in the pub. Neil told me that he's a dealer, also, his father is a policeman. He's really tall and good looking, but he's got a kind of uncontrolled air about him that makes me nervous. Sylvia is crying and Mary gets up to give her a hug. "What's wrong?" I ask. Craig gets up, knocking his chair over and starts pacing around. I lift his chair up and sit down at the table. "Is it Andy?" Sylvia nods miserably. Mary stands up and gently moves a silvery blue silk scarf away from our friend's long, pale neck to show the finger shaped bruises her husband has left. Celia looks at me nervously. She knows about Andy already; I told her that morning after we took the mushrooms, then I told her after I met him at the picnic in the park. She hasn't met Andy yet, but she and Rod have both told me that I'm to phone the police if he comes anywhere near me - they were very insistent about that.

"I don't understand why he feels he has to force himself on me." Sylvia sobs. "He's my husband, and I want his children, but not this way." - "He's a rapist," says Mary. "And you should leave him." - "It's not actually rape if you are married," Neil says. None of us had noticed him standing behind us, helping himself to another cup of punch. "I mean, legally, a man is allowed to have intercourse with his wife, with or without her consent." Mary throws him a look of total fury. Celia puts her head in her hands and groans.

"I'm not saying it's right," Neil protests, raising his hands up in a gesture of innocence.

Craig stops pacing, stands, hands on hips staring at Sylvia. "He's right. It's not against the law." - "Aye well we all know who writes the laws don't we?" Mary growls. "It's fuckin' rape, whatever the law says." Mary is angry but Craig looks even more so. "Those bastards wouldn't do anything about it even if it was illegal. If anyone knows it, it's me. I've watched my father beat the shit out of my mother my whole life. And all my so called uncles down at the station know all about it - fawning over her, telling her what a doll she is - *if you were my wife...*" He stands shaking his head, fists clenched. "None of them ever did anything about it."

Someone has put on *1999* by Prince and I feel the need to get away from this misery. I go through to the living room and start dancing with Hamish. I've never danced with him before. He looks kind of funny with his cropped hair, leather jacket and combats - dancing to Prince. It makes me laugh and he grabs me and starts tickling me. "Are you laughing at my dancing?" He holds me very close. "No I wasn't. Honest. I wasn't!" He stops tickling me and we start kissing, but it feels too public, there are about twenty other people dancing or standing around us drinking and chatting, so we go to my room.

When I get up in the morning Neil is in the kitchen making tea. Dot is lying sleeping on the sofa. I stand for a while looking at her. She looks like a china doll, totally unblemished, like a child. Neil must think so too because he says, "I'm too old for her really. But I'm completely in love with her." - "Oh well, just make sure and treat her well eh?" We wander back into the kitchen. "What about you and Sam then? Is that all off?" - "I don't know if it was ever on." We sit at the table, light our first cigarettes of the day. "I don't know if he really likes me, if he thinks of me as his girlfriend. He never tells me." - "He's not over Cathy," says Neil. "Cathy's the only woman Sam will ever love. I told you that."

We are quiet for a bit. There's snoring coming from Mary's room. "It's Craig," Neil says and we both make a funny face; Craig and Mary are such an unlikely couple. "Were there mushrooms in the punch?" I ask him. "Briefly. I put some in but Mary made me take them out." - "How long were they in there?" - "Seconds," he says. "If you were out of it, it wasn't the punch you were feeling - Dot put a wee bit of hash in the cake." - "Oh no – that's mad, not telling people." - "I did! I thought everyone heard. You must have been too busy snogging Hamish to hear it." - "Well, thank God he didn't eat any. He could have ended up back in hospital." I tell him about Hamish's experience with LSD. He shakes his head sadly - "You'd be better off with Sam, even if he isn't in love with you."

"What about Mary?" I ask him. "It was her birthday cake and she hates drugs." - "Yeah, she was a bit pissed off. But hey - she'd better get used to it - she's sleeping with a dealer." We both laugh at the very idea of it. Mary is always lecturing us about the dangers of illegal drugs, tut tutting, furiously knitting her little baby clothes, for the unknown baby.

Stratheden Psychiatric Hospital
Ward 6 Psychogeriatrics
November 1984 – January 1985

The chairs are arranged around the walls, as if some kind of performance is going to happen in the middle of the room. Nothing ever happens. There are no patients hallucinating that they are in the pub here, no one pacing up and down smoking their pipe, chuckling nonsensically. The patients don't get out of their chairs unless coaxed. Most of them can't anyway, even if they want to, because they are in bar chairs. Bar chairs are not like bar stools; they are more like big metal baby chairs with a tray at the front which is locked in place so the patient can't escape. Some of the patients spend every minute of their day trying to figure out how to get themselves free of their bar chair.

It's the same routine day after day, but at least there are doctors and visitors on this ward - occasionally even a psychologist. They don't speak to the nurses though; it's as if we are invisible to them. Doctors will speak to us if they have to, but generally it's only the charge nurse they converse with. Val Cooper has been nursing for thirty five years. She's an enrolled nurse - but she knows more than any charge nurse I've ever met. One day I hear her say to our new registrar, "Perhaps we could try him on a wee bit of Imipramine" – "I'M THE DOCTOR HERE AND I'LL THANK YOU TO REMEMBER IT!" Val scurries off, red faced, blinking back the tears. I stand in the office staring at the doctor until he looks up. "WHAT?" I just keep staring. He lowers his head again, writing up the drugs chart. I am wondering what Val's son would say if he'd witnessed what just happened. I've met Val's son a few times; he lives near the cottage. He always stops to offer me a lift if it's bad weather - swinging my bike into the back of his van with one hand. He's big like his mum, but more confident - jovial. He runs his own joinery business. He could squash this man just by leaning on him.

Later on, when we are doing the medicine round, we see that the young doctor has written the patient up for a small dose of Imipramine. "He's a total prick," I say to Val. She flushes pink because it's not the kind of language she would ever use, but I can see she is pleased to hear me say it. She's the nurse I like best on this ward. The charge nurse is okay - Mike Laing - C/N Laing; we are not allowed to call him by his first name. He's cool and distant, but he's always very polite. He hardly ever comes out of his office, no matter how busy we are. We take his tea and coffee into him, with a small plate of biscuits. We also take his meals to him. He never goes to the canteen. We have to go in and ask him what he wants - stand quietly waiting while he takes a look at the menu and chooses, then carries on reading his paper. Off we scuttle to fetch his food and take it through to him on a tray.

We had a classical studies teacher like him at school. At the start of every lesson he would walk round the room giving us each a text book saying, *chapters three, four and five*, or whatever it was that day. Then he would just sit and read his own book until the bell went. None of us minded; he was nice enough to us and we liked the stories we were reading - bible stories or Greek myths and legends. It felt like we were colluding with him in some way though - doing something pleasant and restful for forty five minutes in the middle of a school day. We knew he was a chancer, but we were used to a lot worse than that. It's the same with Mike Laing; he's a lazy sod - a chancer - but it could be worse.

There's a wee joke going round that Charge Nurse Laing can't walk because of muscle wasting. I've laughed along with that, but I'm curious that the nurses are so clearly aware of the dangers of muscle wasting and yet they let it happen to our patients. They limit their movement by locking them into bar chairs. They serve their meals to them on the tray of their bar chairs, so they don't have to get up and sit at the table to eat. They wheel them to the toilet and hook their vests round the lid of the seat so they can't stand up when they are finished.

The patients are all toileted at the same time, it's called *the toileting round*. There aren't enough loos for all the patients, so some are put on commodes that are arranged round the walls of the bathroom, with nurses standing like sentries between them, holding them in place - the door wide open so they can still see the telly.

A couple of patients are still able to walk - a retired colonel who paces round the place, "hunting for cats," - usually naked. Another, 'the Prof,' who taught Philosophy at St Andrew's University many years ago, walks with a stick. He is a thin, fragile man, very anxious and tearful, constantly asking us where he is. We've been told in college to tell our patients the truth when they ask that. It's called *reality orientation*. The first time the professor asked I said, "Stratheden Hospital." - "You mean the asylum?" - "It's only because of your memory." He cried for hours. Today when he asks me I say, "You are in the dining room, but would you like to come outside for a little walk? It's a beautiful day." - "Oh yes please," he says. "Just let me go and fetch my scarf." His scarf is long, stripy, hand knitted. "A Doctor Who scarf!" I exclaim - "Yes!" he laughs - "A young man knitted it for me." Then he looks kind of confused and frightened and I think he's going to cry again, so I take his arm. "Come on then Doctor. Let's get out of here."

We have only been out a few minutes when we meet Ross McGilvery, an enrolled nurse that Neil has recently befriended. I've seen him at the pub a few times and he came to Mary's party. "Are you going out with that guy Hamish then?" he asks me. I tell him yes. "Pity," he says. "Would you like to help with a bit of fundraising at the Christmas Fare this year? I'm on the committee." - "What would I have to do?" - "Just stand in your uniform and let people throw cold water at you." At first I think he's joking, then I realise he's serious. The professor is standing looking like he's wondering where he is again. "Don't you think that's a bit sexist?" I say to Ross. He shrugs, then grabs the professor's stick and starts twirling it around. "Shame on you!" The professor calls out. He dives about trying to catch hold of his stick. Ross laughs. "GIVE HIM HIS STICK" I shout. Ross holds it towards the professor, then pulls it back when he tries to take hold of it. "GIVE HIM IT NOW!" He looks surprised and a bit hurt. "Okay bonny neebs. No need tae get yer tits in a fankle. Bit of a bad temper on ye eh? It's true what they say then eh? Bit of a stuck up bitch - and the rest." He walks off laughing. The professor takes my arm and we wander into a pretty, wooded area, sit on a big log. "Look, red squirrels," I point at the tiny creatures that have become so rare. The professor smiles, but I can see he's too anxious to enjoy being out. I take him back to the ward, at least we know where we are there - well I do anyway.

Hamish has come home with me for the weekend. It's the first time he's met my parents. On Friday night we go along to the Auld Hoose in North Berwick for a Labour party meeting. Everyone is very sympathetic when Hamish tells them that he is unemployed. There is a lot of talk about the impossibility of finding work in Thatcher's Britain and everyone wants to buy him a pint. His unemployment is the main source of conflict between him and his step-father and I can see that he's really moved by people's attitude. "Your parents are fantastic," he keeps saying. "They are really something. My God you are so lucky." He loves the beach and he is very taken with my little brother too. The dog has just had puppies and the two of them sit mooning over the tiny creatures for hours on end. That pleases Mum; she doesn't trust people that don't like dogs. "I like him," she says. "He's very nice." On the way back to Fife I tell him I love him. It just kind of pops out, but it's true. He smiles, and puts his arm round me, but he doesn't say it back.

Because we are in our last year of training we have to practise being in charge of wards, so for the last week of every placement from now on, we make all the decisions - as far as patient safety allows. I'm absolutely terrified when the charge nurse gives me the keys. Sitting in the canteen at tea break I say to Val - "You'll keep me right won't you?" - "You do what you think is right and I'll stand by you," she says. I'm not sure what that means, but I feel better anyway, knowing she's aware of how scared I am.

The first thing I do is change the toileting regime. "They must have privacy," I say. "Put them on a loo, in a cubicle with the door closed. If you think they might fall off then hold them gently by their shoulders. There's to be no more hooking them on to the seat by their vests." Val raises her eyebrows and bites her lip, but she gives me a wink too. The other nurses grumble and swear under their breath. "It's hardly giving them privacy if you're to hold them up on the toilet," someone protests. "Well okay then. Shall we hook you on to the lavvy by your vest the next time you need the toilet?" I don't wait for an answer.

The next day I tell the team that I want them to start helping those patients who are not immobilised by pain to start walking short distances, building up their strength. "What's the point?" Someone shouts. "To keep them fit and healthy,"

I tell her. "For what?" I don't really know what to say to that so I just ignore it. Later, in the canteen Neil says - "She's right though isn't she? I mean, would you want your life to be extended any longer than is necessary if you were in there? Anyway, it sounds like you are doing better than me." - "What's happened with you?" He is looking into his coffee miserably. "I sacked someone." - "WHAT?" I shout, then lower my voice. "You sacked someone? Are you allowed to do that?" - "She was stealing," he says. "Oh," I'm thinking about all the petty pilfering I've witnessed over the last couple of years by almost everyone. "Was it medicine?" If it's drugs then he is right, he had no choice but to sack her. "No - it was half a pound of butter." - "You sacked someone for stealing butter?" - "I had to didn't I? I saw her do it. If I hadn't sacked her I would have been colluding. Then I could be facing a disciplinary - wouldn't I?" He looks like he might cry, presses his fists into his eyes. "She's a domestic. She's got a big family. I guess they are finding it hard to make ends meet." - "Well they will now," I say. I can't believe he's sacked someone. "What did the charge nurse say?" - "He says it's my decision," says Neil. "But they all hate me."

When I get back to the ward after my break everyone is talking about it. "Are you going to sack us?" One of the nursing assistants asks me. She looks genuinely worried. "Only if I see you hooking someone on to the toilet by their vest." I tell her. "Or sitting them in a circle while they are doing their business." - "Okay." She takes off to spread the word. Val looks over at me and we laugh. "I think you're getting a taste for it," she says.

Cycling home I allow myself to imagine how the ward would be if I were really in charge: all the patients dressed in their own clothes; sitting in small groups chatting to nurses and visitors; drinking tea and coffee the way they used to drink it at home; telling us about the things they like to do; playing games; painting; listening to music; being read the kind of books they used to read. I tell Mary about it when I get back to the cottage. She stops knitting and stares at me, eyebrows raised - "Aye right. Like that's ever going to happen."

I'm working the whole of Christmas this year: late shift on the twenty third; double shifts Christmas eve and Christmas day. It feels like a very unfair system, especially for the nurses with young children. I suppose it works out over the years - if you want to work here for years and years and years that is. Most of the students say they would happily work to let the nurses with young children off, but the shift system in this hospital is completely inflexible, there can be no deviation.

In some of the wards the patients get presents, bought by the sisters or charge nurses, sometimes from their own pocket, sometimes from the ward budget. C/N Laing doesn't do either, so some of us decide to buy the presents ourselves. We take four patients each. We don't spend a lot because none of us have much money; wee boxes of chocolates; cheap perfume; plastic beads - that kind of thing. I've got a whisky miniature for the Prof because he told me he was once a member of the Whisky Society. I've knitted some purple bed socks for him too. I used some very soft and fluffy wool left over from a cuddly octopus that my mum knitted for my brother when he was little.

Neil comes back to the cottage with me after our shift on Christmas day with some of the other nurses. Sylvia turns up too, then Craig. Mary is on the A shift, so she's away back home to her family. Sylvia has black eyes and finger marks all over her throat and neck. This time Neil insists that she has to go to the police and eventually Craig takes her there. Neil and I sit for a while drinking and smoking. He gives me a present - his two favourite books - The Electric Kool Aid Acid Test by Tom Wolfe and The Dice Man by George Cockcroft, which is about a psychiatrist who makes life decisions based on the rolling of a dice. I've seen Neil and Rod doing this before, but it's usually only for silly things like: go to the pub or stay at home. Once, I believe, Neil decided to finish a relationship on this basis. I like Neil but he really can be very cold.

Craig and Sylvia come back to the cottage about an hour later. The police have filed a report, but made it clear that it was their policy not to get involved in 'domestics' - so it's unlikely anything will happen. Everyone stays the night; Craig and Sylvia in Mary's bed, because Sylvia says she only feels safe with him. Neil starts off sleeping on the sofa but ends up in with me because we don't feel safe on our own either.

In the morning Craig and Sylvia are gone; there's a note on the kitchen table addressed to Mary but it's not in an envelope so we read it.

Dear Mary,

I am sorry not to be telling you this in person. For some time now I've been in love with Sylvia and I've been determined to leave Cupar and take her to a place of safety. I know this won't be a surprise to you. I also know that you think Sylvia will always attract trouble. I don't believe that and I really think I can help her. I hope you can forgive me. I know you will because you are one of the best people I have ever known.

Sincere love and apologies from both of us.

Craig

Hamish comes to see me on Boxing day evening. It's my twenty first birthday the next day and he's meant to be coming back to Gullane with me. I tell him about Sylvia and Craig. He is very quiet and thoughtful, then he says, "So they slept in Mary's bed? Where did Neil sleep?" I feel myself blushing and he guesses. "I thought you were different," he says. "Look. Just forget about us. You've ruined a good thing, the best thing that's happened to me in years, but just forget it."

Stratheden Psychiatric Hospital
Ward 7 Acute Psychiatry - Female
1985 February

We are in the modern part of the hospital, separate from the main buildings which were built back in 1866 - well, for the most part. Part of the old hospital was destroyed in a fire after being hit by a bolt of lightning in 1888. How terrifying that must have been for the poor souls locked up here - although, apparently, our patients have never been locked up. Dr Tuke, who founded the asylum, was very forward thinking and all the patients were free to roam the grounds as they pleased. I guess Dr Tuke forgot about the Behaviour Modification Unit which, as far as I'm aware is always locked.

Our tutors and the older nurses tell us these stories of the old days very proudly - as if the hospital has an unblemished record of care and compassion right from it's very beginnings and they all deserve to take some credit for it. All their sentimental tales say to me is, that there's lots of ways of keeping people prisoner besides locking them in.

This wing feels different though, built at the turn of the century; it is whiter, fresher - single storey. It is less imposing, less pessimistic - on the outside anyway. Inside feels pretty much the same as the older sections; dormitory style sleeping areas and huge bathrooms with no privacy except a flimsy curtain; long cheerless corridors that are constantly being polished by miserable looking domestics who can barely afford to buy food for their families. Mind you - it isn't uncommon to find half bottles of vodka secreted between the starched white bedding in the linen cupboards and that is usually blamed on the domestic staff too. They should get scapegoat bonuses the domestics, they can't all be butter starved alcoholics.

I'm on nights for the first month of Acute. I'm enjoying it because, mostly, I'm looking after a three month old baby whose mum has post-puerperal psychosis. She believes that her new born daughter is her mother in-law reincarnated. Her mother-in-law died the day before the baby was born, and Judy, our patient, was persuaded by her husband to call the child Rose after her. I wonder if he regrets that now. Being on nights I've never met him, though I understand he visits every day, which is unusual in this hospital.

Not so long ago Judy would have been in here by herself, and may well have never got back out. Her husband would have raised their child alone, or re-married like Chrissie's husband - or Rose might have been adopted or taken into care. There's no question of that for Judy and Rose now though; they will live here together until this terrible affliction leaves Judy and they can return to their home and get on with their lives.

Every evening when I come on duty I help Judy bathe the baby, dress her in a fresh Babygro, feed her and settle her for the night. Judy can't breastfeed because of the medication she is on, but I try to persuade her to prepare the baby's bottle and feed her herself. "Just this last bedtime feed," I urge her. "I'll do the middle of the night ones." Sometimes Judy just won't do it and sits with her face to the wall refusing to even look at her daughter. Sometimes she co-operates, though she grumbles the whole time. Tonight I thought we were doing well, but just as I put the baby into her arms to be fed she says, "Did you hear that? She called me a lazy bitch." - "No she didn't Judy. She's only ten weeks old. She can't speak." - "She's not ten weeks old. I know exactly what age she is and the old bag called me a lazy bitch." She pushes her daughter back into my lap and turns her face to the wall.

I sit and feed Rosie and talk to her in a soothing way. I wonder how anyone can be so deluded that they believe this wonderful little being is an old bag and I wonder if Judy always talks like that. She is a probation officer and surely must have to set an example to others. I wonder about her mother in law too - would she really have called her son's wife a lazy bitch? In any case I've learned already that there's no point in arguing with delusional people; it just makes them suspicious and resentful and you lose any chance of a trusting relationship.

I feel very sad for Judy. I hope it's true that people don't remember their psychotic episodes. I feel very sad for Rose too. I'm glad that babies don't remember anything, though we've learned in college about attachment theory, so I know that Rose won't be unscathed by her mother's illness. I wheel her crib into the office at night and we talk in hushed voices. When she cries I pick her up quickly before she wakens all the patients. Staff Nurse McKutcheon lets me tend to her. She's had four of her own and says the practice is good for me. She winks when she says that last bit. I don't tell her that there's no chance of me having a baby anytime soon - not if I can help it anyway. Getting pregnant is my worst nightmare, however much I love babies. Motherhood is a distant dream - way way distant.

Staff Nurse McKutcheon and I are both knitting for baby Rose. I'm knitting a matinee jacket and Nurse McKutcheon is knitting a dress. My mum is making a matching bonnet, bootees and mittens. Nurses from other wards come in during their break, male and female, bringing little presents and hoping to get a cuddle. Even Mary gives up a few things for her. "Who are you knitting them for anyway?" I ask. She shrugs, and looks out the window. Then she says - "Well I might have my own baby one of these days." - "What? Like sometime soon?" She nods. "You mean you're..?" - "No. I'm not. But it's not for want of trying." - "You mean you'd have a baby even if you're not married?" She looks at me as if I'm a bit mad - "Ye really think ye need a man around tae bring up a bairn?" I nod - "Yes I do to be honest. I mean - how could you live? You wouldn't be able to work at all - unless you moved back to your parents." - "There's no chance of that!" She looks genuinely outraged. "No. I'll manage just fine if it ever happens. Don't you worry about me." She puts together a bag of stuff anyway - some stripey jumpers and a funny wee knitted teddy.

Judy takes Mary's presents with a disinterested thanks,

throws them in the pile with all the others. I feel like a parent myself - and Judy my ungrateful teenager. "DON'T YOU KNOW HOW PRECIOUS THESE GIFTS ARE?" I want to scream, but I keep my mouth shut, remember what my dad told me when I was doing a lot of babysitting: reward the good behaviour; ignore the bad.

Someone arranged everything nicely in Rose's room anyway. Folded all the little clothes, put Mary's wee teddy at the bottom of her crib. It can't have been her father, because he's been told to take a break from visiting; Sister and the consultant are worried about his well being. It must have been one of the nurses. It's like someone prescribed love for Rose - to fill the gap that her mother's illness is making. Nurses prescribed it - not doctors; they would never have thought of it, and if they did it would be pulled up into a syringe and injected IM.

I hate going to the canteen for my break during night shift but sometimes Staff Nurse McKutcheon insists. She says it's because I need proper food, not just biscuits, but she only makes a fuss about it when one of her pals is coming to cover for me. I think she wants rid of me so they can get a proper gossip. I wish she would just say that because I wouldn't mind. I wouldn't want them listening to my chat either.

To get to the canteen I have to unlock the door to a very very long corridor that leads to the male acute wards and eventually the exit - and I have to lock it behind me - so I'm locked in there all alone. I wouldn't mind so much if it was just the corridor, but it has rooms coming off it: the kitchen; the dining room; the dentist; the library; the hairdressers. Every door has a window. I try not to look at them in case I see a shadow flitting, or even worse, a face looking out. My heart pounds as I fumble with the keys, locking the women's side, unlocking the men's and quickly locking it up again. One of the male nurses generally comes out to check who is coming and we stop for a chat. It's always done, whatever we think of one another; a quick check in, like soldiers in the trenches. "All quiet down your end?" - "Yes. No problems tonight. And yourselves?" - "Old Winters is going downhill. We're keeping a close eye on him. Needs a bit more ECT if you ask me. Not that anyone has. Give him a blast myself if I could, poor sod. Bloody doctors, barely out of short trousers and they think they know best. Still they're the bosses - ours is not to reason why." - "Theirs is not to reason why." - "What?" - "No, sorry - nothing. See you in half an hour. Want anything from the canteen?"

Sometimes the canteen is empty and I sit in the big dining room by myself eating Findus cheesy pancake and chips from the vending machine. Tonight Neil is there smoking and drinking diet Coke - nobody drinks proper Coke now. I tell him about Hamish and he puts his head in his hands - "I'm sorry but the guy is an arse. Honestly you're better off without him. He's never going to stick with you, anyone can see that." I protest because I feel that the fault lies entirely with me. "Give yourself a break," Neil says. "You told him you loved him - he couldn't say it back. Why don't you find someone that actually wants to be with you?" I feel hurt and nettled but a little bit of me thinks he's right. Perhaps he sees how hurt I am because he offers to chum me back to my ward. He knows I'm terrified of the corridor, he's scared of it too, but apparently he quite enjoys that.

Stratheden Psychiatric Hospital
Ward 8 Acute Psychiatry - Female
1985 February - April

I've been switched wards now that I'm back on days. I'm still in acute psychiatry, just a different ward, right next door to the other. I won't see Judy or baby Rose any more, except in passing when Judy is well enough to go to the dining room for her meals. The Sister in this ward is a big motherly sort of woman in her early sixties working towards retirement. This means they will make her a Matron soon, so that her final year salary is higher and she can get the most from her pension. She's humming and hawing about retiring though, or maybe she just doesn't feel very matronly. I'm not sure which.

There's an enrolled nurse called Patsy who never leaves Sister's side. The two women have worked together for decades and are apparently inseparable - though they are as different as can be. Sister is very tall, over six foot, with slightly bulging light blue eyes and a pale, powdery complexion. Patsy is short and sturdily built with dark, deep set eyes and a ruddy, weather beaten look about her. Sister is calm and thoughtful. I can't imagine her ever being rude or raising her voice. Patsy seems to live in a state of permanent rage.

We stand in the office at the beginning of each shift and wait for our orders: admissions; discharges; big baths; injections; medicine rounds; enemas; ECT. Patsy isn't issued with any orders; it's her job to make sure that we carry out ours effectively. If we don't she'll make sure the whole hospital knows about it. She thrives on the humiliation of others. Sister sits at her desk calmly surveying us, kind but authoritative, dishing out instructions. Occasionally she stops and gazes, in a contemplative kind of way, through the big office windows that look onto the day room on one side and the patient's sleeping area on the other.

We come and go from the office as we please throughout our shifts. When Patsy isn't there it's kind of a haven. We don't have to knock, Sister is always welcoming and pleasant. Sometimes she will be particularly kind to us - if Patsy has been excessively mean, but she never intervenes.

After the lunch time medicine round we do *Relaxation Therapy*. Patsy rings a bell and we trot into the dormitory area like Pavlov's dogs, then she picks one of us to read the relaxation script. She struts around the ward in her short uniform with it's dark green Enrolled Nurse epaulettes, and her green striped cardboard hat screaming at the patients - "INTO THE DORMITORY. NOW! RELAXATION! INTO THE DORMITORY. NOW! I SAID NOW!" The women trudge into the dormitory glancing at one another sneakily, lips curled, eyes rolling. They are not allowed to lie on their beds in case they fall asleep. Instead they lie on thin foam mats that have been laid in a line on the cold linoleum floor. Everyone has to participate, even if they have visitors at the time.

Last week Patsy was on holiday and I did the Relaxation by myself almost every day. On the Saturday I laid the mats out in the day room and asked the visitors to join in. One or two started to protest but I insisted. "You're all under stress. It will do you good. You'll see." I could hear some of the patients explaining my position - that Relaxation was not a choice for any of us really. The visitors caught on and started helping me out - closing the curtains, laying the mats down, giving the patients cushions to rest their heads on. There was a bit of giggling now and again, mostly about the snoring; some of the patient's are very heavily medicated and it's hard for them to stay awake. Most people joined in though, and said afterwards, that they felt quite rested and they would definitely like to try it again. When I went in to the office later Sister smiled and said, "Well done. That was super."

Patsy is here full force today though, standing at my back as I sit waiting for the women to settle. Some of them fall asleep right away. I keep my voice soft and slow:

"Close your eyes and rest your hands on your tummy. Nice and gentle. Close your mouth and breathe in through your nose. Steadily. Slowly. Hold your breath... just for a moment... and breathe out through pursed lips. Slow and steady. In... and out. Feel the rise of your tummy as the air comes into your body... and goes out again. Feel your breath going in... and out.... Imagine you are blowing a candle out. Imagine you are blowing your stress away."

"NOT LIKE THAT. JESUS CHRIST!" Patsy rips the script

out of my hands. "YOU!" She marches over to the sleeping women. "WAKE UP! YE'S ARE NO MEANT TAE BE SLEEPIN! THIS IS RELAXATION THERAPY. YOU." She nudges a snorer with her shoe. The woman wakes with a little jump, looks around in confusion. "AYE YOU! WAKE UP AND RELAX!"

When it's over we roll the floor mats away and drift back into the day room. There's a girl called Babs who has been in for several weeks with Anorexia. She is the same height as me and only four stone. She is drinking diet Coke. Patsy comes in and shouts, "YOU!" She's looking at me. "OFFICE. NOW." The women look at one another anxiously. I follow Patsy into the office and she immediately starts shouting. "WHAT DO YE CALL THAT?" She is pointing through the window at Babs. Babs must hear her because she turns and gives a little wave. "WHAT DO YE CALL THAT?" Her saying it twice is not making the problem any clearer to me.

I look at Sister but she is just sitting watching with her usual detached curiosity. "It's Babs," I say, genuinely confused. "IT'S BABS. IT'S BABS," Patsy mocks. "YOU THINK I DON'T KNOW IT'S BABS? YOU THINK I DON'T KNOW MY OWN PATIENTS NAMES?" I feel like I'm going mad myself because I really don't understand what's expected of me right now. Babs is watching us through the window. She sticks her tongue out at Patsy and wags her finger at me; she seems to find it all very amusing. "AND WHAT IS BABS DRINKING? BABS THE ANOREXIC LASSIE - WHAT'S THE ANOREXIC DRINKING?" - "She's drinking diet Coke."

- "AND THAT'S ALL RIGHT WITH YOU IS IT? THAT'S ALL RIGHT WITH YOU? LET THE LASSIE STARVE HERSELF TO DEATH. NEVER MIND SHE'S ONLY FOUR STONE. IT'S NOT OUR JOB TO GET SOME CALORIES INTO HER IS IT?" She charges out of the office and into the day room.

"I didn't give Babs the diet Coke," I tell Sister. "I know," she says. Babs has finished her Coke and turns the empty can upside down to show us. Patsy tries to grab the can from her but Babs is too quick. She hides it behind her back, then chucks it over Patsy's head shouting, "FETCH." Patsy's face is crimson with rage. She picks up the empty can and comes charging back into the office, stands leaning on the desk looking down at Sister. For a minute I think she might have a heart attack. I find myself hoping that it will be a bad one and she won't survive it. Sister doesn't seem remotely concerned. She offers her friend a cigarette. Patsy takes it, lights it with a long draw, then turns to me, "Just get out. Give Mrs McKerracher a bath - A PROPER BATH." - "But…" She glares at me. I look at Sister but she's looking out the window again, so I leave.

Mrs McKerracher is a small, very gentle lady, just turned sixty, who has severe dysphasia after having had a stroke. She was admitted with anxiety and depression. She is extremely thin, though she hasn't been diagnosed with Anorexia. Mrs McKerracher is terrified of the bathroom. I've tried to get her in there before and she resists with all her meagre strength. I've spoken to Sister about it and she said she would talk to the doctor - until then we could sponge bathe her.

I'm very fond of Mrs McKerracher who I call Eileen. She seems not to mind. Her face lights up when I approach her. She takes my hands, "You, You..." She stutters, nodding her head and smiling. I tell her I've been told to give her a bath. Her face crumples and the tears start. "Please trust me. Nothing bad is going to happen I promise. Please just come and look. I won't run it. Just come and see the room." She gets up reluctantly and takes my arm but she is crying pitifully. I lead her to the bathroom and we stand at the doorway. "Look, see." The bathroom is empty because most of the women bathe in the morning or evening. "Nobody else will be here, just you and me." Eileen stands, clutching the doorway chewing her fingers. She looks at me and shakes her head. I wonder what on earth she is seeing in there.

Patsy comes up and says - "YES THAT'S RIGHT, IT'S A BATH AND YOU'RE GETTING IN IT." She pushes Eileen into the room. "I'm sorry Eileen," I say, gently pushing her down into a seat, taking her shoes off. She is sobbing loudly but she lets me undress her then she stands up and steps into the bath. She makes no attempt to wash herself so I do it, as quickly as I can. I wash her hair too, despite her protests. When she is out and on the chair being dried she makes a fist and waves it at me, her face all screwed up in anger - "You. You."

Cycling back to the cottage in the dwindling light that

evening, I let my own tears flow. I let my nose run, wipe it on the sleeve of my black nurse's coat. I know I will have mascara all over my face - I don't care. The cows are frolicking in the field. That means there's a storm coming. I hope I get caught in it. I hope I get struck by lightning.

Chrissie has been admitted with depression. Agnese brings her in, greeting me with a quick hug. She smells of hairspray and expensive perfume and cigarettes. "Where's Hendry?" I ask her. "He's at my house with Oscar." - "I hope he doesn't mistake him for a cat." - "I never thought of that." Her face clouds for a moment, then she grins - "Oh but they do love each other."

I can't believe the change in Chrissie. She's completely oblivious to the world around her. She paces up and down the corridor wringing her hands, wailing every now and again. We have to sit her down and spoon-feed her at meal times. She takes a small amount then closes her mouth tight so we can't give her any more. I try to coax her into conversation, talking about Hendry and his tricks, but there is no response whatsoever.

The nurses are all a bit low because someone hung themselves in the toilets a couple of nights ago. It wasn't our ward, but it's the second suicide in the last three weeks and it has cast a depression, a sense of futility across the whole unit; as if we are kidding ourselves that we have any hope of getting anyone better. The patients know it too, though the nurses are very discrete; word always gets out. I wonder what they are thinking. I don't think anyone talks to them about these things. I don't know if anyone talks to the patients at all really. Psychologists come and go, but I have no idea what they do. I've sat in on a few psychiatrist's interviews. They ask a bit about childhood history and family life, but it's tick box enquiries really. I've never heard any of them ask a patient to go into any detail, or try to establish what's gone wrong for them, from their perspective:

"How would you describe your childhood?
"It was okay."
"Got on okay with your mum and dad?"
"Okay I suppose. They were okay. My mother was allright."
Tick
"Any problems at school?"
"Not really. I wasn't the brightest maybe - but not the daftest either."
Tick
"And how about married life, any problems there? ... Any problems between you and your husband Mrs T? ... Would you say yours is a happy marriage? Mrs T?"
Patient unresponsive
"And how about work. I understand you lost your job recently. Why was that?"
"Nobody liked me."
"What makes you think that?"
"They told me."
"And why do you think they didn't like you?"

"Because I'm a bad person?"
Tendency to paranoia
"What makes you think you're a bad person?"
"The voices."
"Hmm, yes, now about these voices - do you hear them when there's nobody else in the room with you?"
"I hear them all the time."
"Even when you are completely alone and nobody else is around?"
"They never stop. I wake up to them every morning. I fall asleep to them every night. Sometimes I can't sleep at all because of them"
Tick
"There's a devil inside me Doctor."
"You mean that sometimes you behave badly? Maybe you think bad things - think you're a bad person?"
"No, I mean there's a Devil inside me, an actual Devil. I can feel him moving around inside me."
"Okay Mrs T that's all for today. I'll see you again in a week or so."

I think Chrissie must be hearing voices because every now and again she stops dead in her tracks and shouts - "NO!" Her condition is deteriorating rapidly. This morning we had to physically lift her out of bed. She sat on the commode like a mute child while I washed and dressed her, muttering under her breath from time to time; random half words, frowning as if she was trying to work out what someone was saying even though no one was talking.

I sit spooning soup into her at lunch time, small amounts, trying to tip it rather than push it in. A consultant psychiatrist comes over with a bunch of medical students. They stand staring at us for a while. I wish they would go away. I feel very self conscious. Chrissie stops eating the soup. I try her with some sweet milky tea from a cup with a spout. Some of it goes down but most of it just dribbles back out. The consultant talks about tube feeding and ECT. The students nod sagely, as if they knew it all along. Just before I think they are going to leave the consultant steps forward and says, "Observe." He takes Chrissie's hands and raises them above her head. When he leaves hold of her she stays in that position. There is a murmur of surprise from amongst the students. The consultant looks at me as if I too should proclaim my wonder. Who does he think dressed and bathed her? Who does he imagine puts her on the toilet and takes her off again? I sit back smiling politely nevertheless.

There are five women for ECT besides Chrissie. They are not all from our ward. When you are on ECT you have to look after all the patients that are there that day. You must look after them for their treatment and get them back to their ward safely. Chrissie is the easiest. I just take her by the hand and lead her along the corridor, sit her down in the waiting area; there's no danger of her trying to escape or wandering off anywhere. Some of the other women I need help with; they have to be dragged along the corridor kicking and screaming. Patsy helps me. I'm worried she will shout at them, but she doesn't. She isn't mean to me either. She doesn't say anything at all. Maybe she's imagining it happening to her, putting herself in the patient's shoes. I don't fancy my chances wrestling her down a corridor.

The noisiest patients are taken in first. Wedding rings are covered in tape, any other jewellery is taken off. They are given a general anaesthetic and a doctor administers the shock. Some patients get uni-lateral shocks, others get bi-lateral - on both sides of the head. It depends on the severity of their symptoms and their consultant's preferences. There's no particular voltage prescribed. We have to watch our patient's toes; if they curl when the shock is administered then we know they've had a seizure. You have to watch very carefully because their toes only curl a tiny wee bit. If they don't curl the doctor will say - "Let's shock her again, just to make sure. I think I'll make it a bit higher this time."

They come round pretty quickly after the general, but they need supported going back down the corridor. They stagger about as if they were drunk - red and bleary and disorientated. I take them back to bed to wait for their breakfast. They are fed well, with hot milky coffee, freshly prepared scrambled eggs and buttered toast, not the tepid, rubbery fare that is served in the dining room. They are good patients - compliant. They have done what is required of them and are suitably rewarded.

Chrissie trots in front of me in much the same state as she was before her treatment. But as I am tucking her into bed she looks at me and says - "Oh, it's you!" - "Yes it's me Chrissie. How are you feeling?" She doesn't answer, but it's a good sign. I feel hopeful as I leave to fetch her breakfast. Three days later I take her for her second treatment and, even though I hate doing ECT, I can't deny it's helping. As I set her breakfast tray before her she says - "Thank you nurse. What day is it?" It's an uncanny feeling, as if she was there all along, quietly waiting. It's like hide and seek when you can't find somebody for ages and ages and then they step out from their hiding place, a bit sleepy and rumpled looking, saying - "Here I am. I was in there all the time, right in front of you. I can't believe it took you so long to find me."

Chrissie is pretty much back to her old self after twelve doses of ECT, but she has been prescribed another four just in case. She's not very happy about it and complaining bitterly about her memory, but she is still under section so she really has no choice in the matter. I hope and pray that she won't start fighting about it.

Agnese brings Hendry in and Chrissie cries with happiness. So do I and several others too, nurses and patients. The wee dog runs round the ward yapping and begging, rolling over and playing dead. He has us all in stitches. Nobody wants him to go but Agnese has to get back home. She says - "Oscar will be missing him too." Chrissie wants to meet Oscar but I doubt that will ever happen.

A case conference is being arranged for Chrissie. I'm to attend because she is my case study; also Agnese has requested it. She has told Sister that Chrissie and I got on very well while I was doing my community placement. She's stretching the truth because I only met Chrissie a couple of times. I think she is just trying to help me out. Perhaps she's heard from Patsy that I'm a rubbish nurse - she's told me it often enough, once in the pub in front of lots of other people. She was sitting up at the bar, on her own, very drunk. I had greeted her quite politely, trying to keep things nice. "You're rubbish," she said to me through gritted sparkling white false teeth. "Rubbish." She turned to the barman, Ted. "She thinks she's good, but she's a rubbish nurse." - "I think you've had enough," Ted said coldly. "I'd like you to leave now." She staggered off her stool and across to the door, turned and shouted, "YOU'RE RUBBISH!" She drew her finger across her throat as if to say I should do everyone a favour and finish myself off now. "Another one of your fans?" Neil said, laughing. Ted shook his head and tutted. "What a mess. I hope I never have to be looked after by her." He poured a pint of beer, pushed it towards me - "On the house. I'd rather be looked after by you any day of the week."

The case conference is to be held in the dining room. Sister has me set the tables and chairs up, then I have to make up a trolley of teas and coffees. I have to use a special china coffee pot and a silver tea pot that usually sits in Sister's office. We don't add milk and sugar to the pots, like we do with the patients. We have a pretty little jug of milk and a bowl of white and brown sugar lumps. Two kinds of cake are sent over from the kitchen and we use mugs, not the patient's cups - none of the staff would drink out of them.

The consultant psychiatrist is there; the registrar; two medical students; Agnese; Sister; a staff nurse; a pharmacist, and a social worker - that's ten of us in total. Agnese and the social worker have been to Chrissie's house to check her mail and start preparing for her discharge. They found a letter from her son, asking for a meeting. It was open, lying on the coffee table; they think that this might be what precipitated Chrissie's relapse. The consultant nods sagely, stroking his chin. "Best get this sorted out now then," he says. "Let's bring her in." Sister nods to me and I scurry off to find Chrissie. I'm a bit worried about her having to meet all these people but when I go to her she seems ready for it. She's washed and brushed her hair and put some makeup on. "You look very nice," I tell her. She smooths down her skirt, "Good enough to go home?" - "I don't know Chrissie." - "Well a do. A'm bloody going whether they like it or not." - "Chrissie, you're still under section. And there's things that need talked about first." She stops and looks at me, pales a little. "Aye well, let's talk about them then." She charges ahead and I trot after her.

"Good afternoon Chrissie. How are you feeling today?"
"No sae bad Doctor. A hell of a lot better than a was a few weeks ago anyway."
"And why do you suppose that is?"
"I suppose maybe the ECT Doctor. Maybe."
"Hmm yes. No regrets about that then?"
"Well a'd rather no have had it if that's what ye mean. A mean it wouldnae have been ma choice. But still - needs must

when the devil drives."

"Quite so Chrissie. Quite so. Now about this letter from your son."

"Oh aye. Aye - a'd kind of forgotten about that Doctor. Aye, the letter, right enough."

"Well - do you want to meet the lad?"

"I think so Doctor - don't you? A mean, it seems like a should."

"And do you feel strong enough for such a meeting. How do you think you'd cope if something were to go wrong?"

"A would be okay if a wis back home and a had her beside me."

"Agnese?"

"Aye. A would meet ma laddie in ma house wi her beside me, and ma wee dog Hendry."

"Well I rather think you should meet your son here Chrissie, in the hospital, with Sister and the other nurses around too. Just in case eh? Be on the safe side."

"Well ad rather meet him in ma ane wee house Doctor."

"No I think you'll meet him here. Then a week or so to assess the impact. Then we'll see about home. Okay? Nice to see you Chrissie. I hope it all goes well. Sister will keep me informed."

Agnese and I are taking Chrissie to Dundee to buy a new outfit for her son's visit. She's to have her hair done too. Patsy grumbles about that, saying she could just as well get her hair done by the hospital hairdressers. "It's bad enough she has to meet him in the hospital," Agnese says. "The least we can do is get her looking her best." She looks at Patsy in a cool, appraising kind of way. She doesn't look very impressed. I am very proud of Agnese. It's as if she's my mum or something. I'm losing my fear of Patsy day by day. Since the episode in the bar she hasn't been so horrible to me. I've seen her looking at me a bit nervously sometimes - or maybe it's suspiciously - I'm not sure. I'm wondering if she only half remembers the incident - she was very drunk. I'm just pretending it didn't happen and being extra polite to her. It gives me a sense of power. I hope she remembers being asked to leave. I hope she only remembers that and just has a bad feeling about the rest - a really bad feeling. I like the idea of that.

We have a lovely day in Dundee; shopping, then lunch, the hairdressers, then tea. Sitting in the car driving back to the hospital Chrissie swings between excitement and anxiety. "A wonder if he looks like me - poor lad. A wonder if he's clever like his father. What if he doesn't like me? What if he doesn't come? What if a say something daft? He might think a'm a daftie!" - "CHRISSIE STOP!" Agnese is stern. "He wrote to you because he wants to meet you. You are his mother. You are very important to him. AND YOU ARE NOT A DAFTIE." It sounds so funny hearing Agnese say that last bit that Chrissie and I start giggling. "She's right though Chrissie." I put my hand over hers. "You just have to see what happens. It might be a bit difficult at first. You might have to be a bit patient. It's just the beginning." - "Aye, aye," she says. "A jist need tae calm doon a bit. Have faith in the laddie eh?"

I set the dining room up for their meeting using the same pots and jugs that we used for the case conference, but I put out the patient's cups and saucers. I'd be in trouble if I put out the staff mugs; the cups and saucers are nicer anyway. Agnese has brought in a box of cakes and a fancy table cloth. Sister brought a posy of flowers from her garden, so the table looks very pretty and festive. The social worker will settle Chrissie's son into the dining room then she'll come to the day room to fetch Chrissie, Agnese and Hendry.

Chrissie looks younger in her fitted blue dress and her new hair style. She's wearing pearls too, and a small diamond ring that I haven't seen before. "My engagement ring," she tells me when she sees me looking. "Might as well wear it eh? Naebdy else is going tae gie me diamonds." - "You look lovely Chrissie," one of the other patients says. Quite a few people have gathered round - patients, nurses, domestics. There is a general air of excitement. "What if he doesn't come?" Chrissie calls out to Sister as she walks in. Sister takes her by both hands. "He's here Chrissie. He's waiting for you in the dining room. You look wonderful. Any son would be proud to call you his mother. And may I say how beautiful the table looks." She throws an approving nod in my direction.

Agnese leads Chrissie through, like a bride to the alter, myself and several other nurses following behind, but we don't go in to the dining room, we stand at the window watching. Agnese goes in, a little ahead of Chrissie and shakes hands with a dumpy, middle aged man who has the same sad eyes as his mother. He stands awkwardly, reaching out to shake her hand, then changes his mind and embraces her. They stand holding each other quite a long while and when they break apart we see that they are crying. They are not the only ones, even Patsy's eyes are watering. "Mr Kiplings!" We hear Chrissie say, as they sit down at the table. "What braw! Do ye like a Mr Kiplings? There's nae yin better than another." - "Oh Aye," says her son. "A like Mr Kiplings allright." He holds the plate up for her to pick first, takes one for himself then bends down and gives the wee dog a bit. "Ye need tae make him beg," Chrissie says. "BEG Hendry! BEG! ROLL OVER! PLAY DEAD!" Her son's laughter echoes down the corridor and we leave them to their tea.

Eileen, is not doing well. She doesn't put up a fight about the bath any more, but she doesn't respond to anyone either. She sits slumped in her chair with her eyes cast down for the most part. She refuses to eat and drink and there's talk of force feeding her. We all try to coax her, nurses and patients, but she keeps her mouth closed tight. I'm hoping with all my heart that we don't have to force feed her.

Sam turned up at the cottage last night and stayed over. We have arranged to meet Neil, Rod and Celia in the pub. He's only just back on shore and I'm pleased that he came straight to me, but it still doesn't feel like I'm his girlfriend. I have a suspicion he sees other women too. I know I should ask him, but it just doesn't feel polite, especially since I was seeing Hamish for that stretch of time. I know he knows about that because Neil made it clear he had told him, though I'll bet he didn't tell him about the night he and I spent together when we were scared of Andy coming to get us.

Sam and I talk about lots of things. We talk about motor bikes and mutual friends and his mother who he lives with when he's on shore. We talk about his dad who died of a heart attack. We talk a lot about that, because Sam tried to resuscitate him. We never talk about our relationship, but I do enjoy his company. He makes me laugh, and he's very attentive and thoughtful.

Hamish comes in to the pub and nods in my direction. I smile back and Sam puts his arm around me. The pub gets busier and busier and when it's my round I end up standing at the bar next to Hamish. We are pushed together so our bodies touch. "I've missed you," he says. "I've missed you too." - "You're with Sam again though eh? He seems like a nice bloke." - "He is. He's very nice. I'm sorry about what I did." - "I'm sorry too. I know I was sitting on the fence a bit. That can't have felt very good for you." - "No it didn't. Well, bye then."

When I get back to my seat Sam is talking to a guy called Tony who is an engineering student in Glasgow. He is home visiting his parents for the weekend. He has a motorbike and

Sam and him have met a few times at rallies. "So you're from Cupar?" I ask him. "Born and bred. Born and bred." He laughs as he says it. "How long have you lived here?" - "Too long," I tell him. "I'm training to be a psychiatric nurse up the road." - "And yer no enjoying yer labours at ye old asylum?" - "Are you joking? Have you ever actually been there?" - "I have not. Not yet anyway - though I do have an old auntie whose been in there donkeys." - "Your auntie? You've got an auntie up there? What ward?" - "Oh I don't know. Her name is Gianna Barone." - "Gianna? Wee Gi Gi Barone? Are you kidding? That's your auntie?" - "It certainly is - though I've never heard her called that before." - "But why don't you visit her? She's such a lovely wee thing and nobody ever visits her." He shrugs - "Don't know. Never really thought about it. She's my dad's sister and he's always really busy." - "Too busy to visit his own sister!" - "Okay. Okay. I surrender!" He holds his hands up, laughing, "Jeez! Are you always this bossy?" - "I'll be even bossier if you don't visit your aunt. She speaks to no one and no one speaks to her - poor wee soul. Does she even understand English?" - "Probably not." He looks a bit sheepish now. "Look she's better off there than she was back in Italy. People used to call her a witch, said she dried up the wells - turned their milk sour." - "SHE IS NOT BETTER OFF!" I tell him. "Go and visit her, see for yourself. And take her some sweeties, chocolates - nice ones. And some perfume - she'd like that." - "Aye Aye boss." He salutes me and turns to Sam, "Jeez! You've got your hands full with this one eh?"

I've been off for four days and when I get back to the ward Eileen isn't there. My heart thumps violently as I make my way to the office, stand in front of Sister's desk. She is writing up the Kardex, ready for handover. I watch as she finishes her sentence then looks up. She smiles, "Yes dear?" - "Excuse me Sister, where is Mrs McKerracher?" - "Oh, don't panic. She's safe enough. She's been sent to psychogeriatrics. They'll be able to look after her better than we can." I feel an enormous sense of relief, but I feel troubled too. Sister must see that, because she says, "You can always go and visit her. I'm sure she would enjoy that. But try not to worry, they're a kindly bunch over there. You know that don't you? You were happy enough there weren't you?" - "Yes. Kind of. Thank you Sister." I don't understand Sister's reasoning. I'm thinking: Mrs McKerracher is younger than you, how would you like to be in psychogeriatrics? It's hardly the same - working there and being a patient there. I should have phoned Mrs McKerracher's family and said don't let them send her to psychogeriatrics. But nobody ever visited her, so they probably wouldn't have done anything anyway.

After my shift ends I go to see her. Val is on duty but she's really busy because someone had a fall and then died the next day. That means a police investigation, even if a doctor says the cause of death is nothing to do with the fall; all the staff who witnessed or recorded the incident have to be interviewed. The police are always very nice about it, assuring us it's just a formality, but it's a nerve wracking process and it takes a lot of time.

I wander through to the day room and see Eileen straight away. She stands out because she is so much younger than the other patients. She's trying to work out how to get out of her bar chair. "Eileen!" I call as I walk towards her. When she looks up and sees me she looks surprised and relieved. She motions with her hand at my appearance; it's the first time she's seen me out of uniform. I'm wearing a long lilac tiered skirt, a pale blue mohair jersey, black tights and monkey boots. My hair is down but pinned at the sides with cheap pink grips. I stand back and do a little twirl then curtsey. "Do you approve?" She kind of nods and shakes her head at the same time, but she is laughing.

She grabs my hands as I sit down - "You… You…" She rests my knuckles against her cheek, then starts shaking the tray of her bar chair to show me that she's trapped. "You can't get out of it," I tell her. "You won't manage it, and you might hurt your fingers." - "You… You.." She is pointing at me, begging for my help. "I can't Eileen. I'm just a visitor here. I can't do anything." She looks at me in disbelief, then tips her head back and howls like a dog. The old man sitting next to us starts shaking and making funny noises. I lean over and pat his shoulder, trying to reassure him. Eileen is crying bitterly. I sit back down and take her hands in mine. "I'll speak to Val tomorrow. I promise. You know Val? The big lady with the red hair, very tall?" Eileen makes her circular nod. "She's very nice, but she's very busy today. There's been an accident and the police are here - look." I point down the corridor to a police officer who is chatting up one of the nurses. Eileen looks a bit sceptical but she seems to understand. "I promise

Eileen. I'll do what I can. But you must promise me you will eat yes? You have to eat." She nods, but not convincingly.

Val is still with the police so I leave without talking to her, go straight to the nurses home and up to Dot's room - guessing that's where Neil will be. She is playing Al Stewart - Year of the Cat, one of Neil's favourites. That's something else we don't have in common - our taste in music. No way would I have put Al Stewart on for him. I bang on the door. "Just a minute," Dot shouts.

I turn and look out the window, see a patient from women's long stay kissing a man I don't recognise behind the hospital shop. He is raising her skirt up at the back. Some of the women have sex for cigarettes. I don't want to watch so I turn to face Dot's door again. She opens it just a little. She's wearing Neil's jumper and a long hippy skirt, bare feet. "Fancy getting drunk?" I ask. "Yep," Neil's voice calls out. "We do." Dot opens the door a bit wider and I see Neil bare chested, fastening his jeans. "Yay!" Dot shouts and throws her arms around my neck.

We go to the staff Social Club and order some Findus pancakes and three pints. Dot and Neil have pies too. Sitting in the big bay window we have a good view of the woods: the red squirrels and big Lackie Johnston, a barrel chested man in his fifties from Ward 4. He is running up and down a small hill flapping his arms, up and down. His legs are long and spindly. Dot looks at him quizzically. "He's trying to fly," Neil explains. "Who can blame him." I say. Neil nods. Dot lets out a little noise of dismay. Then she turns to me, her eyes full of concern - "Bad day at the office?"

I tell them about Eileen. "That's shit." Neil says. "But you do get overly fond of them, it's true." - "But it's so hard not to." I hate the sound of my own, whiney voice. I look into my pint, trying to remind myself what Dr Chowdhury said back in General Medical - It's not your tragedy, it's theirs. You are not the ill one. You are the well one. You can be strong, that's what they need of you. "You can't help people if you are over involved," Neil says. "Just bide your time and wait 'til you get an opportunity to change the system." - "That's not going to help Eileen is it?" - "Yeah, well. You can't help everyone can you?" I'm thinking, we don't help anyone, but then I remember Chrissie. Maybe I'm being overly negative. I take a long drink then put my pint down. I look at Neil - "I'm globalizing, aren't I? Or am I catastrophising?" I put my head in my hands. "I don't know what I'm doing."- Neil looks at me long and hard - "General cock up on the cognition front I reckon." That makes me laugh. I get up and go to the bar, order another round. I'm working tomorrow but who cares.

Sitting in the staff room at tea break time Lara, who I worked with in women's long stay, comes in. She's working in women's acute now too. I'm too hung over to pretend I like her so I just say hello then ignore her, pretend to be engrossed in an out of date People's Friend. Patsy comes in and it's all I can do not to groan out loud.

Patsy usually has her breaks in Sister's office so I don't know what she's doing here, but she's in a foul mood. I'm guessing she was asked to leave the office, probably by the new psychologist - no one else would dare. I feel terrible after all the alcohol last night. I'm drinking coffee with three sugars and eating stale digestive biscuits. It's the first food I've had since my cheesy pancake. "You look hellish." Patsy stands with her hands on her hips. I just keep reading the People's Friend, blank her as if she doesn't exist. "Are you on heroin or something?" I don't answer her. "You'll end up with Aids."

"There's a patient on the Sick Unit with Aids," Lara says. "Aye," says Patsy. "You'll no catch me working there, that's for sure." - "Me neither," says Lara. "I don't think anyone should have to work with them. They should just look after themselves. Why should our lives be put at risk for a bunch of junkies and perverts." I throw the magazine down and leave.

I'm on admissions today. I go to Eileen's bed space to check it's clean and tidy for our new patient. Then I go into the office to see if the notes have arrived yet. It seems they have, but Sister is reading them. I sit quietly waiting for her to finish. "What a shame. Poor lass." She hands me the notes. I open them up and look at the patient's name - Samira Moran. Samira? I look at her date of birth, 27th August 1963. It's the right year. Could there be two Samira Moran's living in Fife, born in the same year? I read the first page, the only page with any actual notes on it.

15 March 1985 - Home visit:
Husband raised concerns with GP when his young wife became excessively pre-occupied with cleaning the house. Refusing to go to bed, refusing to prepare meals for her husband, refusing food, not answering the door to visitors or talk to her parents who are extremely concerned about this change in their daughter's character. Lack of libido, extreme emotional lability, a series of urinary tract infections and weight loss following spontaneous abortion November 1984 at 12 weeks.

17 March 1985 - Emergency admission:
An attractive young Asian woman, presenting clean but dishevelled, midway through RGN training. On interview patient is unresponsive. Husband, anxious but attentive, reports that he has had to lock up 'all things sharp' or she will cut herself. Night of admission husband awoke to a crashing noise downstairs, when he got downstairs she was cutting herself with broken glass. Ten stitches, wound clean, dry dressing applied. Evidence of multiple, previous, superficial cuts to R and L inner thighs.

"Are you all right dear?" Sister is looking at me with concern. She has taken her glasses off and she looks older. Her eyes have deep dark circles below them. "I don't feel very well Sister. I think I need to go home." - "You certainly don't look too clever. I think maybe we'll get Dr Turner to check you over." I start to object but she's on the phone already calling the doctor. "You go into the treatment room dear and wait for the doctor there, he'll not be long." I'm too tired to argue so I go through and sit in the treatment room, pull a blanket from the trolley, take off my hat and close my eyes.

I've never spoken to Dr Turner before. He always seems very serious. He never smiles or jokes with the nurses like the younger doctors in the general wards sometimes do. He pulls up a chair and sits looking at me for a few moments. "I'm alright Doctor Turner, really. I've just got a hangover." - "Hmm. I see - I think I'll just take your blood pressure anyway." He wraps the cuff round my arm. His fingers feel dry and warm on my skin. I lay my head back, let him get on with it. It feels very strange to be doing this at work. It's like being ill at school, though I was usually pretending when I did that - to get out of Maths. I suppose I'm doing the same thing now, one way or another.

"It's pretty low," Dr Turner says. "Are you sure you're alive?" I laugh a little bit. "It's always low." He nods, sits back looking at me thoughtfully. "You are very thin. Are you always this thin?" I sigh, I kind of love it and hate it when people say I'm thin. I want to be thin, I try very hard to keep myself that way, but I know that what comes next is a lecture on eating or a jibe about me being anorexic or a drug addict. "You're not very happy here are you? You never look very happy." I didn't think he would have ever even noticed me. I start crying, really crying, like a child that's hurt themselves. The doctor gets up and gathers together a blood testing kit: a long needle and a few small syringes. "I'm going to do some bloods okay? I'm pretty sure we're going to find that you are anaemic."

He holds out a tissue for me and I press it against my eyes until I manage to stop crying. "Okay?" He smiles and I nod, hold my arm out, turn my head while he pushes the needle into my vein. I don't like that bit, but I do quite like watching the blood flowing into the syringe. I love the colour of it. I sniff a bit and say - "The new admission, the lady that's coming in today, is a friend of mine." - "Mrs Moran?" - "Samira, yes. We started our training together, before I switched to Psychiatry. We used to go to clubs together, Jackie O's and Bentleys, you know." - "I wouldn't have had you down as a clubbing sort of girl." He sounds so old fashioned I can't help but laugh. "I hate them. But the others like them. I just go because there's not much else to do. Samira loves them, but her husband doesn't like her going." - "Hmmm. Well, she's not been clubbing for a while I don't think. Am I right?" - "She hasn't been with me anyway. We've not seen each other since I came here."

We are quiet while he sorts out the blood tests, fills out the forms and puts everything into a small polythene bag. "I'll drop this off at the lab myself," he says. "No need for everyone to know your business eh? And I think you should take a couple of weeks off. Go to your GP, tell him what's going on. I'll arrange for these results to be sent to him. But you need to eat more - red meat, leafy greens, lots of dried fruit. You need the iron and it will help you put on some weight. You should stop smoking too. Have you any idea what it does to your lungs? I think we'll send you for a chest X-ray. I don't like the sound of your cough. I'll tell Sister that Mrs Moran is your friend. We'll have to make some other arrangement, get you onto another ward. You can't be nursing your pals, it isn't ethical." I feel like crying again, but this time with relief. I stand up, smooth down my uniform, start putting on my hat. "You won't be needing that." He plucks it off my head. "You're going home now, and you'll be off for a week at least, ideally two. I'll talk to Sister."- "Thank you Dr Turner." - "You are most welcome." He stands up and opens the door, leans towards me as I am about to leave, gives me a little smile - "Let's get you away from the dreaded Patsy eh?"

Stratheden Psychiatric Hospital
Ward 7 Acute Psychiatry - Female
May 1985

My GP signed me off for two weeks and started me on a high dose of ferrous sulphate. I've given up smoking and I've put on a little bit of weight. Some of the other nurses and the patients who have been in a while are telling me how well I look. That feels quite nice, though I know they mean I'm fatter. I've only a week of Acute left; its my last placement and it's my management week. After this it's back to college for a fortnight, then the final exam. If I pass, my training is complete and I will be a registered nurse.

I've been moved ward just as Dr Turner promised. I'm sitting in front of the Sister in the office I used to look after baby Rose in. It feels different in the daylight; more like the glass box that it is. I am facing the window that looks onto the day room. Judy is in there, playing with Rose, tickling her, singing little rhymes and rubbing her tummy. Some of the other women sit around watching. They are smiling but their eyes look sad. "You'll be making the decisions about nursing care this week," Sister tells me. "But they will be approved by me. If you make any bad decisions I will intervene." - "Yes, thank you Sister" - "You are welcome - and for God's sake relax. My name is Fiona and I'm not going to eat you."

I've been pretty anxious about this week but I'm kind of looking forward to it too. Because I'm in charge I don't have to do any of the day to day duties. I will attend the ward round and case conferences, but I won't have to set up the teas and coffees - Lara can do that. The doctors, psychologists, OT's and social workers might even start acknowledging me a little - so all in all things are better.

It seems Samira has been moved to Dundee, because she knew some of the other nurses too. She asked to be moved. I think that's a good sign - her still caring about her privacy. I would have liked to see her, but I wouldn't like to have seen Donald coming and going. I might not have been able to be very polite to him. I'm not sure why I've been changed wards when Samira isn't here anymore, but I'm guessing that Dr Turner told Sister it would be better for me not to have to work with Patsy. I saw her in the locker room earlier. She sort of growled at me, but I completely ignored her; as if she was invisible - like Tooje would do. It works - it feels powerful.

We have a new admission on Ward 7 today; a young woman called Ruth, about my height, thinner than me, but not full scale anorexic. She is wearing a leotard with footless tights and a short, frilly skirt which I think is called a ra-ra skirt. Her feet are bare and her light brown hair is so long it reaches her waist. She has been brushing it for ages - it looks very full and glossy. She is a student at the Royal Ballet School in London and was sent back home for a while because of her weight and *bizarre and inappropriate behaviour* towards her fellow dancers. She wanders about the ward singing quietly to herself, stretching in graceful poses from time to time. She has a menacing air about her. "We need to watch her don't we?" I say to Fiona. She nods slowly. "So what are you going to do?" - "I think I'll put Lara in there to keep an eye on things." - "Really?" Fiona raises an eyebrow. "Well, she likes a fight right enough. Maybe we should sell tickets?" I turn to look at her, "Oh my God you've just had to intervene on my first decision!" I laugh as I say it though, because I know she's right. "Maybe I'll just go in myself, monitor the situation for a while." - "That sounds better." She pats me on the shoulder, wanders back over to her desk smiling.

I go and sit by Judy. She remembers me from nights, but she doesn't really remember the details of that time. "Did I do anything bad to her?" She is looking at her baby. "No, of course not. No, you just weren't able to care for her, that's all." She gazes at her daughter dreamily, her eyes full of love at last. "But I would have, wouldn't I? If you guys hadn't been around to stop me." - "Don't think about it," I tell her. "It's all in the past. You're going home tomorrow. You're going to have a lovely time with your gorgeous wee baby." Judy smiles. "She is gorgeous isn't she? I mean, I know all mothers think their babies are beautiful, but she actually is - isn't she?" I look at her baby long and hard then I say - "You don't think she looks a bit like your mother in law?" I keep a straight face while I say that, then I start laughing. Judy thumps me on the arm. "You're a right little devil you are!" She's laughing too. "Actually my mother in law was quite a good looking woman - and she wasn't so bad. I don't really know why I took against her like that." She asks me about all the gifts. She can't believe that my mum knitted the bonnet, bootees and gloves.

"I really love those," she says. "And those stripy jumpers - and the wee teddy. Who made them?"

I am watching Ruth from the corner of my eye. She's standing at the tea trolley waiting for her turn to get a drink. "I think you should go to your room Judy." Judy looks at me quizzically. "Now - take Rose to your room." Judy follows my gaze then jumps out of her chair and grabs Rose so quickly she gets a fright and lets out a loud wail of distress. Just as Judy is running out the door with her daughter, Ruth grabs the giant tea pot and throws it across the room towards me. Warm, milky tea splashes over the women who were waiting at the trolley. Some of them cry out in alarm, others just stand there looking down at their wet clothes trying to figure out what just happened. The teapot lies on its side by my feet. Ruth is going for the coffee pot now but Sister has appeared and manages to grab it first. Ruth starts going really crazy, fighting Sister for the coffee pot, grabbing at her hat, scratching her face, and neck. I run over and press the alarm and almost immediately nurses come running from all directions. We wrestle Ruth off Sister and lay her flat on the floor. I issue instructions: who is to keep hold of which limb; who is to protect her head as we lift and carry her to her bed. She kicks and bites and screams at us. "WHORES! FILTH! SHAMELESS SUDUCTRESSES! YOU ARE VESSELS OF SIN AND CORRUPTION AND I WILL RULE OVER YOU!"

Lara and I run to the treatment room to draw up an injection. When we return there are two male nurses helping to hold Ruth down. Sister pulls the ra-ra skirt right up above her waist but Ruth has her leotard on over the footless tights. I try to pull it up and her tights down but I can't manage. "Oh for God's sake," I groan and look at Sister apologetically. Sister and I start trying to get Ruth's leotard off her, which means someone has to let go of one of her arms. She grabs Fiona's hat, pulls it off, along with a fistful of hair. Fiona yelps in pain. When we let go of her right arm she grabs my hat and does the same. I grit my teeth, put my head down and pull her leotard down past her hips. Her tiny, teenage style bra slips down as well, leaving her whole upper body exposed. The male nurses turn their faces away. I stick the needle in to her hip, worrying that there won't be enough fat.

I am horrified by this situation which feels wrong in so many ways. I'm worried that the needle will be too long and that it will scratch against a bone, though I don't actually think there is a bone in that part of the body. Images of text book skeletons float through my mind as I push the needle in, surely it couldn't hit the back of the ilium. It feels okay. It feels like muscle there. My heart is pounding, my head is aching, my hands shake as I pull the needle out and drop the empty syringe into the shiny metal kidney dish. Four nurses, including the two men sit holding Ruth until the drug takes effect. Sister pulls the sheets and blankets up and over her as I rummage in her locker for a nightdress.

I feel bad for Fiona. She is the first Sister I've really liked for ages - since Sister Bonnyface really. I feel terrible when I look at the angry red scratches all down the side of her face. "I should have been standing closer to her," I say. "I should have got between her and the trolley right away." - "You did fine," says Sister, dabbing at her face with a wet swab. "You sat by the baby. It was a natural choice. And how could you know what was going to happen?" I'm thinking - I sat by Judy because I like her and I like her baby. Next time I'll be right beside the person that's posing a risk. That's where I should have been all along. I say, "Do you think, since I'm in charge this week I can make this ward a no hat zone?" Fiona stands looking at my bashed up hat, her own still lying in a frilly crumple on her desk. "Abso-bloody-lutely," she says. "And definitely while Ruth is on the ward." - "What do you think that was all about, the things she was shouting at us?" - "Och just rubbish. She's completely psychotic. It's just nonsense." I nod politely, but I'm not so sure.

Ward 6 seems very quiet in comparison to the acute unit. Val is in the office with the doctor so I just go right through to the day room. I feel terrible that I haven't been to see Eileen since before I was off sick. She won't know I was off, but I think she will remember my promise to help her. I am bracing myself for a re-run of my last visit, or worse, but to my surprise she is up and pottering around the big table in the corner. She seems to be arranging some flowers in a vase. "Eileen!" I call. She looks up in surprise. "You… You…" She is smiling, pointing at me. She makes her way over, holding on to the table. There's a walking frame next to me and I guess it's hers. I carry it to her and she grabs hold of it. We walk together to a brown vinyl wing back chair by the window. I put my arm round her as she sits down. "You!" She takes hold of my hand, looking up at me smiling. "I was off sick." Her face clouds, "I'm fine now, honest."

She tugs at my skirt, "You, you?" - "Oh yes!" I jump up. "It's the same skirt as last time, but I got my mum to turn it into a ra-ra skirt. Do you like it?" I'm standing now, holding the edges of the lilac peasant skirt out at each side. "My sister got the bottom half. Mum made a new waistband. Wasn't that clever?" Eileen is laughing, holding her hands together under her nose. I sit down smoothing my skirt over my legs, it reaches just above my knees. "It feels funny wearing a short skirt but I think it looks okay?" Eileen shakes her head but I know from her eyes she is trying to nod.

As I leave I go into the office to see Val. "Well, what do you think?" She beams at me. "No bar chair for Eileen." - "How did you know?" I ask her. "The girls told me, and you're right, she shouldn't have been in one." - "But she seems so happy and settled too?" - "Oh yes, well I dared to suggest it to his nibs again - a wee bit of Imipramine, and you know he didn't say a word, he just went right ahead and prescribed it."

Hamish and I are back together; we bumped into each other at the doctor's when I was off sick and he's spent nearly every night with me since. I haven't heard from Sam. I'm sure he'll arrive one day and I'll tell him then, if Neil hasn't already. We have been cycling around the countryside a lot, eating picnic food, and lying around in the sun. "I love you," I tell him, as I stroke his stubbly cheek with a daisy. He sits up and puts his head in his hands then stands, his arm extended to pull me up, "Well you are one of my favourite people."

I've passed the final exam, but there's a problem with my medical. Even though I've put on a bit of weight my iron levels are still very low. The occupational health nurse says - "Old age pensioners have better iron levels than you. Don't you feel tired at all?" I honestly don't feel tired, except at the end of a twelve hour shift. Even then I'm usually fine if I haven't been out drinking the night before. It seems they won't give me a permanent contract for a staff nurse post - on health grounds. I'm invited for an interview anyway. There are three nursing officers, all men, looking intense and dishevelled; they've been interviewing all day.

"Ideally where would you like to work?"
"I'd like to work in the children's unit."
"And what do you think you have to offer in the children's unit?"
"Well it was my favourite placement and I got along well with the team there. I love working with children and they seem to like me. My own childhood was stable and happy. I think I'm starting from a good base. My father is a social

worker and he talks to me quite a lot about domestic violence and neglect - the impact of those things on children, their development and how their adult life may be affected. It's something I really care about and I'd like to learn more and maybe be able to make a difference".

Stratheden Psychiatric Hospital
Sick Unit - Female
1985 June - September

I've been given a six month contract on the Sick Unit - where anyone who requires medical care is sent to. I'm back on A shift so everything feels quite different. I wonder what it's like for the patients - this parallel universe feeling that our system provokes. There are only five patients in our ward: two in the late stages of Huntington's Chorea; one in the late stages of Parkinson's; one with severe epilepsy, and a very quiet woman in her thirties, diagnosed with schizophrenia, who keeps setting fire to her legs. Mona - she is called, which is a quite strange because she looks a bit like the Mona Lisa. She sits watching telly all day with a funny little smile on her face; a nice looking woman, with long brown hair and round, dark eyes, but her complexion is pale and waxy looking from all the anti-psychotic meds. Even though she's on a huge dose of those - you can tell something big, and not good, is going on in her head. Nobody is allowed to bring matches or cigarette lighters on to the ward. They must be taken to the office and locked away. She doesn't move around much because her legs are so badly burned - it must be agony for her. If she sees someone on TV with a lighter, or matches, she leans forward and watches them very closely. However dopey and drugged she looks she would be up and out of that chair like a shot if there was any opportunity to cause some more damage to herself.

Three of us work here: Sister Henderson; Enrolled Nurse Shand and me. Sister and Nurse Shand are both approaching sixty and they are planning a trip to Egypt together when they retire next year. They want to see the pyramids. Sister and I get along okay but Nurse Shand doesn't seem to like me at all. I don't like her much either. She is very nervy, watching me all the time with her huge watery eyes. She raises her eyebrows at almost everything I do. I see her looking at Sister sometimes as if to say *can you believe how stupid this girl is* - even if I'm just making toast and scrambled eggs or something. Clearly I don't make toast or scrambled eggs the way she thinks they should be made.

I talk to Sister about it and she says, "She's just a very anxious person, especially since her husband died. He died right in front of her you know. He was only young, and not even ill. It was such a shock." I feel guilty for disliking her, but I do - even more than I disliked Patsy, which isn't rational because Nurse Shand is kind to the patients.

Sometimes I'm lent to the men's sick unit which is right next door. They are busier and often short staffed. It's fine by me; I like it through there much better. The charge nurse, Paul, and the staff nurse, Sandy, are both very interested in poetry and philosophy. They like to talk about madness too. The ward is very full and the work is hard. A lot of the patients are near the end of their lives and need half hourly turning to prevent bed sores. There's a lot already have bedsores and we spend hours every day dressing and packing wounds. I don't mind because I like learning how to do these things well and it's interesting trying out all the latest creams and lotions with their various methods of application. Recently we have been trying a synthetic skin substitute, a kind of clear plastic covering that acts like a second skin - it was featured on Tomorrow's World.

We have a new patient - a lively old man from a titled family that own a lot of land in Fife - a castle and several farms. This new patient fell off his horse a few months ago and was in a coma for some time. He's been brought here because it was difficult to manage his behaviour in a general ward. He lost his eye and suffered some brain damage. It's not clear yet what the long term impact of his injuries will be but he has been experiencing violent seizures and visual hallucinations. Sometimes he thinks his arm is on fire. He flays around wildly trying to beat out the flames. Other times he sees everything upside down. He is complaining about this to his wife today. "It's like I'm still hanging by my arse from the damned horse," he shouts. "Damned inconvenience. How's a chap to take a drink when he's upside down all the time?" - "Well you could try standing on your head," his wife retorts, slapping her thighs in amusement. She tips some snuff in to the crook of her hand and snorts it, then sneezes loudly, wipes her nose on the rough brown tweed of her jacket. She is a tiny woman with short tightly curled hair. She wears a waistcoat, a checkered hat with a feather in it, a narrow knitted yellow tie and plus fours. She also smokes a pipe, though Paul doesn't let her do that on the ward. Yesterday, when her husband was trying to extinguish the imaginary flames from his arm she threw a jug of water over him, laughing uproariously. It didn't help - it just enraged him further. "WHAT THE BALLY HELL!" He roared, so long and so loud his face turned purple. We thought he was going to hit her but he restrained himself at the last minute, which, clinically speaking, is a good sign.

This morning his wife has brought in a framed picture of her husband standing outside their mansion house home with the Queen and the Duke of Edinburgh. She arranges it on his locker, sweeping the sweetie wrappers, used tissues and orange peel onto the floor, then she stands back and salutes. "She's just as mad as him," I say under my breath to Sandy and Paul as we sit round the table for tea break. Paul tips his head back in a thoughtful way. "No. I don't think so. I'd say she's NFF. Wouldn't you Sandy?" The staff nurse hesitates, snaps his biscuit in two, looks over at the old couple then nods. "Yep. NFF. I'd say so." - "NFF?" I have never heard this acronym before. Paul leans back, stretching his arms behind his chair. He has a very long, lean body, blonde curly hair and the bluest eyes I've ever seen. "NFF," he says - "Normal For Fife. When I meet a new patient who is supposedly mad, I ask myself - is this person's behaviour normal for Fife? Because Fife people you know, being separated on one side by the Firth and the other by the Tay - well we have our own particular characteristics. We are quite different to Edinburgh people or Dundonians. Edinburgh people are generally reserved, a bit cold and arrogant - present company excepted of course." He smiles politely at me before he continues. "Dundonians are far more self effacing. They're a joyless bunch - hospitable enough but pleasure doesn't come easy. Fifers on the other hand - well Fifers are warm hearted folk if they know you, or you're part of their family - but they are a fierce, mistrusting breed too. You see we were isolated so long - we're not used to strangers. You know the Romans turned back because of us. They got past Edinburgh and up as far as Falkirk - but the Fifers defeated them - we saw them off and they didn't come back. So there's a general rule - any behaviour, before it's judged to be a sign of insanity, must be considered in the context of that persons cultural norm - whatever that may be. I like to refer to this principle as Normal For Fife."

I ask him and Sandy if they've ever worked in men's long stay. They both shake their heads, looking at me with interest. I tell them about the daily routine which never alters. I tell them about the money being taken off the men's paltry wages for their funeral - about the bathing, and the mice, and the communal clothes. I tell them that nobody's birthday is recognised; that the men have no phone, no visitors, no personal possessions. I tell them about the button sorting and the ball throwing and Bobby shouting HOOF. I say - "What kind of cultural norm is that for the men to conform to? Who can blame big Lackie Johnstone for trying to fly? Running up and down that hill, flapping his arms all day. In the scheme of things it seems quite rational. I mean - what are we doing to these men?" I hear my voice getting high and distressed, lower the tone to calm myself, sit back in my seat and light another fag. "Who wouldn't try to fly away, or escape into madness, trapped in that kind of hell." There is a short silence while the two men contemplate

my speech then Paul leans forward, puts his hand over mine. "That was an unfortunate first experience for you. I hope it hasn't put you off the job. That would be a great pity."
Later, when we are checking the controlled drugs together I ask him - "Do you have a patient here with Aids?" - "No," he says, standing back, looking at me curiously. "If we did would it be a problem for you?" - "No - I don't think so." I shake my head. "It's just that someone told me you did." - "Hmm," he nods, sticks his bottom lip out, then points at me with his index finger - "A good friend will always stab you in the front." Apparently it's an Oscar Wilde quote.

Today I've been sent to the Aids and Prosthetics factory in Dundee with two patients, Jenny and Ron, who are both in late stage Parkinsons. They are having chairs made that will fit the shape of their bodies perfectly and reduce the risk of pressure sores. There's only me taking both patients, but there are two drivers, Brian and Pete, who will do all the lifting and carrying, so I feel pretty relaxed. Pete looks like Elvis. I am trying not to think of that terrible night with Maggie and Jake, but Pete looks nothing like Jake; he's a much younger, slimmer Elvis. He sits in the back with me and the patients singing *Since my Baby left me*... He wiggles his eye brows and his top lip, his leg trembles. He raises his arms, clicks his fingers and tilts his hips suggestively. Jenny and Ron can barely move their faces but I can see from their eyes that they are laughing."

When we get to the factory two staff come out and watch as Jenny and Ron are brought out of the ambulance. They immediately take charge of their wheelchairs. Brian and Pete shrug resignedly, start to climb back into the seats at the front of the vehicle. "No! No!" shout the Aids and Prosthetics people. "Come inside and see our factory. And you must have some tea with us."

It's an enormous place and the staff seem very proud of it; long, low ceilinged rooms with rows and rows of false limbs hanging from metal beams, hundreds and hundreds of them all different sizes and colours. The workers stop what they are doing as we come in, smiling, shaking our hands, nodding politely to Jenny and Ron. "I didn't know they come in different colours," I exclaim, staring up at the brown, pink and creamy coloured limbs. "Well of course," our tour guide protests. "You think a black man would want a pasty pink leg?" - "Are these just for Fife and Dundee?" Everybody laughs, "You must think there's an awful lot of amputees in Fife and Dundee! We supply to countries all over the world."

All the staff come along and join us for tea. There are nine of them and they are very friendly and polite with each other. The man who seems to be in charge, a tall, thin man called Derek who looks like a TV scientist, offers me and the ambulance drivers tea or coffee, but he offers our patients diluting juice. "They'll take tea actually," I tell him. He holds up his hands and says, "I beg your pardon. Do forgive me. I was worried about them scalding themselves. Is that not a risk?" I bring two, non spill feeder cups from my bag and hold them up. They are pretty discoloured and chewed up looking. Derek takes them from me and starts filling them with tea. "Lots of milk please," I say. I don't want to burn my patients either.

They all watch as I feed Jenny. She looks at me, moving her eyes only, to see if I'm noticing. I give her a little smile, think I see the flicker of one back. One of the Aids and Prosthetics team has started feeding Ron. He copies me, breaking tiny bits of cake off and putting it on a tea spoon - a tiny bit of cake then swig of tea, a tiny bit of cake, then a swig of tea, slowly slowly, giving time for our patients to enjoy the taste. When we're finished the Aids and Prosthetics man who has been feeding Ron holds the plastic beaker up for everyone to see - "The design is basic but it does the job. We could certainly improve on the appearance, and handles might enable the patient to hold it independently."

After tea we are invited back through to the factory to see our patient's chairs being made. First they have to sit on big clear plastic bags filled with polystyrene beads. The air is sucked out of these, the patient still sitting in them, until they became hard. The final product will be made of a soft rubber like material based on this mould. All the staff have gathered round to watch because it seems that this is the first time one of these chairs has ever been made. Ron and Jenny look different on their white bobble thrones, like a pair of long married monarchs, though neither of them have met until today. You can see that they have both been rather good looking people before illness struck.

Jenny isn't well this morning. She refuses her scrambled egg and doesn't want to get out of bed. I leave her to lie, but when I get back from my tea break Nurse Shand has got her up. I go over and ask her if she wants some breakfast now but she closes her eyes in refusal. I ask if she wants her jewellery on. She closes her eyes again. "Are you sure?" She closes her eyes tighter and longer. Her husband is coming to visit. He will makes a fuss if she isn't wearing her jewellery. He is very attentive, but sometimes I think I see Jenny kind of flinch when he touches her. I mentioned it to the others one day and Sister looked thoughtful. Nurse Shand just kind of snorted. "For heaven's sake the woman can barely move." Later as we were doing the medicine round Sister said, "You never know what goes on between married people."

When I first got here Jenny's husband asked me if I would like to work for him on my weekends off, so he could take Jenny home for those days. I saw her eyes flicker up towards me during that conversation. "You do her hair so nicely," her husband said. "And you know - you have an old head on young shoulders. That is a very special thing. I'll pay you well. You could save the money, put it towards your own home. I imagine you live in rented? You'll want your own home eventually, everybody does." - "Thank you for asking," I tell him, "but I think I'd rather not."

He's not so friendly today. He wants to know why Jenny isn't wearing her jewellery. He isn't happy and he asks me where I've put it. I have to go and get it from the safe. He wants to speak to Sister. When I tell him she's on leave I hear him saying something about NHS workers getting too many holidays. I wander over towards the television and pretend to watch that for a few minutes. I can hear him talking to his wife as he puts her jewellery on. He says, "There now that's a pretty lady."

He stays several hours and Jenny is struggling to sit upright. She leans more and more to the right. She always leans a bit, but by the end of his visit she has three pillows propping her up. As soon as her husband leaves I put her to bed, she's so small and light I'm able to do that on my own. I ask Nurse Shand to take her blood pressure while I phone the doctor. While I'm on the phone Nurse Shand comes in to the office and says, "She's gone."

We have to wait a while to give Jenny's husband time to get back to his house. "You know you mustn't tell him that she's dead," Nurse Shand reminds me. "Would you like to talk to him?" I ask. I'm not trying to be cheeky when I say that - but she purses her lips tightly and scuttles off.

"Mr Pearson?"
"This is he"
"Mr Pearson I'm phoning from the sick unit. I'm afraid Jenny has become very gravely ill."
"Yes I'm very well aware of my wife's condition thank you

very much."

"Mr Pearson, I think she is very near the end of her life."

"Is this some kind of joke?"

"Mr Pearson you need to come back to the ward now."

"Oh, I see, okay, well... If you insist."

Nurse Shand stands in the doorway staring at me. "It's ridiculous not being able to just say it," I grumble. "I know but people would complain if you told them on the phone, and besides, the doctor hasn't been yet." We go back down to wash Jenny, brush her hair and make her look nice for her husband. "Will you stay with me while we tell him?" I ask Nurse Shand. "No. It's your job to tell him. You're the staff nurse." - "I know, but don't you think it's a bit silly, all this staff nurse/enrolled nurse nonsense? I'm only twenty one - you're almost sixty. You've been doing this job for forty years, I've been doing it three. I mean, who would you rather hear it from?" She looks at me with her giant eyes - "It's your job. You tell him."

The doctor comes pretty quickly and does all the checks then signs the death certificate. I wait for Mr Pearson at the ward entrance so he won't go down to Jenny's bed and get a shock. When he arrives I reach out and take him by the arm, ask him to come with me to the office. He looks confused and irritated and as he sits down he says, "Now what's this all about?" - "Mr Pearson I'm afraid Jenny passed away shortly after you left today." His face turns grey. He looks like he can't believe what I'm saying. "But she was fine," he stutters. "She was fine when I left her. Are you sure she's dead?" - "Yes Mr Pearson. The doctor has confirmed it. I'm so sorry. It was very peaceful – it was just like she went to sleep." He starts crying. Nurse Shand appears with a tray of tea and biscuits. She looks at me like I made him cry out of badness. After she leaves he lifts his head and looks at the tea tray. I wouldn't blame him if he picked it up and threw it at the wall. I take him down to sit with his wife. He takes her hand, sits stroking her fingers, rubbing her engagement ring. "There's a pretty lady," he says between his sobs.

It's my weekend off. I'm just out of bed, though it's past midday. Sam has turned up with Neil. Neil knows I have to talk to Sam alone so he says, "I just need to talk to your landlord about something." He disappears over to the farmhouse. I stand in the kitchen stirring the tea, thinking how glad I am that Hamish isn't here, though I am going out with him this evening, to the cinema in St Andrews - he's picking me up at six.

"There's something I need to tell you," Sam says. I put the teapot on the kitchen table, stick Mary's knitted cosy over it and offer him some toast. He takes a slice, puts some of my mum's home made marmalade on it. He chews his toast for a bit then says, "You've put on weight. It suits you. You look good." - "I've given up smoking," I tell him. "And I'm on a mega dose of iron. Don't come near me with a magnet for God's sake." He laughs, then flushes, drops the half eaten toast on to his plate. He looks embarrassed. "I've been seeing someone else, a girl from Dundee - Pam. I haven't known her for very long but I really like her. She's lovely and, well - she's pregnant." I stop eating. I hold my toast in the air and stare at him. He looks right at me, eyes wide, trying to judge how his news has gone down. "Congratulations." My voice sounds hollow and false. I clear my throat and say it again, with a bit more enthusiasm.

I want to behave badly. I want to shout, "ARE YOU FUCKING JOKING?" I want to hit him, throw crockery round the room like a Ward 1 geriatric who has been served salad for tea. But I don't feel I have the right to say or do anything given that I was going to tell him about Hamish. So I just smile and ask when the baby is due and make a stupid little joke about quiet nights in from now on. He is visibly relieved, starts telling me the details, as if I'm actually interested: the scan; the due date; the house his mother is buying for them all to live in. I just keep nodding and smiling and looking concerned at what I hope are the right times. When he leaves he puts his hands on my shoulders, strokes the back of my neck with his thumbs then kisses me full on the mouth. He says - "I'm going to miss you. You're one of my favourite people."

I thought Neil had gone with him, but he comes in and sits at the kitchen table, starts rolling a cigarette. "You okay? Stupid question. Come on, you can't really blame the guy - he's only doing the decent thing. You were going to chuck him for Hamish anyway weren't you?" - "Yes. Yes - it's fine. Of course. It's fine. He'll be a lovely dad." Neil looks at me suspiciously but I manage a smile. "It's fine. Honest." - "Well in that case," he says, "lets take some mushrooms."

I resist for a while, telling him I'm going to the cinema with Hamish later. "What to see?" - "Purple Rain" - "Well Jesus that's perfect. You should definitely take mushrooms for that. It might actually be interesting if you're tripping." Neil is not a Prince fan. "You'll be coming down by then, anyway. Come on, it's our weekend off. Let's do it." Dot arrives and she wants me to take some too. I compromise by taking twelve. They both take forty. We walk through the town centre then along a farm track towards the old Sugar Beet factory. We tell Dot about the gypsies. Neil says he thinks they were ghosts - it's not like him to be so whimsical.

It's a bright, sunny day and we are hot despite our light clothes. Neil brings some beers out of his bag and we stop for a rest in a pretty meadow that sits alongside the train track. There are lots of wild flowers and butterflies. Dot is laughing like a child. "Oh my God, the colours are amazing." Neil watches her fondly. I lie back and look at the clouds. "Look that one is like a whale!" - "Moby Dick?" Neil asks. He knows I have been reading it - well trying to read it. "I'm not getting very far with that book." I am disappointed in myself. "Yeah. It's not the easiest." Neil says. "What is it all about?" I ask him. "I thought it was about whales," Dot says. Neil laughs - "It is superficially. But I think the consensus is that it's about man's struggle to control his destiny and the natural world." Dot sighs, "It's all about men then? Wanting to control this." She gestures out to the meadow and the sky. I throw a buttercup at her and when she looks I raise a thumb of approval.

"I wonder why Adam is so obsessed with it though." Neil says. "Well he's certainly not the master of his own destiny. Is he?" I respond, though I don't feel that that really explains it. I feel silly now for not asking him that day when I was making his bed. I remember the passage he'd underlined. I've underlined it in my book too - in pencil. Maybe it's as well I didn't ask him. I might just have stirred things up.

The train to Edinburgh passes and we all wave. "Bye," Dot shouts. "Thanks for coming. Come back soon!" Neil and I are lying down again, looking at the sky. I turn to look at him and am surprised by how dazzling and vivid the colours around me are. "If you focus on the blue of the sky, then turn your head quickly to the ground with the green grass and buttercups, it's really good." We all do that for a while, swishing our heads between the sky and the grass. Then Dot sits up and says, "I love you both very very much." - "We love you too," Neil and I say in unison. She jumps up and runs around the meadow whooping. Neil and I exchange glances. She really is a very lovable girl.

"Do you think that when they gave psychotic people LSD they were hoping for a double negative?" I ask Neil. "You know - two negatives make a positive? Hallucinogenics cancelling out hallucinations?" We have opened some more beer and Neil is rolling a joint. I don't think we'll be walking any further today. He looks at me thoughtfully. "Nah. I think they just thought they'd give them it and see what happened." - "Pretty scary you would think. Tripping when you are psychotic." - "Who knows," Neil says. "I hope to God none of us ever have to try it. Though I suppose, if you were very distressed they could knock you out with Melleril." - "Hmm. I suppose they could - but whether they would - I'm not convinced." - "Come on. There must have been some good intentions there," Neil protests, but he doesn't look convinced either. We wander back to the cottage. Irish and his new girlfriend, Hazel, are standing on the doorstep knocking. "Come in," I shout and they both jump and turn around looking confused. We sit inside the kitchen for a while, then drag the chairs out the back and sit in the sun looking across the fields, drinking mushroom tea.

It's Neil that reminds me at half past five that I've only half an hour to get ready. I run to my room and change into my lilac rara skirt and a white lacy top. I keep my canvas baseball boots on; their whiteness makes my legs look brown. I sit at my dressing table and put some make up on, one eye at a time. After I do the first one I sit back and stare. It looks huge and the other looks tiny. Neil comes in and looks at me and laughs. He pulls up a stool and sits down. I put some eye make up on him, then some blusher and lip gloss too. We sit looking into the mirror giggling. I do my other eye, brush my hair, weave it into a French plait, spray myself with Roses Roses and I'm ready. "Do I look okay?" I ask, turning to Neil. "I think so. I have no idea. Do I look okay?" - "You do actually." I say. "But you better not go to the pub like that. You'll get beaten up." I squeeze some baby lotion onto a cotton wool ball and start cleaning his make up off.

Hamish doesn't seem to notice anything at first, in fact he says - "Wow look at your eyes." His sister is giving us a lift. She turns her head and smiles, says, "You look amazing." She drops us off at a pub on St Andrew's High Street. "I'll pick you up same place at 10.30pm." She toots her horn as she drives off. "She's lovely," I say to Hamish. "She says the same about you." He smiles and puts his arm round my shoulders.

We are meeting some friends of his; a guy called Simon who he was at uni with, and his girlfriend Sheena. They are living together in St Andrews. It all seems very grown up, though they are only a couple of years older than me. They are very friendly, tell me they've been dying to meet me. I'm surprised and pleased that Hamish has even told them about me. As we leave the pub I stop and stare at a neon sign across the road. It says Fish and Chips, but it looks so pretty I find myself smiling at it. Simon stands next to me looking. "Have you partaken of something illegal young lady?" I nod sheepishly. "Don't tell Hamish, he'll go nuts." - "Well, yeah, literally eh? Tell you what - I won't tell him if you give me some." He's only teasing, but I take a small bag out of my pocket and slip it into his. "Honestly? Really?" He looks delighted. "Well tonight just got a lot more interesting."

Simon disappears into the toilets before the film has started. When he comes back into the cinema he gives me a nod and a wink. "What's that all about?" Hamish says, looking a bit suspicious. "Nothing." We watch the film and even though I like Prince, I can't help but think it would have been a bit boring without the mushrooms. When it's finished we go back to the pub. Simon leans towards me and says - "I think you had the best idea taking the 'shrooms a few hours before the film." - "I knew you'd taken something!" Hamish shouts. We hadn't noticed he was standing right behind us. "I knew it. How could you? After what happened to me? How could you be so ignorant?" - "Hang on mate," Simon says. "I've taken them too - not just her." - "You're not my girlfriend," Hamish retorts. It's the first time I've ever heard him call me his girlfriend.

The rest of the night is really awkward, despite Simon and Sheena's efforts to keep things light. Hamish is furious. He can barely look at me. On the way home his sister tries a bit of small talk. I answer her as cheerfully as I can, but it's just too difficult and we lapse into an unhappy silence. She drops us off at the cottage.

It's cold and dark in the cottage. Mary's bedroom door is closed. She's on a twelve hour shift tomorrow so she'll be sleeping. I move the fire guard out the way and put a couple of logs on the smouldering fire then sit down on the multicoloured rag rug - another of Mary's creations. I stretch my hands out towards the heat. I don't feel like I'm tripping at all now. Hamish sits in the armchair looking at me, like he's trying to decide something. He sighs and starts rubbing his head in an agitated kind of way then says, "I can't do this. I like you. I really do. It's been one of the best years of my life - but you're such a child." He looks down at me, like an exasperated parent. "I kind of like that. It's one of the reasons I like being with you. But it drives me nuts too. I'm just not the right person for you. I'm not what you need and you're not what I need. I've tried - but I'm not in love with you."

I sit staring into the fire, the logs were quick to catch light and the heat is beginning to get uncomfortable. I'm crying and my nose is running, but I don't care. I could do with a drink but I can't be bothered getting up and going into the kitchen. There's a pack of Mary's cigarettes on the coffee table. I take one and light up. "Don't do that - you've done so well with giving up," says Hamish. "I've been smoking all day," I tell him, taking another drag. I want him to go away - but I want him to stay too. He gets up and walks to the door, turns and says, "I'm sorry." I hear him talking to Mary in the hall, we must have woken her. "Is she awful upset?" Mary sounds concerned, Hamish mumbles something and the door closes. Mary bolts it fast.

I hear her in the kitchen; the kettle being switched on, the squeaky fridge door opening. I hear the rattle of ice in glasses. She comes through with two long black drinks. "Vodka and Coke - the real stuff, not that diet crap. I was going to make tea but then I thought better of it." She hands me the drink, puts a blanket round my shoulders, lights a fag and says - "Two in one day. Not bad going - even for you." I look up at her, with my snotty tear stained face. She sits on the chair that Hamish just vacated. She's wearing a pink flowery dressing gown and mad fluffy high heeled slippers. There's a strip of redness across her top lip - she must have waxed it before she went to bed. "Neil told me about Sam." I start crying again. She leans forward and rests her head against mine, rubs my back soothingly, then wipes my face with a tissue, gets up, takes my empty glass and heads for the kitchen. "Put some music on," she shouts. "Me and you are gettin' pissed."

Goodmayes Hospital London
Psychogeriatrics
1985 September

I wasn't really thinking about leaving yet but I spotted an advert in the Scotsman for a job in London that said *interviewee travel expenses will be reimbursed*. My brother is living in London now so I thought I could pay him a visit - if I don't get the job at least I'll have had a free holiday.

I am half an hour early for my interview. The nurse who answered the door asks me if I would like to look round the ward where I may be working. It's an elderly care ward. I'm steering clear of Acute because I don't like forcing people to have ECT or injecting them with horrible drugs against their will - however unwell they are. I always enjoyed looking after older people anyway. For some reason, that I don't understand, it makes me happy.

The patients sit around the walls of the ward in their bar chairs looking at the faded swirly green linoleum. The telly is off and there is no music playing. An old man on a bean bag in the corner is trying to get up. He is calling out for help. There's a wet scrunched up draw sheet at his feet. He picks it up and throws it into the room. An old lady looks at me and waves. I wonder who she thinks I am. "Would you like to see the dormitory?" The nurse asks. I nod, though I know that it will be exactly the same as every other hospital dormitory I've seen. It is the same - but they have no proper mirrors on the lockers; they have squares of what looks like silver coloured plastic. I look in one and see a vague pink shadow. "Why don't they have mirrors?" I ask the nurse. She looks at me as if I'm completely stupid. "They are psychiatric patients." She shakes her head in disbelief as we leave.

I sit for another half hour in the ward waiting for the nursing officer to come and fetch me, thinking I should leave because there's no way I'm going to work here anyway. Then I remember Neil saying - "You have to wait until you're in a position to change things." I look around again. The old man on the bean bag is still shouting for help. The old lady waves at me again. I wave back. I think - I could change things here, for these people - even just by putting on some music. That old man must have wet himself, why doesn't anyone come and help him?

A small, harassed looking man comes in. His shirt is grey/white and there's a button missing just below the neck. His suit is cheap and ill fitting. He looks very young for a Nursing Officer, though I guess that's what he is. He doesn't introduce himself - "Are you for interview?" I nod and stand up, but he says, impatiently, "Well sit down then."

"I'm telling you now, the budget's extremely tight. There's hardly any money for anything - definitely not training."
"Oh, I see."
"Well, what do you think?"
"I think the ward could be made a lot more homely without spending very much money."
"There's no money."
"Well we could get donations, from relatives - local businesses?"
"Do you want the job or not?"
"No thank you."

Littlemore Hospital
Oxford
1985 September

It's just an hour and a half on the bus to Oxford from London so I've come to visit my friend Eddie; he's studying Philosophy and Theology at the university. Eddie's twin sister, Alexa, was at school with me; North Berwick High - not the boarding school that her brothers went to. That's what wealthy families do apparently - send their boys to private and their girls to the 'local school.' Alexa and I have similar views on that tradition.

I like Oxford much better than London. It's so ancient and dreamy. I feel like a character from a novel walking round here. Eddie takes me to a pub called *The Lamb and Flag* where CS Lewis and Tolkein used to drink. He introduces me to his friends who are mostly students too. They are very interested to hear about my work as a psychiatric nurse. One of them, who has just graduated in politics is working as a nursing assistant at a psychiatric hospital just a few miles away called Littlemore. "They're having a recruitment day tomorrow. Why don't you go up there, have a chat with them?" - "That's very fortuitous," Eddie says. "And I'm leaving Lake Street in a month or so - you could take my room. I'm sure my landlord would enjoy having a nurse for a tenant."

Littlemore is about the same size as Stratheden and probably built about the same time, though it looks quite different -

being built with red brick. I have a walk around the grounds. It's less austere than Stratheden - the fire escapes aren't ringed with barbed wire. I wander into a courtyard with pink and light grey concrete paving slabs arranged like a chequer board and a huge mural with trees, toadstools, rabbits and rainbows. There are toilet bowls propped up against the wall opposite, with flowers growing in them.

A small, slender man with a fresh, pale blue blazer and very big glasses comes over and asks if he can help. "I'm here for the recruitment day." He looks so surprised that I think I must have the wrong day. "No, no," he says. "You've got the right day. It's just that you're the only - I mean, the first person here." He smiles broadly, extends his hand for me to shake. "My name is Bill Drake. I'm the nursing officer in charge of recruitment. Would you like a coffee?" He leads me through the admin building, introducing me to every member of staff that we meet. They greet me with wide, open smiles, as if I'm a new neighbour and they can't wait to get to know me better.

Bill's office is long and narrow, sunny and warm. He asks me about my current job and he asks me what I think of Oxford. "I think it's an amazing place. I went to this pub yesterday called The Lamb and Flag where Tolkien and C.S Lewis used to drink." He laughs at my enthusiasm. "Yes, that's right, Graham Greene too. And Thomas Hardy is purported to have written Jude the Obscure there. Have you read much of Hardy?" - "I've read Tess of the Durbervilles and Far from the Madding Crowd - I love those books." - "Ah yes - the old faithfuls. You should try Jude the Obscure if you're planning to live here. Though I will warn you - it's not a cheerful read. I'm more of a Graham Greene man myself - not that he's particularly cheerful either mind you."

He sits looking at me, head tilted, smiling. "What's your sick time like?" I feel myself blushing. "It's not great. I've been off a lot. I hate it at Stratheden. I've been very tired because I was anaemic and didn't realise it. But I'm on iron now - so I'm okay really." - "Hmm, but would I be right in saying that when you're not happy you go off sick?" He is looking at me a little sternly. "Yes." I nod. He laughs and shakes his head. "Well you are refreshingly honest. And perhaps we'll manage to cheer you up a bit eh? Mind you - you will have to have a medical. If your iron levels are still low it will not be a permanent contract. I'm afraid we have no vacancies in Acute at the moment. It will be Rehab or Elderly Care." - "That's where I want to work - Elderly Care." He looks surprised. "Really?" It's like he can't believe what he's hearing. I nod enthusiastically. "Yes. Really. My two favourite placements when I was a student were the children's unit and Elderly Care. "Well we don't have a children's unit here I'm afraid. But we have lots of vacancies in the geriatric wards. So come along and see what you think." He jumps up and opens the door, stands back to allow me through. "There's someone I want you to meet."

We march along the corridors quick-smart, through grubby glass verandahs, past gaudy sixties murals and even more plant filled toilets. A middle aged woman comes skipping towards us in denim dungarees and a plaid shirt. She is carrying a teddy. She stops in front of Bill and says in a babyish voice, "Can I have a lolly?" He starts pressing his jacket like a man that's lost his wallet, saying, "I don't seem to have any today." She stands before him pouting. "Off you go Belinda," he says, kindly but firmly. "You know full well I don't have any lollies." The woman sticks her tongue out and runs off.

"I just need to go into Rohan first," he says, pushing open the door of what looks and smells very much like a geriatric ward. The nurses wear light blue uniforms but they are not wearing hats. The patients are arranged around the walls of the day room staring into the middle at some coffee tables with magazines on. Radio one is blaring and we hear someone singing along. Bill leads me over in that direction and opens a door. We see a tall skinny woman in a dark blue sister's dress, without the puffy sleeves, hooking a patient on to a commode by his vest. "Oh I do beg your pardon," Bill says to the patient, backing out the door. "Irene may I have a word?" She stops singing and smiles, follows us out into the day room, bellowing at one of the other staff to take over from her with the toileting as she leads us to her office. "Irene is the Sister here in Rohan," Bill tells me. She looks me up and down - "Are you coming to work with us?" - "That's yet to be decided," Bill says. "I'm just here to give you this." He hands her a slim brown envelope from his inside jacket pocket, there's nothing written on the front of it at all. "It's your new budget. Read and digest. We'll discuss it in a week or so." Irene opens the envelope and frowns, sits down at her desk to study the budget. "Bye for now then," shouts Bill as he ushers me out the door. She waves her hand absently, doesn't look up or say goodbye.

As he leads me up a flight of narrow, sloping stone steps he says, "Now, the choice will be yours, but I have a feeling you'll fit in better up here." There's a green sign with gold writing above the door saying Rivendell in gothic style lettering. Bill pushes the door but it's locked. He tuts and rolls his eyes at me, knocks loudly. We hear a voice on the other side shouting - "HELLO. HELLO. WHO IS IT? HANG ON A MINUTE. I CAN'T GET THE DAMN DOOR OPEN." The handle goes up and down frantically on our side. We hear another voice, lower and gentler than the first. "Out the way then my duck, let's get it open, see who's come to visit." The door opens and two men are standing there. One of them is elderly - short and a little stout, with a hopeful kind of look on his face. The other is very tall, well over six foot, probably in his forties. He is broad and bulky, with a big friendly grin, long unkempt hair and shaded glasses. "You're not supposed to lock the door Rex," Bill says, shaking his head as we enter. "I know, I know," the tall man says laughing. "It's these fucking patients you know. They are very disobedient. They won't do anyfink I tell 'em." He gives me a wink and steers me into the office.

Bill sits down at a big old desk, strewn with the usual debris: cigarettes; lighters; broken specs; hearing aid batteries; newspapers open at the crossword page; marshmallows; jam, and a pen that looks like a syringe. "I haven't seen one of these before," I say, picking it up. "Drugs company," Rex says. "You can 'ave it if you want? Go on you 'ave it. A present from Rivendell. Wiv lots of love. Now, would you like a tea or a coffee? I can do you an Irish coffee?" I laugh and thank him for the pen. "Just plain coffee will be lovely."

We sit quietly while Rex goes off to get our drinks. There's a list of patient's names on a whiteboard fixed to the wall - strange, old fashioned names that you wouldn't get in Scotland: Hyrem; Dilwyn; Grenville; Cecil; Maisie; Dorothea. Rex comes back and perches on the desk, folds his arms and looks at me. "So come on then, who are you? Are you a new medical student? Or have you been abducted by this wicked old man to work on the slave ship Littlemore?" - "She's your new staff nurse Rex," Bill says. "Oh I was right then." He turns to me, " 'E 'as abducted you, you poor little fing." Bill ignores him. "As long as she passes the medical and her paperwork is in order - and she doesn't prefer Rohan." - "Rohan? You must be joking? Bloody 'ell, if she prefers Rohan she should be admitted 'ere not employed. Anyway…" He looks at me with his big friendly grin - "You look 'elfy enough to me. Can you start today?" - "I'm here on holiday," I tell him, laughing again. "I only heard about this place yesterday. I'll have to work my notice back in Scotland." - "Why don't you just call in sick?" Rex is looking genuinely bewildered. Bill puts his head in his hands and groans.

"Something for you," Bill says, handing Rex a slim brown envelope just like the one he gave to Irene. "For me? Aw! You shouldn't 'ave." - "It's your new budget." - "Oh. Yeah, right.

You really shouldn't 'ave." Rex throws the unopened envelope on to his messy desk. An old man comes staggering in looking distressed. "Has anyone seen my Jane?" - "She's at work Syd," Rex says, patting him on the shoulder. "On a Saturday? She don't work Saturday." - "Well she does now. Why don't you just you put your feet up and relax eh? There's no work for you today." - "Well she'll be needing a lift 'ome at the end of 'er shift," the old man says, looking worried. "What time did she say I must fetch 'er?" - "She's got the car Syd." Rex lights another cigarette. Syd walks unsteadily towards the window, peers out. "Well I'll be buggered. She 'as taken the car too. That's a first. When did she start working Saturdays then?" - "Today Syd. She started today." - "Well I 'ope they're giving 'er overtime. Do you think they'll give 'er overtime?" - "I 'eard she's getting double time," Rex says. "Well I suppose that's something anyways." The old man sighs, then walks over to the door. "I'll be off down the pub then I reckon. Tara." - "Tara my duck," Rex says, closing the door behind him. Bill looks at me - "Rex doesn't do reality orientation." - "Yeah well, who wants reality?" Rex says. "Over rated if you ask me - reality. He's quite happy now, aint he? Finkin' 'is Jane is out working, gettin' double time? Rather that than me tellin' 'im she's five years dead. Breaks 'is 'eart every time, poor old love. No. Reality can go fuck itself far as I'm concerned."

He shows me round the ward while Bill makes some phone calls, arranging my medical. There are three other nurses; two wearing uniforms, without hats, the other, who introduces herself as Mo, wears a T shirt and loose cotton trousers. "She calls herself Mo," Rex mutters to me, as we walk down the day room towards the women's dorm. "But 'er real name is Immaculate Conception. Can you believe it? Fuckin' magnificent if you ask me. Now if that was my name I'd 'ave everyone say it, in full, every time they addressed me. Still, we've all got our little ways eh? 'Orses for courses. No accountin' for taste. She's a sweet little fing though, very kind to the patients. She's not one of my staff - more's the pity. She's just doin' overtime to 'elp us out. 'Ere I tell you what - we'll be bloody glad when you come and join us. You're not going to pick Rohan are you? Rohan's terrible." - "No." I hold my hand out to shake his - "I'm going to work here with you."

We stand in the doorway looking at the day room. It feels much more lively than any other ward I've been in, even Acute. The chairs are arranged round the room in the usual way, but there are no bar chairs. Quite a few of the patients are milling around, looking out the window, whistling or humming along to the music that is coming from a radio at the bottom of the ward. "Elgar," Rex says - "Imperialistic crap." He tuts and laughs. "Still, this lot seem to like it." There's a man standing by a fish tank waving his hands about like a conductor. Three other men, Syd amongst them, stand, hands in pockets, watching. One of them is whistling and the would be conductor encourages him enthusiastically, as if he was a member of the orchestra. A skinny black cat sits on the fish tank behind. His little head is following the old man's movements. "A cat!" I shout. I'm so surprised to see anything so homely. Rex grins, walks over and picks the cat up, rests him on his shoulder like a baby. The cat purrs loudly. "This is Moog. My wife found 'im in a bin. Kind of apt - don't you fink?"

Syd turns round and says, "'Ere, when we goin' down the pub?" - "After lunch Syd. About three. That okay?" Syd looks a bit disappointed but he nods and carries on listening to the music. Rex takes me over to the window, points to a low building sitting just beyond the hospital wall. "That's our local there." - "Will you really take him there?" - "Not me, no. But the students will take 'im. They come on at one. Nice lads. They'll be more than 'appy to take a few of 'em down the pub, knock a couple back, 'ave a nice game of Aunt Sally." - "Aunt Sally?" - "Aunt Sally - you know - skittles. By God lass you've got a lot to learn. The sooner you start the better."

Stratheden Psychiatric Hospital
Sick Unit - Female
1985 October

It's my last week in the sick unit, my last week in this hospital. I've been to visit Eileen and I'm feeling pretty down because she's had another stroke. She was slumped in a bar chair propped up with pillows. Her eyes were open but she didn't seem to register my presence at all. Sister puts a cup of tea in front of me - "You can't afford to get too attached to them. You know that don't you?" Nurse Shand sits down, puts her hand on my shoulder. She says, "I'm exactly the same. I find it impossible to not get upset. Sometimes it's best just to have a good cry." I smile at her. I know that she's only being nice because I'm leaving, but I'm grateful. I feel the tears start, wipe them away quickly. "Or a big drink," Sister says.

A man comes wandering in to the ward and I look at him in surprise. He's one of my brother's friends from the art school in Dundee. He looks as surprised as me. He smiles, but he seems to be kind of disorientated. "I had forgotten you work here. I think I'm lost. I was looking for Ward 15. I'm visiting a friend." He looks around the ward curiously. We have some new hammocks for nursing people who are dying. They look a bit old fashioned, though we were very excited when they arrived earlier in the week. They are like stretchers, made of fine, flexible netting. We turn the poles every half hour to redistribute the patient's weight - hopefully preventing pressure sores. It saves us disturbing them and it saves our backs too. I suppose they look a bit odd though - maybe a bit wartime. "So this is your ward then?" - "Yes. I'm glad your friend isn't here. It wouldn't be good." He nods politely, taking it all in. He's very good looking - black curly hair, nice eyes. I take him gently by the arm - "Come on, I'll show you the way." As we leave I hear Sister and Nurse Shand giggling, Sister saying, "Well that perked her up." We chatter all the way to Ward 15, my brother's friend and I. I tell him I'm moving to Oxford. He tells me he's moving to London - "It's quite near London isn't it - Oxford?"

After lunch Paul comes in with a present from the men's ward - The Complete Works of Oscar Wilde. He asks Sister if he can borrow me for an hour or so. She smiles rather knowingly. I have a feeling they have something planned. Sure enough he leads me right past the male sick unit and along the corridor to Men's Long Stay. "What's going on?" I ask, trotting along beside him. I'm a fast walker but so is he, and he has very long legs. He smiles mysteriously - "There's someone I want you to meet."

My heart gets heavier as we approach Ward 4. I start to feel kind of shaky. "Don't worry," Paul says, his back against the door, looking down at me. "Your friend Bobby doesn't work here anymore." We walk along the veranda, past the room where Jackie Lowe died and into the dining room. The nursing staff are having their tea break. Jim gets up and holds his arms open for a cuddle. Sheila, the domestic, stops knitting and shouts - "Ahoy there my lovely." A few patients are sitting around the table too; Dougie Short, Willie

Somerled and Adam - all looking quite settled and happy. Adam smiles at me shyly. There's another man in a white coat who I've never met, bearded, probably in his forties. "This," says Paul gesturing towards him, "is my very good friend Tom Holligan. He is the new Ward 4, A shift, charge nurse."

Tom gets up and shakes my hand. "A pleasure to meet you, though I understand that you are soon to be leaving us?" He sits again, pours me some tea from the pot. "Littlemore then eh? You'll have to know your stuff down there. Therapeutic community isn't it?" I kind of shrug and bite my lip - I hadn't known that. "Still you've had a good teacher in this man these past few months." He nods towards Paul. "So Paul - is she normal for Fife?" Adam and Willie Somerled laugh. Tom turns and winks at them. "Most definitely not," Paul says, smiling. "Oh well, we'd best pack her off to Oxford then eh? Maybe she'll be more at home down there in the dreaming spires. Mind you…" He leans towards me, wagging his finger - "I know your type. You're the type that'll come back and tell us all how to do it properly." My face flares red despite his obvious good will. "No," I tell him. "Not me. I won't be coming back."

I'm going through to Kirkcaldy for one last night with Linda and Shona. When I arrive at five o'clock they are getting ready. "Oh my God! Look at your hair!" Shona shouts. When I was in Oxford I had it cut short, really short like a boy's haircut. "Are you absolutely sure?" The barber looked me square in the eyes. I swallowed then nodded and he switched his razor on; some of the other barbers gathered round to watch. "It's even shorter than mine!" Shona shouts. "Ye look great though. It really suits ye." - "That's not what my mum said. She went completely mental." - "Ach ye dinnae want to go by yer mum. As far as I'm concerned if ma mum likes something I'd better change it quick!"

I pull my coat off and throw it on the bed. I've got a new outfit on; red jeans, loose at the top, pulled in with a wide leather belt, a tight black jersey with buttons at the shoulder, and monkey boots. "Aw my God! No they bloody monkey boots!" Shona yells - "Ach but ye look great, ye really do." - "So do you," I tell her, because, as always, she does. "What about me?" Linda says, raising her arms and turning slowly, wiggling her bum from side to side - "Weight watchers! I've lost seventeen pounds." She's wearing an off the shoulder sequinned top and a ra ra skirt. "You look amazing. But will you not be freezing?" Linda and Shona laugh. "I telt ye," Shona says to Linda, then turning to me - "I telt her you would say that. Some things never change."

Jackie O's is mobbed and we fight to get to the bar. I order three Vodka, Malibu and Cokes. It's not a drink Linda and Shona have ever tried. Linda has hers with diet Coke. It comes with silver straws and little umbrella cocktail sticks stuck into a cherry. We drink greedily. "Peacock Pie - that's ma drink from now on," says Shona. Linda nods and smiles in agreement. We have another round then get up to dance in a threesome. Linda and Shona put their handbags in the middle of our wee group. I don't have a handbag. I've got my dad's old camera bag looped across my body - my money and makeup rattling around inside it.

Someone taps my right shoulder. I turn round but I can't see who would have done that. It happens again on my left and I quickly turn. Samira is standing in front of me laughing. She is wearing a very tight, short red dress. Her dark hair is shiny and sleek. She is the picture of health. She holds one foot up to show me, at the end of a long, slender leg - "Monkey boots!" Shona shakes her head in disbelief. "What about Donald?" I yell to Samira, still holding her hands after our hug. "I LEFT THE BASTARD!" She spins around me, clapping her hands, laughing, her teeth dazzling white in the neon light. I laugh too and we hold one another as we dance, singing along to the music - *We'll always be together -Together in Electric Dreams* - and I think I could dance with her all night - and I don't give a damn what I look like.

Queen Charlotte Rooms
Leith Edinburgh
2020 December

It's been two years since I was here last. Well, just under two years, since my mother's funeral - 30th December 2018; four year's since Dad's - 30th December 2016. Cancer killed Mum in the end, a second episode in her later years. She lived just short of 82.

Our friend Boris wasn't so lucky. We are still in shock at the news of his death, just before his 60th birthday. Everybody says it's terrible to lose people at Christmas time, but I think it's not so bad; it's a special time, when we are all trying to be nice to each other anyway and most of us don't need to worry about work. I don't need to worry about work. It's been a long time since I was a nurse, doing twelve hour shifts on Christmas day.

My brother in law, the social worker, comes over with a young man I haven't met before. "This is Boris's nephew, Charlie. He's a junior doctor working in Stratheden." I shake the doctor's hand. "I was there this morning," he says. "Not Ward 4 was it?" - "As a matter of fact it was." A wave of anxiety courses through my body. "That was my first ward at Stratheden. It was awful - but it was a long time ago. A lifetime really - before you were even born. Long before they built the new hospital. I suppose the men I knew will be dead or discharged years ago." - "You might be surprised," the young doctor says. "It seems to me there's some patients been in there since the dark ages." He laughs, takes a swig of beer. "No, really," I say - "It's been, what - about thirty seven years since I worked there." - "Try me with some names." I reel off three names, surprised myself to have recalled them so readily. "Stop!" He shouts, holding his hand up - "Two of those men are still there."

"Jesus Christ!" My brother in law looks horrified. "People do less time for murder." I don't say anything. I feel like time is slipping around beneath my feet. I feel like I've got motion sickness. "I'm getting a bad feeling," the doctor says. "Are you telling me you knew these men when they were in their twenties?" I nod, laughing a little. My hand shakes as I raise my glass to drink. "God I'd love to have known them then. What were they like?" I shrug. "I mean - were they violent?" He is looking at me with concern now - "They weren't were they?" I shake my head, try to gather myself. "Is there still a charge nurse called Tom Holligan there?" Charlie smiles. I guess this feels like safer territory. "Oh, yes. Well he was - he retired last week. What a lovely guy eh?" - "Yes, he was lovely - but still..."

Thorngrove House Sheltered Housing Complex
Aberdeen
2023 February

My sister and I are visiting Mum's old pal in Aberdeen. She lives in sheltered housing. We are in the guest room, tucked up in bed, though it's not very late. We aren't really sleepy, despite drinking a lot of wine. We lie in the dark whispering:

"I can't believe I'm staying in sheltered housing,"
"I know - a taste of things to come. Does it remind you of your nursing days?"
"Not really. This place is a lot nicer than anywhere I ever worked."
"You weren't very happy when you were a nurse were you?"
"Not in Fife I wasn't. Especially not Kirkcaldy."
"Yes, I think I remember that. I think Mum and Dad knew that. Dad used to make us wave to you, you know. We'd all stand at the living room window looking across the sea, Dad with the binoculars, 'Wave to Catriona,' he'd say, and we'd all stand there waving."

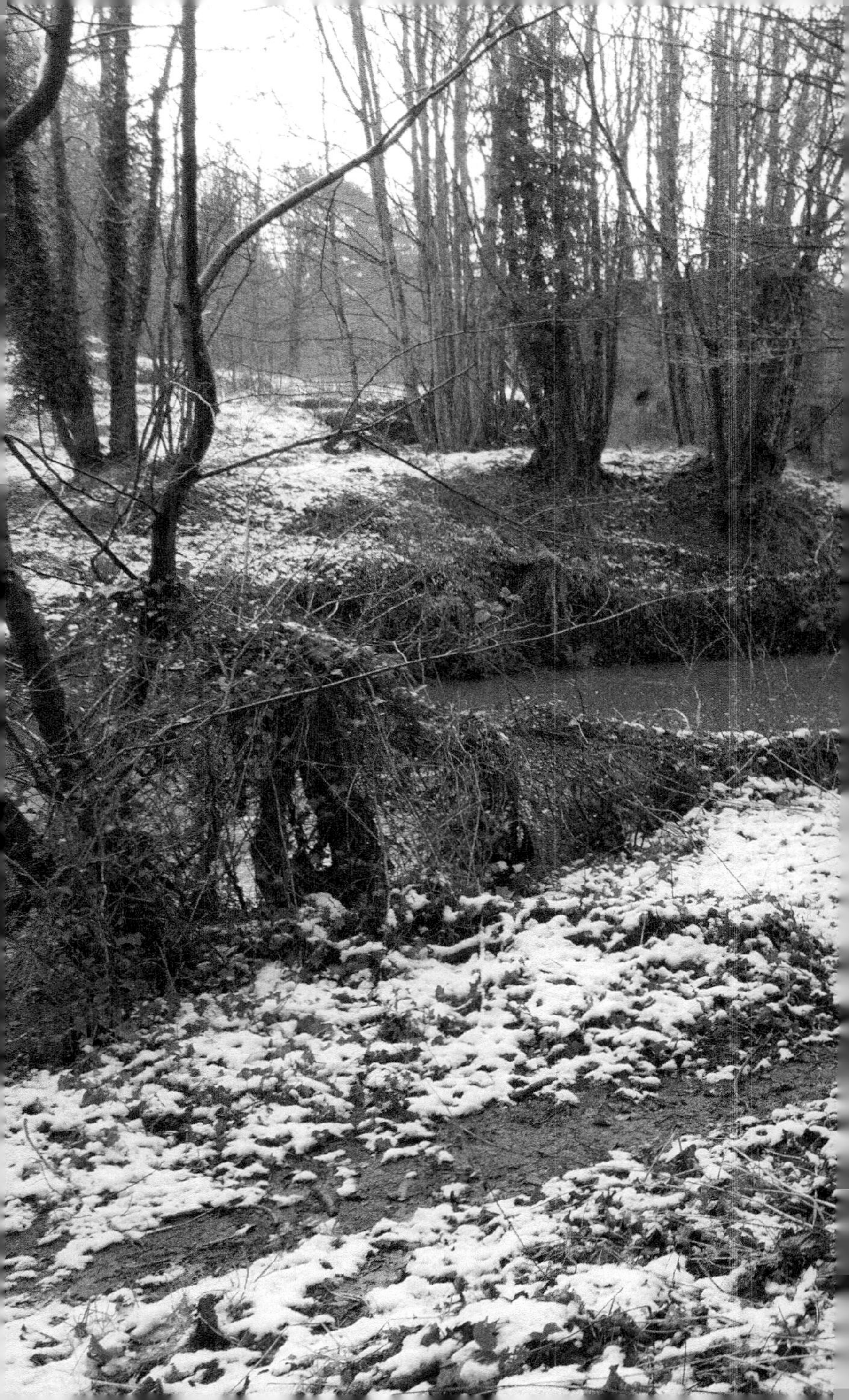

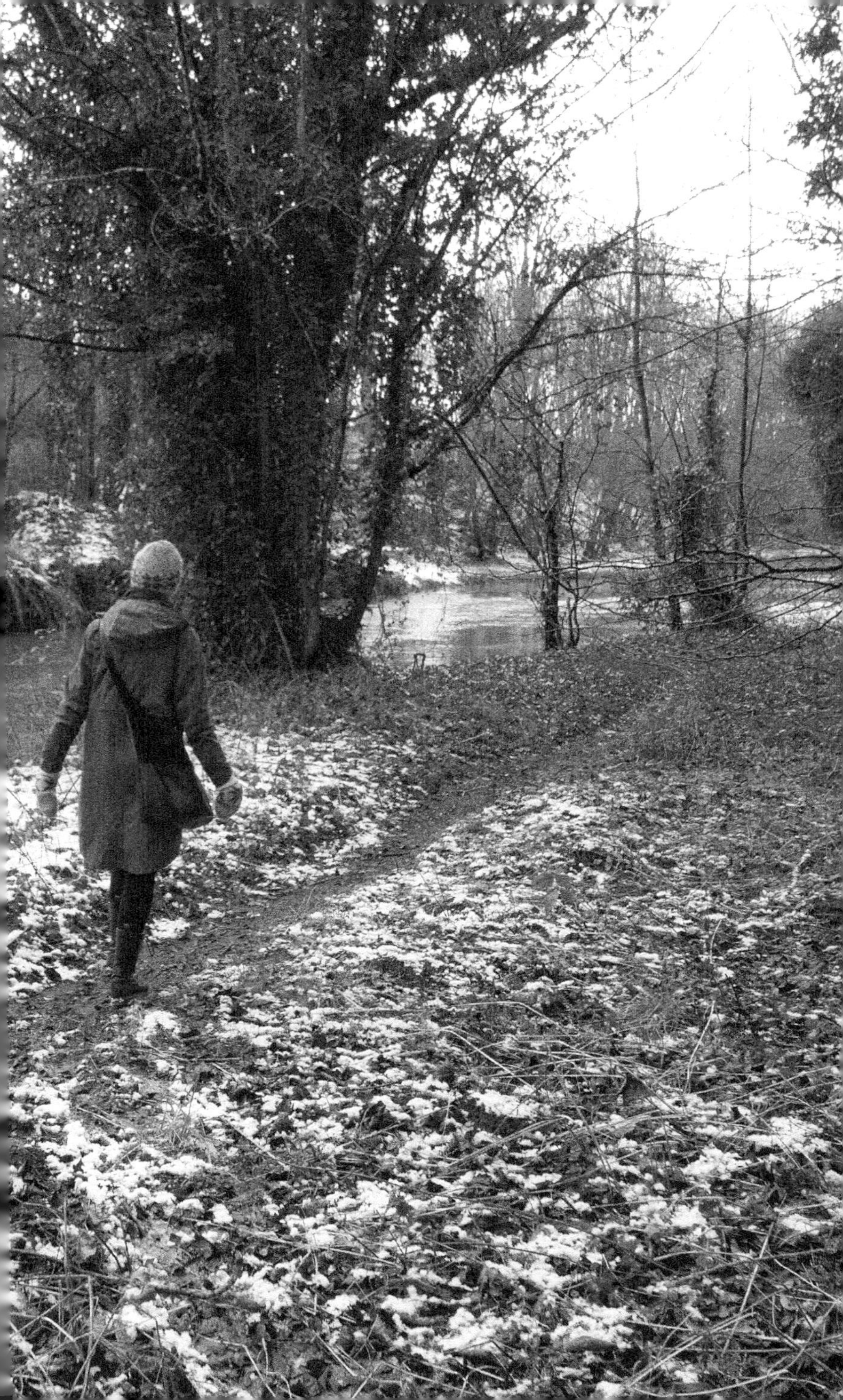

Glossary

Acute Psychiatry - the care of people who are acutely ill, requiring close observation generally because they are a risk to themselves or others.

Anti-psychotic drugs/major tranquillizers - drugs that are designed to reduce hallucinations and delusional beliefs eg Melleril/ Chlorpromazine.

Apgar score - the condition of a newborn at birth.

Behaviour modification - positive and negative reinforcement for good behaviour/bad behaviour eg. an electric shock for looking at an image relating to homosexuality.

Catastrophising (in CBT) a tendency to view situations in a very negative and dramatic way.

Cheyne Stoking - a pattern of breathing associated with the last stages of life.

Cognitive Behavioural Therapy (CBT) a talking therapy focusing on thoughts, beliefs and attitudes and how these affect our ability to function and maintain mental well being.

Controlled drugs - medication that is addictive or that may be sold for street use. Always kept in a non-transportable locked cupboard with limited staff access.

Diazepam - Valium, used to stop people having seizures during alcohol withdrawal.

Dysphasia - inability to form words, often following a stroke.

Electroconvulsive Therapy/ECT - an electric current through the brain, used to treat depression which is not responding to medication.

Endogenous depression - depression that is not attributed to any particular cause.

Entinox - gas and air for labour pains.

Folie a deux - a delusion that is shared by two people who are closely associated to one another.

Foot drop - damage to the nerves of the muscles that control the feet, in this case due to limited movement because of overly tight bedclothes

Globalising - In CBT - overgeneralising eg. I *always get everything* wrong.

Hydrotherapy - a treatment used in psychiatry 1930-1950. Patient is immersed in water for long periods of time to calm them down. The hydrotherapy pool was a different treatment - simply encouraging closeness and relaxation.

Industrial therapy - physical labour, generally repetitive and demanding little thought or problem solving etc. Earning a small amount of money in this way was believed to be therapeutic.

Insulin shock therapy - used in 1940's-1950's. Patient injected with large doses of insulin to put them in a coma, mainly used for people diagnosed with schizophrenia.

Kardex - a recording system for day to day patient care.

Legal detention - patient is held in hospital under the Mental Health (Scotland) Act. Also called *sectioning*, relating to the section of the Act that they are detained under. If they leave they may be brought back by the police.

Lobotomy/Leucotomy - generally used interchangeably, the severing of connections between the frontal lobe and the thalamus. Following this procedure patients were more docile and easier to care for.

Minor tranquillizers - drugs designed to treat anxiety eg. Diazepam/Valium.

Modified insulin therapy - smaller doses of insulin given for people with anxiety/depression etc

Obs/observations - pulse; blood pressure; respiration; temperature

Post - puerperal - following child birth

Prn - pro re nata - as required

Psychosis - the presence of symptoms such as auditory or visual hallucinations; delusional beliefs; inappropriate or bizarre behaviour

Rational Emotive Therapy - a form of CBT, focusing on unrealistic expectations of ourselves and others.

Reactive depression - depression following a life event - bereavement; break up of relationship; unemployment etc

Sphyg - sphygmomanometer - for measuring blood pressure. At this time a stethoscope was used to listen to the rate at which the blood was pumping through the patient's artery.

Tachycardia - fast pulse/heart rate

Tardive Dyskinesia - involuntary, abnormal movement of jaw, lips, tongue. A side effect of anti-psychotic drugs

Total hysterectomy - removal of both uterus and cervix

Transactional Analysis - a talking therapy, focusing on communication/social interaction.

Uni-lateral ECT - Electroconvulsive therapy delivered on one side of the head only, possibly helping to reduce the memory loss associated with bi-lateral ECT where the patient receives a shock on both sides of the head

Upper, outer quadrant - IM injections must be delivered within a hand span of the hip bone, avoiding the sciatic nerve

Voluntary detention - patient is not held under section. Technically they can leave if they wish

Stratheden 2022

Poems & Songs

Not waving but Drowning - Stevie Smith (Not waving but Drowning 1957)

I walk the Line - Johnny Cash (1973)

Fergus and the Druid - William Butler Yeats (The Rose, 1893)

Little Grey home in the West - Hermann Frederic Lohr and D. Eardley-Wilmot (1911)

The Song of the Mad Prince - Walter De La Mare (Peacock Pie 1913)

A Song of Enchantment - Walter De La Mare (Peacock Pie 1913)

Together in Electric Dreams - Philip Oakey & Giorgio Moroder (1985)

With thanks to: Iona Colvin; Al Gray; Lesley Gordon; Marie Hayes; Anne Jones; Clare Sutherland; Maysoon Sutherland.

A special thanks goes to my husband Mike (a Fifer born and bred) for ongoing book production. He has a collection of sayings about the Kingdom. His current favourite is...
"You can always tell a Fifer, but you can't tell them much"

Catriona Windle 2023
www.linktr.ee/catrionawindle

Jackie O

KIRKCALDY
Telephone 4496 or 65483
For details of party discounts

Kirkcaldy's Most Popular Licensed **DISCOTHEQUE**

Open till 2.00 a.m. every Wednesday, Thursday, Friday, Saturday and Sunday.

Featuring the famous Jackie "O" **HAPPY HOUR** ON WEDNESDAY, THURSDAY AND SUNDAY NIGHTS, when all drinks will be e.g. LAGER 30p (pint) GIN & TONIC 31p (one-fifth gill)

PLEASE DRESS APPROPRIATELY

Bentley's NIGHTSCENE

OPEN 5 NIGHTS — **LICENSED — 5 BARS** INCLUDING LATEST AMERICAN COCKTAIL BAR

BENTLEY'S HILARIOUS BEACH PARTY
SUNDAY, August 23
Show off your summer tan!
Bikinis — Shorts — Wet Suits
Fun — Games
Candy Floss — Toffee Apples

WORLD DISCO DANCE CHAMPIONSHIP
Sponsored by
HONDA
Final of local heats tonight
Friday, August 14

SAVE YOUR MONEY WITH OUR HAPPY HOUR
Every Wednesday, Thursday and Sunday
9.30 p.m. to 10.30 p.m.
ALL DRINKS ½-PRICE

Bentley's help you celebrate. GIRLS' NIGHT OUT!
50% admission discount EVERY...

ABBOTSHALL HOTEL

MILTON ROAD, KIRKCALDY
TELEPHONE 60803

Friday, August 28, afternoon —
GO-GO DANCERS
3 p.m.-5 p.m. in the Caroline Lounge
Evening — RADIO FORTH DISCO
Admission £1. 8 p.m.-midnight

Saturday, August 29, afternoon —
GO-GO DANCERS
3 p.m.-5 p.m. in the Caroline Lounge
Evening — RADIO FORTH ROADSHOW

Printed in Great Britain
by Amazon